International Review
of Health Psychology

Editorial Board

International Review of Health Psychology

VOLUME 2

Edited by

S. Maes
Leiden University, The Netherlands

H. Leventhal
Rutgers University, USA

and

M. Johnston
University of St Andrews, Scotland

JOHN WILEY & SONS
Chichester · New York · Brisbane · Toronto · Singapore

Other Wiley Editorial Offices

John Wiley & Sons, Inc., 605 Third Avenue,
New York, NY 10158–0012, USA

Jacaranda Wiley Ltd, G.P.O. Box 859, Brisbane,
Queensland 4001, Australia

John Wiley & Sons (Canada) Ltd, 22 Worcester Road,
Rexdale, Ontario M9W 1L1, Canada

John Wiley & Sons (SEA) Pte Ltd, 37 Jalan Pemimpin #05–04,
Block B, Union Industrial Building, Singapore 2057

British Library Cataloguing in Publication Data

A catalogue record for this book is available from the British Library

ISBN 0-471-93826-2

Typeset in 10/12 pt Sabon by Vision Typesetting, Manchester
Printed and Bound in Great Britain by Biddles Ltd, Guildford and King's Lynn

Contents

List of Contributors

Andrea Abele
University of Erlangen/Nürnberg, Germany

Steven D. Barger
University of Utah, USA

Adrian Bauman
University of New South Wales, Australia

Walter Brehm
University of Bayreuth, Germany

Robert T Croyle
University of Utah, USA

Stewart M. Dunn
University of Sydney, Australia

Theresa M. Marteau
Royal Free Hospital School of Medicine, London, UK

Rob Sanson-Fisher
University of Newcastle, Australia

Charlotte A. Schoenborn
National Center for Health Statistics, Maryland, USA

Jerry Suls
University of Iowa, USA

Annette Swain
University of Iowa, USA

Kenneth A. Wallston
Vanderbilt University, USA

Preface

As mentioned in last year's Preface, *The International Review of Health Psychology* is an annual publication containing review-type chapters covering four health psychology areas: I general concepts and methodology; II health behaviour and health promotion; III illness behaviour and health care; and IV practical and professional issues.

The first area is covered by chapters which present the current state of the art concerning general concepts such as gender, age, social class or ethnicity and health, as well as contributions on, for example, social support, coping, perceived control, compliance, stress or pain. It also includes chapters on methodological issues with regard to measurement and research in health psychology and related disciplines. The second, or health behaviour and health promotion, area contains chapters on various health behaviours (such as smoking, physical exercise, weight, nutrition habits, use of alcohol, sleeping habits and safety) and on interventions aimed at these behaviours, carried out in various settings (including community, health care, school, worksite, leisure and family settings). The third, or illness behaviour and health care, area comprises review type contributions concerning psychosocial consequences and psychological interventions in various groups of patients (including cardiovascular, cancer, AIDS and diabetes patients, as well as patients suffering from rheumatic or chronic obstructive pulmonary diseases). Further chapters in this area concern psychosocial aspects of, and psychological interventions relevant to medical examinations (e.g. vaginal examination or pre-natal diagnosis) and procedures (e.g. various types of surgery). In addition, we aim to publish within this area contributions related to the health care system, including studies on health care processes (e.g. patient–care-provider interaction), treatment settings (e.g. health care organization) and health careers (e.g. stress of health careers or training of health professionals). Within the fourth area special attention is given to practical and professional issues, of health psychology research, practice and training in different parts of the world, as well as to the relationships between health psychologists and other health professionals.

Thanks to the support of my co-editors, the members of the editorial board and many other anonymous but excellent reviewers, we also succeeded this year in publishing a volume containing high quality review papers from different parts of the world and covering all four areas. The chapters by J. Suls and A. Swain on 'Use of meta-analysis in health psychology' and by R. Croyle and S. Barger on 'Illness cognition' fit into the first area. The second area is covered by the contributions of A. Abele and W. Brehm on 'Mood effects of exercise versus sports games: findings and implications for well-being and health'; of C. Schoenborn on 'The Alameda Study—25 years later' and the one by R. Sanson-Fisher on 'Primary and secondary prevention of cancer: opportunities for behavioural scientists'. The third area is represented by the chapters of T. Marteau on 'Health related screening: psychological predictors of uptake and impact'; of S. Dunn on 'Psychological aspects of diabetes in adults' and of A. Bauman on 'Effects of asthma patient education upon psychological and behavioural outcomes'. Finally, the chapter by K. Wallston on 'Health psychology in the USA' represents the last area. This second volume also reflects our international perspective, since four of the nine chapters are from the USA, three from Australia and two from Europe.

While all chapters, are in my opinion, very valuable contributions, I would like to draw special attention to the first chapter by Jerry Suls and Annette Swain on the use of meta-analysis in health psychology. Meta-analysis is a quantitative approach to the assessment and integration of results of different empirical studies, which becomes increasingly popular as an alternative for the more conventional narrative review. As it is the objective of *The International Review* to publish review-type contributions, it is obvious that this chapter may lead to better understanding of chapters which are based on meta-analysis. At the same time we hope to stimulate health psychology authors to produce more reviews of this type. While I consider narrative reviews and reviews based on meta-analysis complementary, it is indeed clear that both approaches have their merits. Narrative reviews are mostly more informative with regard to the aim and the content of studies included in the review, and may—in other words—be of better use for future authors on the topic. Meta-analyses, on the other hand, have great advantages for the average reader, since they permit pooling of small samples of individual studies, thus overcoming the lack of power of these studies and subjective interpretation by the reviewer. While Suls' and Swain's chapter is without any doubt more convincing, I cannot resist giving the readers an appetizer before reading the full chapter. Muldoon et al. (1990) and Newman (1992) published overlapping meta-analyses on the effects of cholesterol-lowering regimes. These meta-analyses confirm the results of several individual trials indicating that these regimes lower heart-attack and related death rates. However they also show that death rates from behavioural and other causes, including suicide, accidents and murders, rise in equal proportions in the experimental groups. Muldoon et al. (1990) report that in the combined trials 197 of the control and 169 of the intervention group died from heart attacks, but only 37 of the controls died of behavioural causes, in contrast to 66 in the intervention groups. The differences in death rates for behavioural causes did not reach significance in the individual studies, because the number of subjects was too small. Many researchers, but not the authors of the meta-analysis studies, overlooked the fact that cholesterol-lowering regimes may have behavioural side-effects, which seriously questions their overall effectiveness.

This example illustrates why I would like to encourage authors from different parts of the world to send us not only conventional review papers but also chapters based on meta-analysis, although I do realize that this is not possible and maybe not even advisable for all health psychology areas. As already mentioned last year, comments on already published chapters (including those on meta-analysis) are also very welcome. It is, however, advisable that people who intend to submit a review chapter, contact me at an early stage in order to avoid overlap with already published or submitted chapters. It should be obvious for every potential contributor that his or her manuscript will go through the same review process as the solicited chapters, implying that at least two independent reviewers will evaluate each manuscript.

I would like to thank my co-editors, the members of the editorial board, many external reviewers, the authors, my secretary Ellen Smelik and the supportive staff from Wiley for the time, patience and effort which they invested in the preparation of this volume.

Stan Maes
Principal Editor

REFERENCES

Muldoon M. F., Manuck, S. B. & Matthews, K. A. (1990). Lowering choesterol concentrations and mortality: a quantitative review of primary prevention trials. *British Medical Journal*, **301**, 309–313.

Newman, T. B., Browner, W. S. & Hulley, S. B. (1992). Childhood Cholesterol Screening Contraindicated. *Journal of the American Medical Association*, **267** (1), 100–101.

Part I

GENERAL CONCEPTS AND METHODOLOGY

1 Use of Meta-Analysis in Health Psychology

JERRY SULS, ANNETTE SWAIN
*Department of Psychology, Spence Laboratories of Psychology,
University of Iowa, Iowa City, Iowa 52242, USA.
Electronic correspondence: BLAJMSWY@UIAMVS*

How does the health psychologist researcher, theorist, or practitioner make determinations about the success of a particular hypothesis or relative efficacy of a given treatment that has been studied over a series of experiments? Traditional approaches to research synthesis have relied on qualitative, narrative reviews of existent studies. These are usually accompanied by simple vote counts of studies favoring the hypothesis. The narrative reviewer then declares a hypothesis proven if most studies demonstrate a statistically significant effect. Quantitative research synthesis, on the other hand, involves the statistical analysis of pooled results from different analytic studies. While this approach was first proposed in the 1930s (Pearson, 1933; Mosteller & Bush, 1954), it was not until it was dubbed "meta-analysis" and formalized by Gene Glass (1976) that it began to receive wide application. By now meta-analyses have become commonplace in social and medical science journals (Wachter & Straf, 1990). However, our impression is that health psychologist readers of the literature are frequently confused about how quantitative research reviews are conducted and how the results are to be interpreted. The present chapter is written as an introduction to the use and interpretation of meta-analysis in health psychology/behavioral medicine.

It is instructive to consider the potential benefits provided by a quantitative synthesis that are not offered by a narrative review. One example comes from Bryant & Wortman's (1984) excellent summary of evaluation issues in medical quantitative research synthesis. Baum et al. (1981) performed a meta-analysis of studies evaluating the effectiveness of antibiotics by comparing patients who received antibiotics prior to colon-rectal surgery with patients who did not. In twenty-six randomized clinical trials published between 1965 and 1980, Baum et al. found there was a general trend for antibiotics to reduce wound infections and mortality rates but no single study served as strong support due to small sample sizes. In fact, after pooling study results, the authors found benefits favoring treatment as early as 1969 and after only five

International Review of Health Psychology. Volume 2. Edited by S. Maes, H. Leventhal and M. Johnston
© 1993 John Wiley & Sons Ltd

studies. Prior to Baum et al.'s quantitative synthesis, however, no practitioners or scientists were willing to draw conclusions on the basis of the separate individual studies because they tended to use small samples. If a synthesis of results had been available to the medical community in 1969, it may well be that practitioners would have earlier recognized the futility of conducting no-treatment controls to evaluate the effectiveness of antibiotics.

In the following sections, the major techniques employed in meta-analysis are described along with examples of their use. First, however, we consider the characteristics of the narrative review and some of its inherent limitations that led to the development and increasing popularity of meta-analytic approaches.

THE CONVENTIONAL REVIEW

The conventional approach adopted in reviews of an empirical literature focuses on the relationship between a set of independent and dependent variables. For any given relationship, the relevant research studies are described, and a "tally" is kept of the number of studies that report statistically significant effects vs.. the number of studies that report statistically non-significant effects. If most of the studies observe statistically significant effects, a conclusion is made about the effect's presence or absence.

The traditional narrative review has several limitations. First, conventional reviews typically ignore the fact that studies differ in their statistical power or capability to detect differences. Consequently, the reviewer essentially gives equivalent weight to studies with both small and large sample sizes. Similarly, such reviews ignore the strength of the effects observed so that equal weights are given to studies with small effects as to those with large effects. The conclusions derived invariably lack information in terms of the strength and nature of the relationship. Moreover, the difference between statistical and appreciable significance is ignored, increasing the likelihood that results which are significant, yet not necessarily meaningful, will be included in the analysis. For example, due to a large sample size a study may demonstrate that a treatment produces gains over that of a control group, but the gains may be quite modest.

An inherent limitation of conventional reviews is that the reviewer draws a conclusion about the null hypothesis based on an overall tally. This is tantamount to using an "intuitive" binomial test of successes vs.. failures. Finally, the traditional narrative review is especially prone to author biases as there are no objective criteria for determining cumulative effects across studies. In such reviews the reviewer may weigh more heavily those studies conducted by reputable authors or may subjectively draw conclusions to fit his or her own *a priori* beliefs about the topic.

Conclusions derived from vote-counting reviews can be in error due to the reasons noted above. A finding may fail to achieve statistical significance due to a lack of power, yet still be in the direction of the hypothesized relation. Nonetheless, in a narrative review the study would be treated as nonsupport. In a revealing demonstration, Cooper & Rosenthal (1980) randomly assigned a group of graduate students and faculty members to evaluate whether seven studies on sex differences in task performance provided any cumulative conclusions. The participants read the same seven studies that the researchers knew beforehand supported the overall hypothesis that females showed greater persistence. Half of the subjects were asked to read and review the studies as they would typically review an empirical literature. The other half were asked to record the significance level of each study and given instructions on how to combine significance levels to obtain an overall test of significance for the entire set of seven studies (the reader will recognize that this is the meta-analytic method of combined probabilities described in detail below).

Afterward both groups were asked whether the evidence supported the conclusion that females were more task persistent, and, if so, to estimate the size of the relationship on five-point scales (definitely yes, probably yes, impossible to say, probably no, definitely no). Although there was a relationship, 73% of the traditional reviewers thought there was either probably or definitely no relationship. Only 32% of the meta-analytic group thought there was a probably or definitely no relationship. Cooper and Rosenthal (1980) concluded from these results that traditional reviewers may be apt to make Type II errors (i.e., failing to reject null hypotheses that are false).

The above demonstration involved a small set of studies. One would anticipate the problems would be amplified when the number of studies is large. Moreover, this difficulty is multiplied when a research literature also involves several cross-cutting moderator variables and/or sample attributes.

The meta-analytic review involves the summation and integration of the empirical literature, building upon the idea that study outcomes may be quantified using a common metric. A major impetus was the work of Gene Glass (1976) who formulated the operationalization of effect size for meta-analysis and also demonstrated the usefulness of quantitative synthesis by reviewing the vast and controversial literature on the effectiveness of psychotherapy (Smith, Glass & Miller, 1980).

There are a number of inherent advantages in adopting a meta-analytic approach. First, it forces the reviewer to be explicit in terms of his or her assumptions concerning which studies are important, which incorporate appropriate methodology and which are flawed in some manner. Second, while still subjective, it allows for more precise methods on which to base judgments and conclusions. Finally, it requires the reviewer to explicitly define the relationship of the variables under investigation.

These comments are not meant to imply that a quantitative review is superior in all cases or that a narrative review is never appropriate. As discussed below, the nature of the data base, the thoroughness with which research authors provide important statistical details, and the general sophistication of the literature determine whether a meta-analysis is a viable and better alternative than a narrative review.

CONTROVERSIAL ISSUES SURROUNDING LITERATURE REVIEWS

There are certain issues that need to be addressed when conducting a review irrespective of the approach adopted. First, the decision of what studies to include is of utmost importance. A selection of poor studies or unrelated studies (e.g. combining "rotten apples") may produce uninterpretable results. The biggest difficulty for both narrative and quantitative reviewers is how to define a "bad" design feature. In some cases, there will probably be little debate about threats to internal validity (e.g. lack of random assignment) and the study should be eliminated from the analysis. But in other cases things may be less clear-cut. One option is simply to include all studies. Unfortunately, the inclusion of fundamentally flawed studies provides no useful information to the reviewer as their outcomes cannot be accurately inferred (Wilson & Rachman, 1983). As there is no one correct strategy to implement to overcome this problem, Light & Pillemer (1984) recommend that a reviewer form decision rules. That is, he or she must explicitly define and justify his or her criteria for study selection with respect to relevance, validity and acceptability. Further, he or she must explain the implications of such a strategy. The reviewer must then take heed, though, as criteria for acceptance necessarily restrict the ability to generalize the conclusions drawn.

The decision to include all seemingly-relevant studies in a review also leads to a separate yet equally important problem, that of integrating unrelated studies. Combining effects of different operationalizations of independent and dependent variables across studies has been likened to combining "apples with oranges". For example, the Smith, Glass & Miller (1980) meta-analysis of psychotherapy studies was criticized on this ground because the results of psychodynamic, behavioral, rational-emotive, etc., therapies were collapsed and averaged together (Presby, 1978).

Glass McGaw, & Smith's (1981) response to the "apples and oranges" criticism was that the critics, usually the researchers themselves, are being inconsistent. If we are willing to generalize over subjects within studies, why should we not be willing to generalize over studies? In addition, apples and oranges are good to mix when trying to generalize to fruit. Some reviewers want the answer to the question, "Is there a general relationship across different studies and different operationalizations of the independent variable (e.g., does psychotherapy produce benefits?)?"

Hunter & Schmidt (1990) further argue that this issue is actually an empirical question of whether a varied operationalization across studies is a moderator variable interacting with the treatment variable. This cannot be answered without a meta-analysis. Thus, in their opinion, it may be viewed as a call for a quantitative review rather than a criticism *per se*.

A related issue concerns the independence or lack thereof of a given study's results. Typically an investigation will employ a variety of related dependent measures. Violations of independence occur when several of these measures are used in a single review analysis or when multiple tests are conducted within the original study. This problematic because results may be correlated due to common methodology, similar subject samples or idiosyncratic laboratory variables (Strube & Hartmann, 1983). For example, several different effect size estimates may be calculated from different outcome constructs or several different measures of the same construct. Or, several effect sizes may be calculated in a study, each of which uses the same control group with multiple experimental groups. A quantitative review is especially vulnerable to this problem. Strategies to overcome this limitation are discussed later in the chapter.

A final source of controversy has been popularly termed the "file drawer problem". This refers to the bias resulting from studies obtaining non-significant findings having a higher probability of not being published than studies reporting significant findings (Rosenthal, 1984). The extremist view of this problem posits published results to be the 5% of studies demonstrating Type I errors (failing to negate the null hypothesis when it is true) while the researchers' file cabinets are filled with the 95% of studies demonstrating non-significant results (Rosenthal, 1979). To compensate for this bias meta-analysts often compute a failsafe N. This is an estimate of the number of unpublished, non-significant studies that would have to exist for the obtained probability level to be rendered nonsignificant ($p > 0.05$).

The major difference between the narrative and the quantitative reviews hinges on the degree to which these concerns are made explicit and explicit operations are used to address them. Meta-analysis appears to require more explicitness than the narrative review. Perhaps Rosenthal (1990, p. 132) said it best:

> We cannot do meta-analysis by reading abstracts and discussion sections. We are forced to look at the numbers and, very often, compute the correct ones ourselves. Meta-analysis requires us to cumulate *data*, not *conclusions*. "Reading" a paper is quite a different matter when we need to compute an effect size and a fairly precise significance level ...

THE LOGIC OF META-ANALYSIS

Since the 1970s, several related, but distinct, meta-analytic procedures have been refined and developed (Glass, McGaw & Smith, 1981; Rosenthal, 1984; Hedges & Olkin, 1985; Hunter, Schmidt & Jackson, 1983). In this chapter we will focus on those two approaches that have the widest applicability in health psychology (see Bangert-Drowns, 1986, for an overview).

Combined probability method

The combined probability approach relies on testing for statistical significance of combined results across studies. The question of interest with this method concerns the probability the pattern of p values observed across studies could result given that the null hypothesis of no effect was true. The meta-analyst using this approach pools p values across independent studies. From this an overall or aggregate p value is derived. Pooling can be done for analysis of probability values based on statistics such as t, χ^2, F, and r. (However, in the case of F and χ^2 statistics, meta-analytic approaches are only appropriate for cases where $df = 1$ for the numerator of the statistical test, or $df = 1$ for chi-square of independence. In situations where $df > 1$ the direction of the results cannot be readily discerned.)

For aggregating p values, the two most popular methods are adding Z scores and adding weighted Z scores (i.e. Stouffer method). When using the former method each statistical test value is converted into a one-tailed p value using the appropriate df. These values are then converted to Z score equivalents using a standard normal distribution table and signed according to the direction of the differences. This use of standardized Z score equivalents allows for an objective pooling of p values. The summed equivalents are divided by the square root of k, where k equals the number of independent studies. Finally, this value, Z', is referred to the normal distribution table from which the appropriate p value is derived. This method is more conservative than the Stouffer method because it weighs all studies equally, including those with small N which typically have larger p values. Although this method of aggregating Z's is applicable under a wide range of conditions, it is limited by the facts that it may increase the probability of Type I or Type II errors and that under certain conditions it assumes equal variance (Rosenthal, 1984).

The Stouffer method is very similar to the method of adding Z's except that each Z score equivalent is weighted by its appropriate degrees of freedom. Differential weighing allows for a more precise summation, with larger studies given greater emphasis than smaller studies. This minimizes the likelihood of Type II error. The Z scores are combined by the following formula:

$$Z' = \frac{\sum_{j=1}^{k} df_j z_j}{\sqrt{\sum_{j=1}^{k} df_j^2}} \tag{1.1}$$

Here k equals the number of studies and j, each study starting with $j = 1$. As with the former method, the p value for Z' is simply read from a standard normal distribution table. It is also similar to the method of unweighted Z's in that it assumes equal variances and thus is prone to error in certain cases.

Table 1.1. Selected results from Friedman and Booth-Kewley's (1987) meta-analysis of disease and personality variables

	No. of samples	z	p	Fail safe N
Ulcer and anxiety	7	4.71	0.000001	51
Ulcer and depression	7	2.85	0.0022	15
Ulcer and anger/hostility/ aggression	8	−0.09	0.4623	—*
Ulcer and anger/hostility	7	0.15	0.4410	—*
Ulcer and extraversion	4	−2.54	0.0044	11

* A fail safe number is not calculated if the null hypothesis was not rejected.

The reader should bear in mind that while these two methods are the most widely used for aggregating p values, they are by no means the only methods available. The reader is referred to Rosenthal (1978) and Hedges (1989) for discussions on alternative procedures.

Friedman and Booth-Kewley's (1987) meta-analysis of the literature on the association between personality and disease is illustrative of the combined probability method. These reviewers wanted to evaluate whether there was a relationship between negative emotional traits, such as depression, hostility, and anxiety, and physical disease in the empirical literature. A large number of relevant studies ($n = 101$) were identified via *Psychological Abstracts, Index Medicus*, and by using the bibliographies of the articles already located. Studies reported results in terms of t-, F-test, correlations, or chi-square comparisons. In Friedman and Booth-Kewley's analysis, a positive Z meant that individuals having more of a personality attribute, such as depression, were more likely to have each of the illnesses being considered. A negative Z indicated that depressed individuals had less disease.

Table 1.1 presents some of the meta-analytic results reported by Friedman and Booth-Kewley (1987) for ulcer and five different personality variables. The reader will observe that there was a positive relationship between ulcer and anxiety, and ulcer and depression and a negative relationship between ulcer and extraversion. For example, the p value associated with a Z' of 4.71 is less than 0.000001 for the studies examining the association between ulcer and anxiety. Hence, it is highly unlikely that the p values from the seven studies, considered as a whole, would result if the null hypothesis were true (i.e., anxiety and ulcer were unrelated).

The reader will also notice a column for "fail safe N". This number, as noted earlier, provides a way to protect against the so-called "file drawer problem". The failsafe N for combined probability can be calculated by:

$$NS = \frac{(\Sigma z_j)^2}{2.706} - k \qquad (1.2)$$

where NS is the number of studies in the file drawer and k equals the number of independent studies on which combined probability is based. Table 1.1 shows that approximately 51 studies with a z of zero would have to exist in file drawers for doubt to be cast about there being a positive relationship between ulcers and anxiety.

Combined estimation

The previous method indicates whether the null hypothesis should be rejected, but it may be equally important, if not more so, to know the strength of the effect. Unlike the combined probability method, combined estimation involves estimation of treatment (or other variable) magnitude across studies. The estimated population effect size should be based on the set of studies as a whole, as opposed to any single investigation.

Indices of effect size

Effect magnitude found in a study can be indexed in several ways. Glass's (1977) effect size indicator is $\triangle$, the standardized difference between treatment and control group means, $(X_t - X_c)/S_c$ where X_t is the mean of the treatment condition, X_c, the mean of the control condition, and S_c is the standard deviation of the control group. Hedges and Olkins' (1985) effect size index is called g which also uses the standardized difference, but the standardization is performed by dividing by the pooled standard deviation of the treatment and the control group (hence $g = (X_t - X_c)/s$). Hedges prefers the pooled s.d. because it has such desirable properties as small sampling error and is often the only standard deviation available. If the means are not reported, a t can be converted to g by the formula, $g = t\sqrt{(1/n_t + 1/n_c)}$. By expressing these effects in standard deviation units, the meta-analyst can directly compare studies that differ in terms of design, methodology or sample size, etc. However, it is important to keep in mind that g is an estimate of the population effect size, δ, and as such, is assumed to stem from subpopulations with equal variances. Thus, in some situations with heterogeneous sample variances, this may not be an optimal method.

Another effect size indicator is the product moment correlation r, whether in dichotomous or continuous form (Pearson's r, Spearman's rho, phi, or point biserial r). This r, however, is not the simple correlation between the treatment and outcome within a given study, though it may be derived from individual study correlations. Rather, it focuses upon the degree to which bivariate relationships may be generalized across studies (Raju et al., 1991). Simple computational formulas using values of t and F statistics have been proposed by Rosenthal (1984). However, they fail to account for such artifacts as errors of measurements, sampling biases and range attenuation. Recently, more flexible, correlation-based procedures have been proposed, accompanied with formulas to account for such study artifacts (see Hunter & Schmidt, 1990 and Raju et al., 1991). Their application in the field of health psychology has not yet been widely used.

The health psychologist reader may be concerned that some research domains do not use t, F, or correlation statistics, but effect sizes can also be calculated from chi-squared values. This may be especially relevant if the meta-analysis uses research from the epidemiology literature. (Einarson, Leeder & Koren, 1988 provide an excellent introduction to meta-analysis of epidemiological studies). Effect size can also be indexed by observed minus expected frequency of some outcome like death or the risk ratio between treatment and control groups (Canner, 1983; also see Yeaton & Wortman, 1984).

Once each study's outcome has been converted to an effect size, a series of adjustments are recommended. First, the study effect size, is slightly biased when based on a small sample of subjects ($n < 10$ per group). This can be corrected by multiplying each study g by $1 - (3/4N - 9)$ (Hedges, 1981), which translates each g into an unbiased estimate of the sample variance. This yields an adjusted value, which Hedges refers to as d.

Analysis of effect size indices

At this point, the meta-analyst is ready to compute a composite or average effect size (d_+) which will yield information about the magnitude, direction, and significance of the effect sizes in the data set. However, before pooling, one should determine whether the studies can be adequately described with a single effect size. If the study effect sizes are homogeneous (i.e. come from the same population) then the average value provides a good estimate. However, if the study effect sizes are heterogeneous, according to a test described below, then the average effect size does not adequately describe the study outcomes in the literature. Therefore, a preliminary test of the homogeneity of effect sizes across the studies is performed. If the null hypothesis of homogeneous effect sizes is not rejected, then it is concluded that all of the studies could come from the same population and that procedural or sample variations across studies did not make a statistically reliable difference. The effect size estimates from all of the studies can then be pooled to obtain a more reliable estimate of the population effect size.

To test the homogeneity of a group of study effect sizes, one requires the adjusted study ds and another statistic, V, which provides a measure of the variability of each effect size:

$$V_j = \frac{n_1 + n_2}{n_1 n_2} + \frac{d_j^2}{2(n_1 + n_2)} \tag{1.3}$$

The test of homogeneity of the study effect size composite is:

$$H_t = \sum d_j V - \frac{\sum d_j V_j^2}{\sum \frac{1}{V_j}} \qquad (1.4)$$

The H_t statistic (also sometimes referred to as Q or Q_t) is approximately distributed as a chi-square with $k - 1$ degrees of freedom where $k =$ the number of studies.

These current tests of homogeneity deserve a word of caution. They are dependent upon individual sample sizes so that a meta-analysis composed of studies with large sample sizes will indicate significant heterogeneity when the differences are trivial. Likewise, a meta-analysis with smaller sample studies will often produce non-significant tests for heterogeneity. A random effects, multiple regression model has been proposed to overcome this problem (see Hedeker, Gibbons & Davis, 1991 and Gibbons & Bock, 1987), permitting variation at both the individual and study level.

Homogeneous effect size situations

If the value, H_t, is not statistically significant, the null hypothesis of homogeneous effect sizes is accepted, that is, the study effect sizes can be inferred to come from a common population. A composite effect size (average effect size, d_+) can be then calculated as an estimate of the true population effect size. Hedges suggests the average be calculated with each d weighted by the reciprocal of its variance; hence, more weight is given to the most reliably estimated study outcomes. The formula is given as:

$$d_+ = \frac{\sum \frac{d_j}{V_j}}{\sum \frac{1}{V_j}} \qquad (1.5)$$

To test for the significance of the average effect size, a 95% confidence interval (CI) is drawn around the mean. If the CI includes 0.00 (no difference) it can be concluded that across studies there is no relationship between the independent and the dependent variables. On the other hand, for example, if the $d_+ = +0.45$ and the CI was 0.21 to 0.78 (does not contain 0.00), then one could conclude that there was a significant positive relationship.

A literal interpretation of a d_+ of 0.45 is that the experimental and control group differ on the dependent variable by more than 4/10th's of a standard deviation. Cohen's (1977) rule of thumb is that effect sizes of 0.3 should be considered small effects, of 0.5 moderate effects, and 0.8 or more, large effects. However, Cooper (1990) notes that effect sizes need to be judged within their substantive contexts. In a field or subarea where most effects tend to be very small, an effect size of 0.4 can be considered large.

Formulas have been derived to deal with the "file drawer problem" for the interpretation of combined effect magnitude estimation. Orwin's (1983) formula provides an estimate of the number of unpublished studies whose d is zero that would have to exist in order to reduce the sample mean d to some specified value. This criterion value might be set on the basis of Cohen's general prescriptions: 0.3 as weak, 0.5 as moderate, and 0.8 as strong; or alternatively, per Cooper's (1990) suggestion relative to the effect sizes of other variables studied in the same field. Orwin's formula is:

$$NS = \frac{k(d - d_c)}{d_c} \qquad (1.6)$$

where NS = the number of studies in the file drawer, k = the number of studies on which the mean sample effect size is based, d = the absolute value of the unweighted mean of the observed d's across the k studies, and d_c = the criterion value.

Unfortunately, this formula is subject to limitations. First, it requires that the criterion effect size, d_c, be greater than zero. Second, it asumes equal N's for the k number of studies. Thus, in cases with largely heterogeneous sample sizes Orwin's formula should be viewed with caution.

A second formula may be used when the data are in the form of correlation coefficients. This is expressed as:

$$NS = \frac{k(Z)}{Z_c} \qquad (1.7)$$

where k equals the number of studies, Z is the Fisher transformation equivalent of the mean sample correlation, and Z_c is the Fisher transformation of the criterion value.

Heterogeneous effect size situation

When testing for the homogeneity of effect sizes, if H_t is statistically significant, signaling variability among the study ds, then the composite effect size is an inappropriate estimate of the population parameter. In such cases, there are a number of options. First, one may conduct a formal hypothesis test based on some *a priori* notion about how variation among studies (e.g. type of sample, particular operationalization of the independent or dependent variable, etc.) may have produced the heterogeneity in study effect sizes. This type of hypothesis-testing is referred to as categorical modeling. Conducting such a test may reveal that subsets formed in accord with a study attribute result in homogeneous subsets. This procedure involves two steps. In the first, one tests whether partitioning study outcomes according to the attribute yields different average effect sizes for the subgroups. If so, then one wants to determine whether the resulting subgroups are homogeneous.

To calculate between-group differences, the formula is:

$$H_b = \sum\sum \frac{d_j'^2}{V_{ij}} - \frac{\left(\sum\limits_{i=1}^{p}\sum\limits_{j=1}^{m}\frac{d_{ij}'}{V_{ij}}\right)^2}{\sum\limits_{i=1}^{p}\sum\limits_{j=1}^{m}\frac{1}{V_{ij}}} \tag{1.8}$$

(where p = the number of clusters, m_i = number of studies in each cluster, d_{ij} = the unbiased effect size of the study j cluster i, V_{ij} = the V measure for study j in cluster i, and d_i' = the average d measure in cluster i). The average d measure in each cluster is given by:

$$d' = \frac{\sum\limits_{j=1}^{m}\dfrac{d_{ij}}{V_{ij}}}{\sum\limits_{j=1}^{m}\dfrac{1}{V_{ij}}} \tag{1.9}$$

H_b is distributed as a chi-square with $p - 1$ degrees of freedom. One should also determine whether there is significant heterogeneity within clusters. The within-cluster variability, H_w is $H_t - H_b$. This value is distributed as a chi-square with $k - p$ degrees of freedom.

If H_b is significant, this indicates that the clusters are different (and that the study attribute is probably responsible for the difference). Non-overlapping confidence intervals of the two study clusters indicate statistically significant differences. If H_w is non-significant, one can infer that each cluster contains homogeneous effect sizes and therefore come from common populations. The question remains whether the average d for each cluster represents a statistically significant effect. This is determined, as in the case of the composite effect size, by whether its confidence interval overlaps with zero, 0.00. In cases, when one or more of the clusters show significant within-cluster variability (again using equation 1.4), then another study feature may be identified as possibly responsible for the heterogeneity. The above procedure (equation 1.9) is repeated using the new variable to form clusters of study outcomes, assess between- and within-cluster variability, etc. (The preceding modeling methods to account for study effect size heterogeneity pertain to outcomes from t-, F-, and χ^2 statistics. Analogous methods are applicable to the case of outcomes based on correlation coefficients. The interested reader is referred to Hedges and Olkin, 1985.)

The above technique is based on dividing studies in terms of attributes into categories (e.g., subjects in some studies may come from high SES while other studies may have subjects with low SES). A similar approach can be used with continuous models in which the study attributes are represented by a scale.

Continuous models are tested with unstandardized regression weights in the model (See Johnson, 1989, pp. 21–22; Hedges, 1982).

Rather than modeling approaches to heterogeneity, the meta-analyst can also take a *post-hoc* approach, analogous to *post-hoc* comparisons in analysis of variance. In essence, study effect sizes from the k studies are rank-ordered, and then transformed to U statistics, i.e. standard normal variates. ($U_j = 2c_j$ ($\sqrt{nj}$), where $cj = \log(d + \sqrt{d + 8}) - 1.0536$ and $n = (1/k \, (\Sigma\sqrt{nj}))^2$ where n refers to the number of subjects per group in a given study (if there are unequal n, a conservative approach is to define n by the small n of the two groups.) Differences between the transformed values are determined by specifying the number of steps, between effect sizes (in the rank order). This is obviously an exploratory approach which should be used conservatively, though it may yield useful information for future hypothesis-testing.

Throughout this discussion, studies were assumed to involve contrasts between a treatment group and a control group (or between two different treatments). In behavioral research, independent variables other than the treatment are often employed, as design (blocking) factors or covariates. Pretest/posttest designs may utilize change scores. If all studies in the data set use the same designs than the effect size metric is uniform and all procedures just described are appropriate. It is more often the case, however, that designs vary across studies so that each study involves a different definition of within-cell variance. In general, studies with more complex designs have a smaller standard deviation than simple posttest scores. In such cases, the meta-analyst should transform effect size estimates so that all values used in the analysis employ the same type of standard deviation. Glass, McGraw & Smith (1981) provide formulas that relate standard deviations in various designs to the pooled within-groups standard deviation. For example, in an experimental-control group design with one covariate, the effect size can be transformed (based on raw posttest scores) if the correlation between the covariate and posttest is known. The effect size derived from ANCOVA statistics is multiplied by $\sqrt{1 - r_{xy}^2}$ to yield the desired g(based on raw posttest scores). (Also, the intermediate statistic, V, the sampling variance, should be adjusted. In the example, the adjusted variance = $V(1 - r_{xy}^2)$.)

An example of combined estimation

Suls and Wan (1989) used the Hedges–Olkin approach to examine what kinds of preparatory information are most effective in reducing pain and distress in response to stressful medical procedures and pain. Observing that previous narrative reviews disagreed about the relative merits of information about sensations, procedures, or combined information preparation, Suls and Wan retrieved relevant studies and then aggregated study outcomes bearing on four separate contrasts: sensory information vs procedural information, sensory information vs control (usually attention-placebo), procedural information

Table 1.2. Meta-analytic statistics for comparisons of sensory, procedural, combined, and control conditions (Suls & Wan, 1989)

Outcome category	Sensory vs procedural	Sensory vs control	Procedural vs control	Combined vs control
Negative affect states				
d_+	0.06	0.35	0.25	0.53
95% confidence intervals	$-0.23-+0.36$	$0.07-+0.62$	$-0.13-+0.63$	$0.13-+0.93$
Heterogeneity				
H_t	2.19, ns	31.06, $p < 0.01$	4.11, ns	6.03, ns
Number of studies	7	9	4	5

A positive d_+ indicates that the first condition was associated with more benefits (i.e., in this case lower negative affect than the second condition).

vs control, and combined sensory plus procedural vs control. Studies varied in the outcome variables assessed. Four general outcome classes were formed: negative affect states (measured on mood scales), self-rated pain, other-rated distress (e.g., physician or nurse-ratings of patient distress) and other outcomes. All studies were between-subject in design. Separate meta-analyses were conducted for each contrast (e.g. sensory vs procedural) and for each outcome category (e.g. negative affect states).

As described above, study effect sizes for each outcome were derived from t or F statistics and corrected for small sample bias to yield d values. In those cases when there were multiple outcomes within a category (e.g. two different distress rating scales), outcomes were averaged to yield a single effect size. Then average effect sizes for each outcome category were computed weighting each study effect size by its variance and tests of heterogeneity were computed. Table 1.2 shows a portion of the data from the Suls and Wan meta-analysis.

Combined information was associated with less negative affect than controls ($d_+ = 0.53$), the CI did not include 0.00, and the composite consisted of homogeneous study effect sizes (H_t was non-significant). Sensory information was also associated with less subsequent negative affect ($d_+ = 0.35$, CI $0.07-0.62$), but the study effect sizes were heterogeneous. The other contrasts were neither significant nor heterogeneous.

Because of the heterogeneity of the outcomes for sensory vs controls, we used categorical modeling to determine whether study attributes accounted for the variability. Several attributes were tested, such as sex of sample, lab vs medical setting, using the procedures described above of testing for between- and, if significant, then within-cluster variability. None of the model tests captured any significant amount of variability. As a last resort, *post-hoc* clustering was employed. Although some clusters did emerge, they exhibited no apparent logic. The authors concluded that reasons for the variability for the sensory information empirical tests were unclear.

Suls and Wan's general conclusion, which also applied to other outcome categories (such as self-rated pain), was that the combined treatment performed better than control information with d_+'s between 1.03 to 0.22 and outcomes were homogeneous. This suggested that a combined treatment has moderate beneficial effects which are also relatively consistent across studies. In contrast, sensory information had a small effect and was inconsistent across studies for unknown reasons. The practical implication drawn by Suls and Wan was that a combined preparation is the preferred option for patients undergoing surgery or other painful situations because of the strength and consistency of the combined treatment's effect.

When to use combined probability or combined effect estimation

Which approach is preferable—combined probability or combined estimation? The answer depends on the reviewer's questions and goals, in addition to the nature of the data base being meta-analyzed. Combined probability answers the question whether the null hypothesis is false (i.e. there is a relationship between the independent and dependent variable). It does not provide an index of the size of the relationship. Combined estimation does provide such information, but makes more stringent assumptions. First, all studies should have similar designs and measure the outcome in a similar way. Second, unlike the probability method in which only the p value is required, combined estimation requires indices of study effect size which means that information about standard deviations and cell sizes is required. Unfortunately, empirical reports may not provide such information. For any of these reasons, the meta-analyst may have to rely instead on the combined probability approach.

The present authors recommend combined estimation whenever possible. Ultimately, researchers want to know more than whether the null hypothesis is rejected (after all this only means that any number of non-null hypotheses can be correct). In an early meta-analysis, we were interested in evaluating the efficacy of avoidant and non-avoidant coping strategies in handling stressful events. It became very clear from the start of the undertaking that study samples, stressors, operationalizations of coping strategy use, and adaptation varied so widely and study statistics were reported in such a cursory fashion (i.e. missing values) in some cases that the best we could do was to estimate the combined probability of certain strategies in that quantitative synthesis (Suls & Fletcher, 1985). On the other hand, the empirical literature on information preparation for surgery and pain was relatively uniform in design and analytic statistics thus permitting use of the combined estimation approach (Suls & Wan, 1989).

The problem of missing values does not pertain exclusively to combined estimation. The combined probability method requires an exact p value in order to obtain an exact Z. Commonly, research reports will simply mention there was no significant effect. Without other information, the meta-analyst must estimate the effect conservatively: $p = 0.50$, or a Z of 0.000. Similarly, mention of a "significant effect" may be conservatively estimated as $p = 0.05$, or $Z = 1.645$. The parallel strategy for effect size estimation when no significant effect was reported (and no means or $s.d.$'s) is to enter a study d of 0.00.

The reader may find this an undesirable situation. Fortunately, there are alternative procedures. One might communicate with the primary study author and request the precise values. Alternatively, if cell means and n's are provided, the meta-analyst can reconstruct the original ANOVA table and thereby obtain the unreported F value for the variable of interest and MS error if the article also reports an F-test or interaction for any other independent variable. Reconstruction of missing values is discussed by Glass, McGaw & Smith (1981). Johnson (1989) has developed software and a manual which facilitates such reconstructions. In some instances, however, meta-analysts do have to settle for some conservative values ($p = 0.50$ for non-significant effects or $d = 0.00$) because reconstruction is impossible.

In summary, both combined estimation and combined probability methods are viable options. The choice of the meta-analyst depends on the specific research question and the way empirical tests have been implemented and reported. We should also note that software is available for both methods. Mullen (1989) has software in Basic that is available for computing study effect, creating aggregates, fail-safe numbers, and conducting focused contrasts to test new hypotheses (see below). Johnson (1989) has provided a software counterpart for combined estimation, which, as noted earlier, also helps to reconstruct study effect sizes when they are not directly reported.

CRITICISMS OF META-ANALYSIS

Meta-analysis is not without its critics and the reader should be aware of objections to this research synthesis approach. In our view, many of the criticisms are based on misunderstandings about meta-analytic aims and procedures. There isn't sufficient space to consider all objections and compensating strategies, but we will discuss procedures to overcome the most common criticisms. (See Mullen, 1989, for an excellent discussion of "The most commonly asked questions about meta-analysis".)

One common objection to any review, narrative or quantitative, concerns the quality of selected studies. When faced with the problem of flawed studies or "rotten apples" in a meta-analysis, however, a remediable strategy is to differentially weigh study effect sizes using quality ratings from a set of judges (this is analogous to weighing study effect sizes by sample size; see Rosenthal,

1984, Chapter 3). Alternatively, the meta-analysis may use quality features or quality ratings as categorical (or continuous) models in the testing of between-study outcome heterogeneity. If certain design features, including quality, are consequential then effects should be manifested in heterogeneity across the study sample. The statistics reviewed earlier permit the synthesizer to identify the sources of variability and learn which study features make a difference in overall conclusions.

In regard to the "apples and oranges" problem discussed earlier we can now suggest statistical tests of homogeneity of within-group effect size and tests of misspecification of categorical or continuous models. These provide the meta-analyst with guidelines to judge whether the average effect size does a good job of summarizing results ("are there really apples *and* oranges?") and help to determine what explanatory variables account for variability across study effect outcomes.

Even if there is homogeneity among study effect sizes, the critic might argue that all studies may suffer from the same design flaw so that all the effect sizes in the studies are consistently wrong. Hedges (1990) observes, however, that not all studies are likely to have the same flaws; therefore, if different studies with different design flaws yield consistent results, it is implausible to explain the consistency of the results as a consequence of consistent bias.

One of the knottier problems in meta-analysis is how to address non-independence of outcomes. When non-independent outcomes are treated as independent, standard errors of parameter estimates are affected (Strube, 1985).

Five "solutions" have been suggested to cope with the non-independence problem. The first, really not a solution at all, is to treat each finding as independent, but report it with the qualification that calculations were performed under the assumption of independence. The use of this strategy, however, invariably weighs more those studies with a larger number of reported measures and inflates Type I error rates through its ignorance of intercorrelations. Another solution is to randomly select only one outcome from each study. In some literatures, because of their small size, however, using only one outcome per study would be extremely prohibitive. Moreover, since within a given study one treatment manipulation may yield different effects on different outcome variables, such a strategy can be misleading. Thus, this solution is not often used.

A third alternative to the non-independence problem is to derive a single study effect size by integrating test statistics for each measurement of the same outcome class (for combined probability this would mean averaging Z's within studies before combining results across studies; for combined estimation this would mean averaging the effects sizes of different outcomes within the same study). This option is not appropriate, however, when the outcomes represent different constructs, unless the construct can be assumed to respond identically to the experimental manipulation (Raudenbush, Becker & Kalaian, 1988).

Another common strategy is to conduct separate meta-analyses for the various outcomes. This limits the generality of the hypotheses the researcher may test, however.

A final solution to this issue, developed by Raudenbush et al. (1988) uses a fixed effects, generalized least squares regression approach. A linear regression model is formed employing a matrix of predictor variables with each effect size represented by a separate row of the matrix and each predictor represented by a separate column. This model allows the researcher to test for the significance of the predictors in addition to individual and mean effects. It is, however, limited by its necessity for values of intercorrelations between dependent variables, which many primary studies fail to include. It is also prone to misspecification if the reviewer does not take into account differences across studies measuring different subsets of outcomes (i.e. does not consider differences in moderator variables). Although no data set may be amenable to all of these approaches to non-independence, it is likely one or two can be used. At the least, the meta-analyst must be cautious when drawing conclusions from non-independent outcomes.

META-ANALYTIC EXAMPLES FROM HEALTH PSYCHOLOGY

Table 1.3 is provided to convey the range of questions in health psychology already examined by meta-analytic techniques. Before concluding, we review the brief history of a series of meta-analyses all devoted to the same question, the association between Type A behavior and coronary heart disease. The example helps to illustrate different types of procedures and decision rules and the consequences they have for the conclusions the meta-analyst draws.

There is almost no literature in health psychology that is more controversial than the one pertaining to the purported relationship between the Type A behavior pattern (characterized by competitive achievement-striving, hostility, and time urgency) and coronary heart disease (CHD). Numerous reviews have appeared, but conclusions have been contradictory (Matthews & Haynes, 1986; Dimsdale, 1988). In 1987, Booth-Kewley and Friedman published the first meta-analysis on the Type A–CHD literature. Using a combination of the estimation and probability methods, the authors identified cross-sectional and prospective studies which assessed Type A either through the structured interview (SI) or self-report questionnaires such as the Jenkins Activity Survey (JAS) and Framingham Type A Scale (FTAS) and assessed coronary heart outcomes (global CHD, myocardial infarction, angina, cardiac death, or degree of atherosclerosis). Magnitude of study effects was evaluated by the r effect size index and significance levels were obtained by adding standard normal deviate Z's. Across all measures, Type A was associated with all heart disease outcomes at a probability of $p < 0.000001$; the average $r = 0.112$. Separate analyses using the SI, considered to be the "gold standard" for measuring Type A, revealed a somewhat higher average effect size, $r = 0.197$, and probability that the null

Table 1.3. Representative meta-analyses in health psychology

Authors	Year of publication	Results
Brown	1988	Patient teaching has positive outcomes for diabetic patients.
Pieper, LaCroix & Karasek	1989	Five investigations of 12 555 men showed that blood pressure was related to job decision latitude.
Shinton & Beevers	1989	Risk of stroke is associated with smoking.
Black, Gleser, & Kooyers	1990	Couples programs for weight-loss are superior to subject-alone programs.
Yarnold & Mueser	1989	Type A instruments possess moderate effect strengths in terms of reliability effects.
O'Connor, Buring, Yusuf et al.	1989	Meta-analysis of randomized trials of aerobic exercise programs for MI patients shows a non-significant trend for benefits, however, at least 4400 individuals are required in future clinical trials to distinguish between no effect and the effect obtained in the present meta-analysis.
Fredrikson & Matthews	1990	Essential hypertensives exhibit greater cardiovascular reactivity to behavioral stressors than do normotensives.
Holroyd & Penzien	1990	Both propranolol and biofeedback and relaxation are effective in treating recurrent migraine.
Muldoon, Manuck, & Matthews	1990	Six investigations of cholesterol reduction demonstrate a non-significant trend to lower mortality rates from CHD yet to significant increase in mortality from accidents, violence or suicide.
Kaufmann, Jacob, Ewart, Chesney, Muenz, Doub, & Mercer	1987	Behavioral interventions decrease diastolic blood pressure in nonmedicated patients but not in medicated patients.

hypothesis was wrong, $p < 0.00000001$. However, smaller, self-report measures of Type A were also significantly associated with CHD.

Booth-Kewley and Friedman recognized that cross-sectional studies are causally ambiguous so they also made separate calculations between study outcomes based on prospective and cross-sectional studies. In general, the cross-sectional values based on all Type A measures ($r = 0.156$) were higher than ones for prospective studies ($r = 0.045$) suggesting relations in cross-sectional studies may be inflated. This pattern was duplicated when separate analyses were made for each Type A instrument. The reviewers concluded that there was a small relationship between Type A and CHD, but observed that even modest effects can have important practical implications. The authors also tested whether there were changes over time in the association between Type A and CHD. Regardless of the Type A measure, the average effect size was smaller in pre-1977 studies than in studies published afterward. Whether this was due to historical trends, instrumentation changes, etc., could not be determined.

It should be noted that Booth-Kewley and Friedman's review (1987) possessed a potential bias; mainly that they excluded individuals with fatal MI and sudden death in cross-sectional samples. Such a possible exclusion of important subgroups of patients with CHD from cross-sectional studies attenuates any true relationship between Type A and CHD. Thus, their values may actually have been underestimates of the true relationship.

Although this quantitative review seemed to provide some closure, a meta-analysis devoted to the same subject was published by Matthews (1988) a year later. She re-opened the case because she questioned some of Booth-Kewley and Friedman's decisions about study inclusion and also wished to include the results of four prospective studies which appeared after the earlier meta-analysis was conducted. Matthews was particularly concerned that the earlier meta-analysis had included both cross-sectional and prospective studies. Due to the general problem of cause and effect in cross-sectional designs, the exclusion of subgroups of CHD patients and other related factors, Matthews employed only prospective studies in her update. A second decision was to include only one report per study sample. Unlike the earlier review, where multiple reports (from say two and a half, four and eight-year follow-up) were averaged, Matthews selected one report, the one with the longest follow-up period and largest sample size. The advantage of using the largest sample is clear-cut; the length of follow-up period capitalizes on the fact that CHD is a slowly progressing disease.

Booth-Kewley and Friedman (1987) also did not distinguish between studies of high-risk samples (e.g. patients referred for angiography) and population samples in their analyses. However, studies of these different groups frequently differ in design. Matthews decided that the differences in samples and design required the calculation of different estimates.

Matthews also segregated studies by Type A measures using only those employed frequently in prospective studies—the SI, JAS, and FTAS. However, because Booth-Kewley and Friedman also considered the role of other emotions—notably depression and hostility, prospective studies incorporating these measures were also examined by Matthews. Although Matthews does not emphasize the point, her analysis was devoted exclusively to estimation of the combined probability; no estimates of effect size magnitude were calculated.

Matthews noted that a variety of statistical approaches—chi square, relative risk, univariate, and multivariate are used in research on Type A and CHD. This poses problems in interpreting significance levels. To cope with this problem, Matthews decided to employ univariate tests, whenever possible, because not all studies adjusted for the same risk factors other than Type A. The earlier meta-analysis ignored these study differences and may have created a biased picture, especially with respect to the average effect size.

Because of Matthews' decisions about study inclusion, she employed a much smaller data base (a total of 16 independent significance tests). The analysis of weighted probability levels showed, in contrast to the earlier analysis, that Type A across all measures was not a predictor of CHD ($p = 0.261$), but there was an association when Type A was measured by the SI ($p = 0.001$). Results also showed that Type A (all measures) predicted CHD in population samples ($p = 0.001$), but not in high risk samples ($p = 0.552$).

The difference in results with Booth-Kewley and Friedman (1987) demonstrate that meta-analytic results can differ substantially depending on decisions regarding study inclusion criteria made by the analyst. As Matthews (1988) observed:

> As with any method of review, it (meta-analysis) depends on the analytical steps determined by the scientist. In fact, meta-analysis encourages the articulation of those assumptions that often go unstated in an enumerative review (p. 379).

Beyond their methodological significance, Matthew's substantive differences indicate that the kind of Type A measure is critical and that the Type A-disease process does not operate in the same fashion in high risk and population samples.

The story does not end here, however, because a third meta-analytic review has recently appeared. Miller et al. (1991) were particularly interested in determining why prior to 1979 the findings of most (cross-sectional and prospective) studies found a relationship between Type A and CHD, but null findings predominated after that time. Miller et al. employed meta-analyses in combination with other techniques to explore reasons for the trend toward null findings and more generally to explain the main contradictory findings.

As Booth-Kewley and Friedman, Miller et al. obtained a sample of cross-sectional and prospective studies and calculated effect sizes. However, instead of using the Pearson r, they opted for the biserial or tetrachoric r; both are more appropriate when either one or both of the variables are dichotomous. Miller et al. were concerned that because the base rate of CHD is generally low, but obviously higher in high-risk study sample and 50% in case-control studies, Pearson r would consequently vary across type of study design even if the actual magnitude of association was the same. The biserial and tetrachoric correlations avoid the base-rate problem because these correlations are estimates of what the Pearson correlation would be if the variables were continuous instead of dichotomous. Miller et al. also weighted Z's by sample size and, unlike prior reviews, tested for the heterogeneity of the composite effect sizes.

The most notable feature of Miller et al.'s review was, however, their testing for disease-based spectrum bias to account for the trend toward null results. This bias refers to the fact that when researchers enroll only high-risk subjects with CHD or suspected CHD, as in high risk samples, the range is restricted, which consequently reduces the possibility of detecting a significant correlation between the two variables, i.e. disease and Type A. To the extent that recent studies have relied on high-risk samples, a recent trend for null effects may simply represent range attenuation.

To examine this notion, Miller et al. evaluated the Type A–CHD association across high risk vs population samples. They also employed meta-analysis to assess the relative percentage of Type A in high risk vs population samples across studies. If disease-based spectrum bias was present then high risk samples should consist of a larger proportion of Type A's. Miller et al. also estimated the reduction in the magnitude of the correlation that would be produced by range restriction in high risk studies. This was done by estimating the likely attenuation in correlation created by range restriction. The range restriction correlation presented in Alexander et al. (1985) was employed to make these estimates. (Other range restriction formulas for meta-analysis are given by Hunter & Schmidt (1990).) The important parameters needed for this formula were the percentage of healthy subjects expected to incur MI's in the future and the correlation between Type A and MI in a healthy population. Both values were taken from the largest population study, the Western Collaborative Group Study (Rosenman et al., 1975). Then Miller et al. compared the correlations obtained from the range restriction formula with the actual correlation between Type A and CHD in high risk studies.

The notion that the disease-based spectrum bias explains the null trend was indicated by the following findings: (a) smaller composite effect sizes were found in high-risk samples than in population samples; (b) there was a higher proportion of Type A's in high-risk studies; and (c) the range restriction formulas accurately estimated the actual correlations found in high-risk sample studies. Miller et al.'s review also found, consistent with their suppositions, that recent studies have tended to be high-risk studies, therefore accounting for the temporal trend observed by Booth-Kewley and Friedman (1987). Miller et al. also found that Type A was a reliable predictor of non-fatal CHD, not of fatal MI. Furthermore, the relationship between Type A and CHD was larger than those found in any other review but space does not permit us to consider these findings in detail.

For present purposes, the most significant implication of Miller et al.'s results and that of the earlier meta-analyses regarding Type A and CHD is that the nature of decision-rules about study inclusions and outcome aggregation are integral to the conclusions obtained. Furthermore, the recent analyses provide excellent examples of how quantitative research synthesis works best when coupled with conceptual qualitative analysis.

QUESTIONS TO ASK ABOUT A META-ANALYSIS

Before concluding, a list of questions is provided to the reader. Although the list is not exhaustive, these are the main issues to consider in evaluating an author's meta-analytic conclusions:

1. What type of meta-analysis was employed—combined probability or combined magnitude—and did the meta-analyst provide a rationale for the approach adopted?
2. If combined estimation was used, what was the index of effect size and why was this chosen?
3. Were study effect sizes adjusted for sample size or weighted for any other considerations (such as reliability of measures)?
4. Did the meta-analyst test for homogeneity of the study effect sizes before calculating a composite index?
5. What was done about missing values, either p-values for combined probability approach or means, $s.d.$s, etc. for combined estimation?
6. Were multiple (non-independent) values included in the meta-analyses, only a single value used, a superordinate value created, or were there adjustments for non-independence of outcomes?
7. Did the meta-analyst provide a fail-safe number?
8. What sort of study attribute coding was conducted to assess whether study features account for across-study variations?
9. If outcomes were heterogeneous, what sorts of modeling were used to identify homogeneous study clusters? And did study attributes capture the across study variability?

The underlying goals of a meta-analysis are test-hypothesis generation and theory construction. The meta-analyst's conclusions concerning these goals are directly related to the decision rules he or she formed and the procedures he or she applied. Thus, answers to the previous questions are some of the key issues in differentiating a good meta-analytic review from a poor review. They are essential issues in deciding if the reviewer's conclusions are valid and justified.

CONCLUSIONS

This chapter has introduced meta-analysis as a viable method for the integration and assessment of the literature in health psychology. The basic logic and techniques used in two forms of meta-analysis, combined probability and combined estimation, were presented in addition to critical issues surrounding such procedures and strategies with which one can adequately overcome the potential shortcomings. The examples of meta-analysis pre-sented illustrated the increased role that this approach has already achieved within the realm of health psychology. Finally, the importance of meta-analysis is demonstrated as a tool for the assessment and synthesis of a given data base to generate new directions and new hypotheses to increase and better define particular areas of study.

ACKNOWLEDGMENTS

The writing of this paper was supported in part by NIH grant 46448. The authors thank Todd Miller, Rene M. Alt and two anonymous reviewers for their helpful comments on an earlier draft of the paper.

REFERENCES

Alexander, R. A., Carson, K. P., Alliger, G. M. & Barrett, G. V. (1985). Further power considerations for the power to detect nonzero validity coefficients under range restriction. *Journal of Applied Psychology*, 70, 451–460.
Bangert-Drowns, R. L. (1986). Review of developments in meta-analytic method. *Psychological Bulletin*, 99, 388–399.
Baum, M. L., Anish, D. S., Chalmers, T. C., Sacks, H. S., Smith, H., Jr. & Fagerstom, R. M. (1981). A survey of clinical trials of antibiotic prophylaxis in colon surgery: Evidence against further use of no-treatment controls. *New England Journal of Medicine*, 305, 795–799.
Black, D. R., Gleser, L. J. & Kooyers, K. J. (1990). A meta-analytic evaluation of couples weight-loss programs. *Health Psychology*, 9, 330–347.
Booth-Kewley, S. & Friedman, H. S. (1987). Psychological predictors of heart disease: A quantitative review. *Psychological Bulletin*, 101, 343–362.
Brown, S. A. (1988). Effects of educational interventions in diabetes care: A meta-analysis of findings. *Nursing Research*, 37, 223–230.
Bryant, F. B. & Wortman, P. M. (1984). Methodological issues in the meta-analysis of quasi-experiments. In W. H. Yeaton & P. M. Wortman (Eds) *Issues in Data Synthesis*. (pp. 5–24). San Francisco, CA: Jossey-Bass, Inc.
Canner, P. L. (1983). Aspirin in coronary heart disease: A comparison of six clinical trials. *Israel Journal of Medical Sciences*, 19, 413–423.
Cohen, J. (1977). *Statistical Power Analysis For The Behavioral Sciences* (Rev. Ed). New York: Academic Press.
Cooper, H. M. (1990). On the social psychology of using research reviews. In K. W. Wachter & M. L. Staf (Eds) *The Future Of Meta-Analysis* (pp. 89–98). New York: Russell Sage Foundation.
Cooper, H. M. & Rosenthal, R. (1980). Statistical versus traditional procedures for summarizing research findings. *Psychological Bulletin*, 87, 442–449.
Dimsdale, J. E. (1988). A perspective on Type A behavior and coronary disease. *New England Journal of Medicine*, 318, 110–112.
Einarson, T. R., Leeder, J. S. & Koren, G. (1988). A method for meta-analysis of epidemiological studies. *Pharmacoepidemiology*, 22, 813–824.
Fredrikson, M. & Matthews, K. M. (1990). Cardiovascular responses to behavioral stress and hypertension: A meta-analytic review. *Annals of Behavioral Medicine*, 12, 30–39.
Friedman, H. S. & Booth-Kewley, S. (1987). The "disease-prone" personality: A meta-analytic view of the construct. *American Psychologist*, 42, 539–555.
Gibbons, R. D. & Bock, R. D. (1987). Trend in correlated proportions. *Psychometrika*, 52, 113–124.

Glass, G. V. (1976). Primary, secondary, and meta-analysis of research. *Educational Researcher*, 5, 3–8.

Glass, G. V., McGaw, B. & Smith, M. L. (1981). *Meta-Analysis in Social Research*. Beverly Hills, CA: Sage Publications.

Hedeker, D., Gibbons, R. D. & Davis, J. M. (1991). Random regression models for multicenter clinical trials data. *Psychopharmacology Bulletin*, 27, 73–77.

Hedges, L. (1981). Distribution theory of Glass's estimator of effect size and related estimates. *Journal of Educational Statistics*, 6, 107–128.

Hedges, L. V. (1982). Fitting continuous models to effect size data. *Journal of Educational Statistics*, 7, 245–270.

Hedges, L. V. (1989). Meta-analysis of related research. In N. Schneiderman, S. M. Weiss & P. G. Kaufmann (Eds), *Handbook of Research Methods in Cardiovascular Behavioral Medicine* (pp. 647–663). New York: Plenum.

Hedges, L. V. (1990). Directions for future methodology. In K. W. Wachter & M. L. Straf (Eds), *The Future of Meta-Analysis* (pp. 11–26). New York: Russell Sage Foundation.

Hedges, L. V. & Olkin, I. (1985). *Statistical Method for Meta-Analysis*. Orlando, FL: Academic Press.

Holroyd, K. A. & Penzien, D. B. (1990). Pharmacological versus non-pharmacological prophylaxis of recurrent migraine headache: a meta-analytic review of clinical trials. *Pain*, 42, 1–13.

Hunter, J. E., Schmidt, F. & Jackson, G. B. (1983). *Meta-Analysis: Cumulating Research Findings Across Studies*. Beverly Hills, CA: Sage Publications.

Hunter, J. E. & Schmidt, F. L. (1990). *Methods of Meta-Analysis*. Newbury Park: Sage Publications.

Johnson, B. T. (1989). *DSTAT: Software for the Meta-Analytic Review of Research Literatures*. Hillsdale, NJ: Lawrence Erlbaum Associates.

Kaufmann, P. G., Jacob, R. G., Ewart, C. K., Chesney, M. A., Muenz, L. R., Doub, N. & Mercer, W. (1988). Hypertension intervention pooling project. Fifth joint USA–USSR symposium on arterial hypertension. *Health Psychology*, 7 (Suppl.), 209–224.

Light, R. J. & Pillemer, D. B. (1984). *Summing Up*. Cambridge, MA: Harvard University Press.

Matthews, K. A. (1988). Coronary heart disease and Type A behaviors: Update on and alternative to the Booth-Kewley and Friedman (1987) quantitative review. *Psychological Bulletin*, 104, 373–380.

Matthews, K. A. & Haynes, S. G. (1986). Type A behavior pattern and coronary risk: Update and critical evaluation. *American Journal of Epidemiology*, 123, 923–960.

Miller, T. Q., Turner, C. W., Tindale, R. S., Posavac, E. J. & Dugoni, B. L. (1991). Reasons for the trend toward null findings in research on Type A behavior. *Psychological Bulletin*, 110, 469–486.

Mintz, J. (1983). Integrating research evidence: A commentary on meta-analysis. *Journal of Consulting and Clinical Psychology*, 51, 71–75.

Mosteller, F. M. & Bush, R. R. (1954). Selected quantitative techniques. In G. Lindzey (Ed.), *Handbook of Social Psychology* (Vol. 1) (pp. 289–334). Cambridge, MA: Addison-Wesley.

Muldoon, M. F., Manuck, S. B. & Matthews, K. A. (1990). Lowering holesterol concentrations and mortality: A quantitative review of primary prevention trials. *British Medical Journal*, 301, 309–314.

Mullen, B. (1989). *Advanced BASIC Meta-Analysis: Procedures and Programs*. Hillsdale, NJ: Lawrence Erlbaum Associates.

O'Connor, G. T., Buring, J. E., Yusuf, S., Goldhaber, S. Z., Olmstead, E. M.,

Paffenberger, R. S. & Hennekens, C. H. (1989). An overview of randomized trials of rehabilitation with exercise after myocardial infarction. *Circulation*, **80**, 234–244.

Orwin, R. (1983). A fail-safe N for effect size in meta-analysis. *Journal of Educational Statistics*, **8**, 157–159.

Pearson, K. (1933). On a method of determining whether a sample of given size *n* supposed to have been drawn from a parent population having a known population integral has probably been drawn at random. *Biometrika*, **25**, 379–410.

Pieper, C., LaCroix, L. Z. & Karasek, R. A. (1989). The relation of psychosocial dimensions of work with coronary heart disease risk factors: A meta-analysis of five United States data bases. *American Journal of Epidemiology*, **129**, 483–494.

Presby, S. (1978). Overly broad categories obscure important differences between therapies. *American Psychologist*, **33**, 514–515.

Raju, N. S., Burke, M. J., Normand, J. & Langlois, G. M. (1991). A new meta-analytic approach. *Journal of Applied Psychology*, **76**, 432–446.

Raudenbush, S. W., Becker, B. J. & Kalaian, H. (1988). Modeling multivariate effect sizes. *Psychological Bulletin*, **103**, 111–120.

Rosenman, R. H., Brand, R., Jenkins, C. D., Friedman, M., Straus, R. & Wurm, M. (1975). Coronary heart disease in the Western Collaborative Group Study: Final follow-up of 8.5 years. *Journal of the American Medical Association*, **233**, 872–877.

Rosenthal, R. (1978). Combining results of independent studies. *Psychological Bulletin*, **85**, 185–193.

Rosenthal, R. (1979). The "file-drawer-problem" and tolerance for null results. *Psychological Bulletin*, **86**, 638–644.

Rosenthal, R. (1984). *Meta-analytic Procedures for Social Research*. Beverly Hills, CA: Sage.

Rosenthal, R. (1990). An evaluation of procedure and results. In K. W. Wachter & M. L. Straf (Eds), *The Future of Meta-Analysis* (pp. 123–134). New York: Russell Sage Foundation.

Shinton, R. & Beevers, G. (1989). Meta-analysis of relation between cigarette smoking and stroke. *British Medical Journal*, **298**, 789–794.

Smith, M. L., Glass, G. V. & Miller, T. I. (1980). *The Benefits of Psychotherapy*. Baltimore: Johns Hopkins University Press.

Strube, M. J. (1985). Combining and comparing significance levels for nonindependent hypothesis tests. *Psychological Bulletin*. **97**, 334–341.

Strube, M. J. & Hartmann, D. P. (1983). Meta-analysis techniques, applications and functions. *Journal of Consulting and Clinical Psychology*, **51**, 14–27.

Suls, J. & Fletcher, B. (1985). The relative efficacy of avoidant and nonavoidant coping strategies: A meta-analysis. *Health Psychology*, **4**, 249–288.

Suls, J. & Wan, C. K. (1989). Effects of sensory and procedural information on coping with stressful medical procedures and pain: A meta-analysis. *Journal of Consulting and Clinical Psychology*, **57**, 372–379.

Wachter, K. W. & Straf, W. L. (1990). Introduction. In K. W. Wachter & M. L. Straf (Eds), *The Future of Meta-Analysis* (pp. xiii–xxviii). New York: Russell Sage Foundation.

Wilson, G. T. & Rachman, S. J. (1983). Meta-analysis and the evaluation of psychotherapy outcome: Limitations and Liabilities. *Journal of Consulting and Clinical Psychology*, **51**, 54–64.

Yarnold, P. R. & Mueser, K. Y. (1989). Meta-analyses of the reliability of Type A behavioral measures. *British Journal of Medical Psychology*, **62**, 43–50.

Yeaton, W. H. & Wortman, P. M. (1984). Evaluation issues in medical research synthesis. In W. H. Yeaton & P. M. Wortman (Eds), *Issues in Data Synthesis* (pp. 43–56). San Francisco, CA: Jossey-Bass.

2 Illness Cognition

ROBERT T. CROYLE, STEVEN D. BARGER
Department of Psychology, University of Utah, Salt Lake City, UT 84112.
Electronic correspondence: Internet, RTCROYLE@CC.UTAH.EDU, Bitnet,
RTCROYLE@UTAHCCA.BITNET.

When John gets sick, he thinks about his illness. He notices his symptoms and uses them to guess the type of disease he might have. He wonders what caused the illness, and how best to treat it. He thinks about how long it will last and how it will affect his work schedule. And, in most cases, he discusses it with others.

Most of us are like John. Rather than being passive victims of illness, we actively process, evaluate, and act upon illness-related information. Croyle and Ditto (1990) defined illness cognition as "any mental activity (e.g. appraisal, interpretation, recall) undertaken by an individual who believes himself or herself to be ill, regarding the state of his or her health and its possible remedies" (p. 32). This definition was derived from Kasl & Cobb's (1966) definition of illness behavior: "any activity undertaken by an individual, who believes himself to be ill, to define the state of his health and discover a suitable remedy."

Although Croyle and Ditto's definition is rather broad, it still does not capture the entire range of research topics that fall under the heading of illness cognition. Many of the studies to be described in this chapter, for example, employ healthy subjects who are asked to form judgments about symptoms or illnesses that they do not have. These data are used to formulate hypotheses about the judgmental processes that are likely to occur when a symptom or sign is discovered. In addition, illness-related beliefs can influence many behaviors that fall outside the traditional definition of illness behavior. Discrimination against AIDS victims, for example, might be related to one's beliefs about the causes of AIDS.

In this paper, we will review some of the recent developments in illness cognition research. We should note at the outset that the review is not comprehensive. The focus here is on basic research conducted by health psychologists. Medical anthropologists and medical sociologists have made significant empirical and theoretical contributions to the study of illness cognition, but these will not be reviewed here (see Chrisman & Kleinman, 1983;

International Review of Health Psychology. Volume 2. Edited by S. Maes, H. Leventhal and M. Johnston
© 1993 John Wiley & Sons Ltd

Farmer & Good, 1991; Mechanic, 1978). Although health psychologists are relative newcomers to the study of illness cognition, the use of experimental research designs and psychological theories has given their work a distinctive flavor. No doubt many of our colleagues in the social sciences would view much of this work as reductionistic and sterile. We hope to demonstrate, however, that the psychological study of illness cognition provides one of the best opportunities for true interdisciplinary collaboration and communication with our academic cousins. Despite our peculiar methods and our interest in the individual level of analysis, the study of illness cognition shares with medical anthropology and medical sociology a fundamental concern with the *meaning* of illness. There is no reason why this common interest cannot bring us closer together in our attempts to understand this fascinating domain of human experience.

This review is organized around two aspects of illness cognition, structure and dynamics. After first reviewing the development of illness representation research, we discuss research that has examined the underlying structure of illness representations. This research includes factor, cluster, and multidimensional scaling analyses of subjects' judgments of illness-related stimuli. We then shift attention toward the dynamic aspects of illness cognition. Studies that have examined illness-related judgments are described. Many of these suggest that illness appraisal is influenced by motives and heuristics. Within this context, we describe work from our own laboratory concerning the cognitive appraisal of risk factor information. Finally, we briefly review findings from research concerning illness-related attribution and social comparison.

A VERY SHORT HISTORY

Skelton & Croyle (1991a) have argued that 1980 was a critical date in the short history of illness cognition. That was the year that Howard Leventhal and his students (Leventhal, Meyer & Nerenz, 1980) published a paper that described a new approach to the study of health and illness behavior. In "The Commonsense Representation of Illness Danger" these authors proposed a framework for understanding health threat appraisal and illness behavior that was quite different than the models that had dominated behavioral medicine and health psychology. They argued that patients' implicit theories of their illnesses mediate behavioral responses to health threats. The problem of noncompliance with treatment regimens was used as a context within which to explain how commonsense beliefs account for apparently idiosyncratic responses to illness.

Leventhal et al.'s advocacy of the study of illness representation as a strategy for understanding the complexities of illness behavior and coping has stimulated much of the work on illness cognition over the past decade (Skelton & Croyle, 1991b). The mental representation perspective provided a welcome alternative to two of the dominant approaches to studying patient compliance. One of these was the Health Belief Model (Becker, 1974; Rosenstock, 1990), originally developed to explain the failure of individuals to participate in screening and inoculation programs. A second was the atheoretical, exploratory approach used by investigators who attempted to relate compliance to any of a variety of demographic and personality variables. The mental representation approach was later incorporated into a self-regulation model of illness appraisal and behavior (Leventhal, Nerenz & Steele, 1984), which will be described in more detail below.

Turk, Rudy & Salovey (1986) described the mental representation perspective in health psychology as follows:

> There is an increasing recognition that the presence of physiological perturbations is evaluated against some implicit or "common-sense" representations of illness. Individuals seem to appraise their condition and decide whether a particular sensation is a symptom of physical disorder that requires medical attention by matching sensations to some preexisting implicit model of illness. These representations of illness are believed to be of major importance in defining the illness experience and in determining the relevance, organization, and interpretation of health, illness, and treatment information. Thus, to some extent, each individual functions within a uniquely constructed reality, based on prior experience, including societal and cultural transmission of beliefs and expectancies concerning health and illness. (References excluded, p. 454)

STRUCTURE AND CONTENT OF ILLNESS REPRESENTATIONS

One aspect of health psychologists' investigations of illness representations that distinguishes them from medical anthropologists is a reliance (some would say dependence) on sophisticated statistical techniques. This reliance has both advantages and disadvantages, many of which have been discussed elsewhere (e.g. Leventhal & Nerenz, 1985). One of the disadvantages is that the output of a structural analysis can depend a great deal on the sample of stimuli chosen by the investigator. This is an especially important problem in the illness domain, where the universe of stimuli is both large and diverse. Investigators' assumptions concerning structural dimensions can influence their selection of the small subset of symptoms, illnesses or diseases presented to subjects. Under such conditions, hypotheses are more likely to be confirmed than not. The present reviewers, along with others, find another troubling disadvantage. Slightly different analysis techniques can produce very different results, and these differences may be difficult to interpret. Given that the relevant studies vary on several methodological dimensions, we are faced with a task similar to that of disentangling one large, confounded experiment. Fortunately, the results of several of the studies are consistent.

One of the earliest investigators was Jenkins (1966; Jenkins & Zyzanski, 1968), who used factor analysis to examine illness representations. He used a semantic differential scale consisting of 16 questions thought to relate to illness (e.g. susceptibility, seriousness, preventability). This work revealed three illness dimensions thought to represent all diseases. These factors were labeled personal involvement, human mastery, and social desirability. Although this work was among the earliest empirical studies of how people think about illness, its reliance on organizing illness information into 16 dimensions and its use of single-item scales to measure higher-order constructs has been criticized (Turk, Rudy & Salovey, 1986).

Around the same time, Leventhal and his colleagues (Leventhal, Jones & Trembly, 1966; Leventhal, Watts & Pagano, 1967) were examining the persuasive effects of a fear-arousing communication. They found that providing message recipients with an action plan for changing a variety of health behaviors (getting tetanus shots, quitting smoking) made the level of fear in the persuasive message irrelevant. Both high and low fear appeals were effective over a relatively long period of time (e.g. three months) if an action plan was included. They subsequently inferred that a change in the way the particular threat was understood or represented must have occurred (Leventhal, 1970, 1975). This implied that understanding how people process information in response to health threats or warnings was crucial in uncovering one's representation of the threat (for a review, see Leventhal & Diefenbach, 1991). This representation has broad implications, from seeking medical advice (is that a swollen gland or do I have a tumor?) to receiving health care (I can't get help because hospital staff are afraid they will become ill).

Leventhal (1980, 1984) and his associates offered a model for the structure of illness representations. The four components they identified were identity, cause, time line, and consequences. Identity refers to the label one gives to the disease, and cause refers to what the person feels is responsible for the disease. Time line refers to the individual's notion of how long the disease is likely to last. Three common time lines observed in these studies are acute, cyclic, and chronic. According to Leventhal & Diefenbach (1991), clustering of symptoms will usually lead to an initial diagnosis or the identity label. Conversely, given a label, a person will expect to experience certain symptoms. For example, a study of people with high blood pressure found that even though 80% of them agreed that people cannot tell when their blood pressure is up, 88% believed that *their* symptoms reflected changes in blood pressure (Meyer, Leventhal & Gutmann, 1985). This difference could reflect an actor/observer bias, or a *post-hoc* search for symptoms that vary as a function of the underlying disorder. (The authors would like to thank an anonymous reviewer for this suggestion.)

Lau & Hartman (1983) provided further support for Leventhal's framework. Undergraduate subjects reported on the last time they were sick ("sick" was not explicitly defined). They described why they got sick and why they got better in both their own words (open-ended) and on seven-point bipolar attribution scales. The open-ended responses were independently coded. Even though participants were not asked to label their disease, 49% spontaneously mentioned the name of the illness or disease. Thirty-seven percent described the symptoms. Lau and Hartman argued that this provides support for the identity and consequences components of Leventhal's model. However, as only 26% of the respondents mentioned anything about the longevity of the disease, they suggested that time line is the weakest component of this model.

Another perspective on illness representation draws from basic research in the field of social cognition. Like Leventhal, Bishop (1991) views an individual's existing cognitive structures as a source of meaning for his or her illness experience. He uses the prototype construct (Rosch, 1978; Cantor & Mischel, 1977) as a model for this cognitive structure. Generally, prototypes refer to organized and reasonably stable knowledge about certain kinds of stimuli. Specifically, prototypes are idealized standards retrieved from memory to which people compare physical symptoms. Symptoms are subsequently interpreted based on a comparison of one's current physical state to memory of other patterns (exemplars) of certain illnesses. The selection of a prototype is not contingent on a perfect fit between the symptoms and the prototype; rather, there need be only enough resemblance to make the selection a plausible interpretation (Bishop, 1991). Again, how an illness is interpreted (am I having a heart attack or indigestion?) can affect decisions by the person experiencing a problem as well as decisions by significant others (physician, spouse, etc.).

Bishop & Converse (1986) pretested the perceived association between various symptoms and diseases to obtain "prototypical" symptom sets. They found that high prototype symptom sets were more likely to be rated as an indication of disease than were low or medium prototype or random sets. These subjects, when asked to identify the disease and state their confidence in their judgment, were more accurate and more confident for the high prototype sets. In a second study (Bishop & Converse, 1986), subjects were presented with symptom sets varying in prototypicality and were later asked to recall the symptoms. Subjects correctly recalled more symptoms for the high prototypical sets than for low prototypical or random sets. Further, low prototypical subjects tended to recall more symptoms congruent with their prototype for the disease in question. This effect was pronounced for those given a label (an explicit diagnosis) for the disease. This recall of prototype-consistent information and neglect of inconsistent information is a central feature of this kind of processing.

Another implication of the prototype model is that a closer fit between a prototype and symptoms should facilitate processing of the symptom information. When subjects were asked to judge whether or not symptom sets varying in prototypicality were representative of a specific disease, they were faster in making these decisions for high prototypic sets than for medium, low, or random sets. This evidence suggests that disease prototypes influence the identification of disease states, the recall of information about illness episodes, and the processing of those episodes (Bishop, 1991). These cognitive structures therefore have a significant impact on what kinds of symptoms are reported as well as on the illness experience itself.

Leventhal & Diefenbach (1991) make explicit the attribution process involved in comparing symptoms to representations in memory. According to Leventhal, if the memorial representation is sufficiently "clear," and the present feels sufficiently like the past, a self-diagnosis identical to the past illness episode is probable. In contrast to Bishop, Leventhal believes that a sufficiently "clear" memorial representation, to which the current symptoms will be compared, will likely be a specific illness episode rather than a more general prototype. He further states that matching to a prototype rather than a specific illness memory would result in more ambiguous outcomes, and that this uncertainty would motivate additional and more active search efforts. Perhaps both investigators are correct. It may be that only frequently experienced illness, such as the flu, stimulate the development of prototypes. Severe or unusual episodes, however, may serve as a direct basis for comparison. These hypotheses await empirical confirmation.

Turk, Rudy & Salovey (1986) provided another look at individual common-sense illness models. They sought to examine the dimensional structure that organizes an individual's commonsense illness schemata. Like Leventhal, they sought to determine if a generic illness representation could be empirically demonstrated, and they also sought to examine its consistency over a variety of populations, diseases, and actual experiences with a specific illness. Across health characteristics (diabetics, healthy nurses and college students) and diseases (flu, diabetes, cancer), their data revealed a four-dimensional structure of illnesses composed of seriousness, personal responsibility, controllability, and changeability. This factor analytic solution was confirmed on a second sample of subjects drawn from the same population. They suggest that this factor structure represents a general implicit model of illness, and that its divergence from the categories of Leventhal, Lau and others argues against a method variance interpretation. However, as Bishop (1991) has noted, the examination of *components* of disease representations relies on different assumptions and methods than does the examination of *dimensions*. The former generally relies on free descriptions of illness, while the latter tends to utilize scale ratings. Further, the two approaches are divergent in that the dimensions (factor analytic) approach examines differences in disease concep-tualization while the components approach examines the shared features of disease representations (Lau, Bernard & Hartmen, 1989, cited in Bishop, 1991). Thus, it is plausible to state that these different approaches do indeed examine complementary aspects of the same phenomena (Bishop, 1991).

This raises the important question of *how* to study illness cognition statistically. Three methods have been utilized: factor analysis, cluster analysis, and multidimensional scaling (MDS). All models generally use Euclidean space (Schiffman, Reynolds & Young, 1981; SPSS^x User's Guide, 1986), but they differ in how that space is organized. Cluster analysis clusters items together based on similarity (or dissimilarity) to one or more variables. Factor analysis and multidimensional scaling both refer to a set of procedures to analyze multivariate data sets. However, factor analysis is based on the angles between vectors (hence we "rotate" factors) while MDS is based on distances between points (Schiffman, Reynolds & Young, 1981). Further, as most factor analytic procedures assume that the observed variables are linear combinations of some underlying factors (Kim & Mueller, 1978), they often result in a relatively large number of dimensions. MDS does not make this assumption, and ". . . normally provides more readily interpretable solutions of lower dimensionality" (Schiffman, Reynolds & Young, 1981, p. 13). Cluster analysis is hierarchical, while factor analysis and MDS are geometric in structure.

DYNAMICS OF ILLNESS COGNITION

Research on the appraisal of health threats has a long history. In this section, we highlight some recent theory and experimental research concerning the appraisal process. We distinguish studies examining reactions to illness or disease *signs* (such as a medical test result) from those concerned with appraisals of *symptoms*. Theory and research in these domains has been influenced by social psychological studies of motivated judgment (Croyle, 1992). As will become clear below, recent research on the cognitive appraisal of health threats has shown that health-related judgments, like self-related attributions, are biased by motives and heuristics.

Appraisal of signs

Clinical observations of medical patients have long suggested that minimization and denial can occur when individuals are first informed about a medical condition (e.g. Janis, 1958). These coping strategies have resisted experimental examination in the medical context because health status cannot be manipulated. From a psychological perspective, however, numerous insights can be gained if *subjective* health status is varied. Many health disorders have no physical symptoms, and in these cases an individual first becomes aware of an illness via the communication of a test result or diagnosis.

Jemmott, Ditto & Croyle (1986) developed an experimental paradigm for studying initial appraisals of illness signs. In several studies, they have examined a variety of factors thought to be important in mediating or moderating reactions to health threat. In their paradigm, subjects are tested for "Thioamine Acetylase (TAA) Enzyme Deficiency." Although the enzyme is fictitious, subjects are told that the condition was recently found by medical researchers to be a risk factor for the development of pancreatic disorders (for a more complete discussion of the paradigm and its limitations, see Croyle & Ditto, 1990). Participants are asked to provide a saliva sample, which is then tested using a "TAA Enzyme Test Strip" (actually a urinary glucose test strip). Because participants are first asked to rinse their mouth with mouthwash containing dextrose, the test strip changes color when immersed in the subject's saliva. The meaning of the color change is experimentally manipulated. Participants who are randomly assigned to the positive test group are told that a color change indicates TAA deficiency. Because the paradigm utilizes deception, it has only been used to examine immediate responses to diagnostic information.

The first study that used the paradigm (Jemmott, Ditto and Croyle, 1986) found evidence of minimization in threat appraisals. Subjects who tested positive for the risk factor rated it as a less serious threat to health than did those who tested negative. The same pattern of results was obtained for judgments of the accuracy of the enzyme test; positive-result subjects rated the test as less accurate. The authors suggested that self-defensive motivational processes biased these judgments, as the tendency to rate the test as less accurate was greater when the subject believed that they were the only ones who received a positive test result.

Follow-up studies have replicated the minimization effect and have ruled out alternative explanations. Croyle & Sande (1988) showed, for example, that lower seriousness judgments were not due to positive-test subjects' inability to uncover confirming symptoms. Labeling actually increased symptom reporting and reporting of risk behaviors, a finding that has been observed in other experimental studies (Baumann & Keller, 1991; Baumann et al., 1989). Ditto, Jemmott & Darley (1988) manipulated information regarding treatability and found additional support for the denial explanation. Whereas a rational processor would be expected to perceive an easily treatable condition as less serious, Ditto et al. found that treatability information led positive-test subjects to appraise the condition as more serious. They argued that treatability information removed the motive for denial. As would be expected, the opposite pattern was observed among subjects who were not threatened with a positive test result. Subjects who tested negative for the enzyme deficiency appraised the condition as more serious when treatment information was absent.

Another bias reported by these investigators is the false consensus effect (Ross, Greene & House, 1977). This effect refers to the tendency to overestimate the commonality of one's behaviors or characteristics, in this case having a particular illness (see Marks & Miller, 1987, for a review). Individuals who have tested positive for TAA deficiency perceived the disorder as more prevalent than those who tested negative (Croyle & Sande, 1988). This effect has been replicated with actual disorders experienced by both college students and physicians (Croyle, Sun & Louie, 1992; Jemmott, Croyle & Ditto, 1988).

In addition to perceived seriousness and prevalence, other components of illness representations are also affected by diagnostic information. Croyle (1990) examined appraisals of hypertension among subjects who received randomly assigned feedback on a blood pressure test. After test results were communicated, subjects were asked to report their beliefs concerning the time course of hypertension. Time-lines were significantly affected by test results. Those who received high blood pressure feedback were less likely to endorse a chronic model of hypertension. Time-line beliefs were also related to seriousness appraisals. Subjects who minimized the seriousness of high blood pressure were also those most likely to endorse an acute model of the disorder (see Croyle & Jemmott, 1991, for a review of other studies of risk factor screening).

Appraisal of symptoms

Given that labeling has effects on various aspects of illness representations, what is the impact of more general cognitive processing on symptoms and their interpretation? To what extent does the individual's history or environment determine subsequent illness judgments? For example, college students asked to judge whether a set of hypothetical symptoms they experienced were due to stress or illness were more likely to conclude they were ill when the judgment was made the day before their psychology mid-term exam than before an open weekend (Baumann et al., 1989). It is clear that higher-order cognitive processes influence symptom interpretation (see also Pennebaker,1982).

Leventhal (1986) offers a bio-psychological model of symptom processing. If one agrees that processing of symptoms is similar to processing within other sensory modalities (Pennebaker, 1982), then we would expect the formation of cognitive structures (illness representations) through integration of sensory and memory codes. Leventhal suggests these representations are coded in three ways: through sensory-motor channels, perceptual memory (in the form of schemas), and abstract semantic or conceptual codes (Leventhal, 1986). The sensory properties of pain, for example, bring with them an emotional and autonomic reaction. Leventhal's model asserts that some of these reactions are a result of memories of previous pain episodes. Further, emotional reactions, having similar autonomic and endocrine activation as illness episodes, can elicit traces of either or both experiences (c.f. Lang, Cuthbert & Melamed, 1986).

The schematic component of Leventhal's model consists of classically conditioned links between symptoms, emotional reactions, external events, and the illness episode. These schemas may be reactivated by symptoms similar to those in a given schema. The key characteristic in this type of schematic processing is that it gives symptom perceptions structure and meaning. It involves concrete elements (current symptoms) and memorial representations (prior illness experience). In contrast, the semantic or conceptual processing element takes a propositional form, and is derived from reflections about experience. It is a "storehouse" of descriptions of symptoms, causes, curative and preventive actions (Leventhal, 1986). They are thought to play an important role in providing a context for the experience and interpretation of symptoms. The schematic process is immediate, structuring the present concrete experience and overlapping similar prior experiences, whereas the conceptual processing of body states is very abstract and produces meanings that combine cause and consequence over time (Leventhal, 1986).

Elements of this framework are exemplified by data from patients with phantom pain and subjects given information in preparation for experiencing noxious stimuli. For example, an individual who has lost a limb has no peripheral feedback from that area. However, they may experience intense pain in that area, accompanied by anxiety and autonomic arousal (Melzack, 1971, cited in Leventhal, 1986). On a sample of dental patients who had been under either novacaine or nitrous oxide, mild electrical stimulation to the previously anesthetized nerve in the drilled tooth recreated the pain of tooth drilling for only the patients who were on nitrous oxide. Novocaine blocks the transfer of sensory information to the central nervous system; nitrous oxide does not. Thus, this suggests that ". . . body regions, symptoms, pain and emotion can be integrated in the type of memory codes we have labelled *schemata*" (Leventhal, 1986, p. 231, emphasis in original).

Leventhal's model, as well as the literature in cognitive psychology, suggests that activation of a particular schema affects the manner in which external information is processed. Therefore, changing the framework (schema) within which physical symptoms are perceived should modify those perceptions. Both Leventhal (1986) and Lang, Cuthbert & Melamed (1986) review research showing that preparing subjects for various noxious stimuli (e.g. cold pressor test, endoscopy) or unpleasant disease processes (e.g. arthritis) can reduce distress and decrease analgesic consumption. Leventhal's intervention achieves this reduction through descriptions of sensations and instructions to monitor them, while the latter uses guided imagery of pleasant, pain-free scenes incompatible with the illness. The first schema could be seen within a "supervisor" framework, where one monitors bodily sensations instead of naively and helplessly enduring them. The second schema is one of optimism, where the negative is discounted and the positive given priority. Under these conditions the subjective experience of something unpleasant is improved.

In a later paper, Leventhal and Diefenbach (1991) suggest that distress reduction operates through (a) the removal of surprise; (b) habituation; and (c) the development of an accurate representation of the stressor. This process allows the person to enjoy decreased distress even after they cease to monitor their body, a long-term effect not obtained by effective short-term strategies such as distraction (Leventhal, 1986). Leventhal argues that this process allows the individual to "get to know" the stressor, forming an objective schema to which it is easier to respond (Leventhal, 1986). This formation of a cohesive cognitive structure for this aversive experience, and being able to "put it behind" them, is similar to the process of closure in other domains (cf. Zeigarnik, 1927; Pennebaker, 1988).

Instead of a schema explanation, Lang, Cuthbert & Melamed (1986) argue that imagery interferes with the normal associative networks of pain that are active in the brain. They argue one cannot have the usual "maladaptive efferents" associated with the disease state (which exacerbate pain) operating and at the same time have a more tranquil physiological state being induced.

Thus imagery has elements of distraction, but the image also contains disease-relevant perceptions that are contrary to the disease process itself. The two perspectives are compatible in that both attenuate distress by preempting threatening interpretations of physical sensations. Interested readers should consult Cioffi's (1991) thorough review of research on somatic interpretation, which includes a discussion of these issues and proposes a hierarchical model of symptom appraisal processes.

ATTRIBUTIONS ABOUT ILLNESS

Another cognitive process involved in illness is attribution. When people are faced with sudden threats or unexpected events, they often search for causal explanations (Wong & Weiner, 1981). Illness is one such threat. This section will outline the conditions associated with causal attributions for serious illness.

Estimates of the occurrence of causal attributions about illness among patients range from 69 to 95% (Turnquist, Harvey & Andersen, 1988). The likelihood that patients will report illness-related attributions varies with disease severity and length of time since diagnosis. (Turnquist, Harvey & Andersen, 1988). For example, recovering cardiac patients with more severe symptoms, compared to those with less severe symptoms, reported a greater number of attributions (Mumma & McCorkle, 1982). When lung cancer and myocardial infarction patients were questioned about their illness attributions both one and two months after diagnosis, 16% more attributions were reported at the two-month assessment (Mumma & McCorkle, 1982). A study of breast cancer patients found that only 28% reported that what caused the cancer was important at the time of diagnosis. However, this figure increased to 41% during recovery (Taylor, Lichtman & Wood, 1984). The differences in the Taylor et al. study were not statistically significant, and the subjects' reports were retrospective, but they are consistent with the general pattern suggested by Turnquist, Harvey & Andersen (1988).

Other illness variables, such as disease severity, impact on attributions (Turnquist, Harvey & Andersen, 1988). For example, terminal cancer patients rated their causal beliefs less strongly than those with benign conditions (Linn, Linn & Stein, 1982, cited in Turnquist, Harvey & Andersen, 1988). Chronic disease patients also rated causal factors as less important if they perceived the outcome of their illness to be a failure (Lowery & Jacobsen, 1984). Thus, illness characteristics relate to attributional activity and content (Turnquist, Harvey & Andersen, 1988). The relationship between disease severity and causal attribution for other illnesses merits further exploration.

The nature of the precipitating event appears to have an impact on attributions. Accident victims, for example, frequently attribute these unexpected outcomes to chance (Kiecolt-Glaser & Williams, 1987), while heart attack patients frequently attributed their illness to "stress" (Affleck et al.,

1987). Evidence for a dominant attribution in the cancer domain is lacking (Taylor, Lichtman & Wood, 1984; Turnquist, Harvey & Andersen, 1988).

Thompson (1991) has suggested that there are three types of attributions, and provides evidence that many attributional studies do not distinguish between them. She distinguishes between causal attributions, selective incidence attributions (why me instead of someone else?), and responsibility attributions (is the person personally responsible for the event?). She measured the attributions of stroke patients and those of their primary caretakers. Adjustment was the primary dependent variable, measured by a depression scale and a purpose-in-life scale. Controlling for the severity of the stroke, "... both patients and care-givers were better adjusted if they reported finding meaning in the experience, if they did not ask themselves 'Why me?', if they did not hold themselves responsible, and if they had identified a cause of the stroke" (Thompson, 1991, p. 92). Searching for a cause did not contribute any variance not accounted for by the above variables. This study suggests that it is important to distinguish between different *kinds* of attributions (not just locus of causality), and that the cognitive theories of adjustment generalize to those involved indirectly in an illness episode.

Actor–observer differences in attributions for illness are also evident, in that observers tend to attribute the cause of illness to the sick person, while the sick person sees situational factors as causal (Turnquist, Harvey & Andersen, 1988). The external attribution on the part of the sick person can have self-protective motives, as their responsibility for being ill is absolved. This raises an interesting question: what are the effects of a spouse or family member's (an observer) advocacy of internal causal attributions? Would the patient's psychological well-being suffer as a result? Clinical research on family interaction suggests that attributions of blame produce a variety of negative consequences (Alexander & Parsons, 1982).

Attributions from the observer's perspective may play an especially important role in determining the behavior of care-givers. The foundation for this approach was laid by Weiner (1980) using college students and judgments of help-giving (actual helping behavior was not measured). He found that attributing the origin of need to internal and controllable causes produced the lowest judgments of aid. Affective responses resulting from perceptions of causality were thought to mediate approach (help) or avoidance (neglect) judgments. The affective responses by subjects toward someone in need (a confederate who fell down in the subway) were obtained. Two different people fell; one appeared drunk (and was therefore personally responsible), and the other was disabled and carried a cane (a state not subject to personal control). In the former condition, the initial feeling toward the confederate was negative while in the latter it was positive. It appears that causal beliefs regarding the origin of need influences affect, and affect promotes or hinders the tendency to help. Later experiments manipulating sympathy and anger independently support this notion (Batson et al., 1981).

The question for the ill individual then becomes "What is the impact of *others'* beliefs about why I became ill?" One has only to think of the way homosexuals infected with the HIV virus have been held responsible for their disease (and therefore less deserving of help) to understand. A less dramatic context in which others' attributions can affect care received involves the variability in the likelihood of drug prescription among doctors. If prescribing drugs is viewed as helping behavior, then these same affective and cognitive players should be at work. Brewin (1984) had medical students rate the likelihood of prescribing antidepressants or tranquilizers to hypothetical patients who had experienced certain life events (drawn from the Social Readjustment Rating Questionnaire; Holmes & Rahe, 1967). They were more likely to prescribe when the patient had experienced uncontrollable events and events that required readjustment. Uncontrollability was more weakly related to prescription than was readjustment, but the suggestion that hard "medical" decisions may include a significant measure of psychology as well as pharamacology restates the importance of attribution theory.

Another study (Sharrock et al., 1990) examined this attributional model within a more specific "helping professional" setting. Using professional staff at a unit for mentally disordered offenders, Sharrock et al. (1990) measured staff optimism and several other variables relating to a specific target patient. These included helping behavior (the amount of extra effort the staff members would exert in helping this patient), emotional ratings evoked by the target patient, and attributions about the major cause of several negative behaviors on the part of the patient. The staff who tended to attribute problem behavior to unstable factors had higher levels of optimism. Of the variables measured, optimism was found to be most clearly associated with helping behavior. The authors conclude that expectations of intervention being successful rather than the emotional reactions generated determine helping. Although these studies do not conclusively outline the effects of observer attributions on people who are ill, they do point to the significance of how others' perceptions of a problem can determine the kind of attention they get.

SOCIAL PSYCHOLOGICAL ASPECTS OF ILLNESS COGNITION

Another theoretical perspective relevant to illness cognition is social comparison theory (Festinger, 1954). According to Festinger, people often evaluate their abilities and opinions through comparison with others. This is most likely to occur when the individual has no objective standard for self-evaluation. Festinger's original social comparison theory states that the desire for accurate information is the primary reason people engage in social comparison. The theory also predicts that people will prefer comparison targets who are doing better on the relevant ability dimension, as this provides information useful for aspiration and improvement. Later revisions of this theory suggest that "persons can increase their subjective well-being through comparisons with a less fortunate other" (Wills, 1981, p. 245). This *downward comparison* is hypothesized to occur in people experiencing negative affect, specifically threats to self-esteem. We suggest, as have others (Affleck & Tennen, 1981; Sanders, 1982; Taylor, 1983) that physical illness is a threatening and sometimes ambiguous experience that is conducive to downward social comparison.

One of the first extensions of social comparison theory was its application to emotional states (Schachter & Singer, 1962). Years later, health psychologists utilized social comparison theory as a framework for understanding how individuals interpret ambiguous symptoms. The first step was to determine the extent to which individuals experienced uncertainty with regard to the meaning of their symptoms. Pennebaker's (1982) landmark book summarized a body of research showing that symptoms are frequently reported by apparently healthy persons, and the interpretation of these depend on a variety of contextual factors. Sanders (1982) describes a questionnaire he administered to 220 undergraduates which addresses this question. These subjects reported that approximately once every five months they had "experienced unusual physical symptoms with mixed feelings and no ready explanation". Only 6% reported no such symptoms. His data also show how common forced social comparison among laypersons may be. On average, these subjects reported receiving unsolicited lay medical advice from others 1.8 times in the past year.

How are these ambiguous symptoms interpreted? The most rigorous theoretical examination of the impact of temporal and contextual factors on symptom interpretation was proposed by Cacioppo et al. (1989). They outline a formal delineation of the process in their psychophysiological comparison theory. This theory maintains that individuals are motivated to maintain an explicable physiological condition. Ambiguous signs and symptoms (the former being detectable by others, the latter being subjective) can lead to evaluation of one's physiological condition. Like the schematic processing described earlier, activation of a sign or symptom can activate or inhibit other pieces of information in long-term memory. These theorists agree with the Leventhal group that current events are compared with representations in long term memory. These *psychophysiological schemata* include "... facts and beliefs about the physiological consequences of (i) normal physiological conditions (e.g. menopause), (ii) transiently disruptive conditions (e.g. fatigue), and (iii) disease (e.g. cancer) ..." (Cacioppo et al., 1989, p. 258). They also have an effect on symptom perception through cognitive processes such as selective monitoring and confirmatory perceptual biases (see also Pennebaker, 1982). The signs and symptoms selected by these cognitive "filters" can alter existing cognitive structures, and therefore influence later perceptions.

Plausible explanations are activated as a result of this comparison process, and the confirmation or disconfirmation process (appraisal) begins. These signs and symptoms elicit and guide the appraisal process, and as mentioned before, shape psychophysiological schemata and behavior (Cacioppo et al., 1989).

Other internal and external elements also shape symptom experience and reporting. These elements involve cognitive and social forces.

Symptoms, by their subjective nature, are more susceptible to misrepresentation. There is also opportunity for suspicion from others ("she's malingering") when dealing with symptoms as opposed to signs (Cacioppo et al., 1989; Skelton, 1991). Biases such as rationalization and denial are more likely to occur with symptoms, other things being equal. Even physiological signs do not merit absolute standards for symptom judgments (Reed, Harver & Katkin, 1991). The best way to understand a symptom, Cacioppo et al. (1989) argue, is to understand where the individual stands in his or her illness history, and to understand the context in which it occurs.

Anchoring effects are one type of cognitive distortion emphasized by Cacioppo et al. One's range of symptom experience provides the context for the symptom report. "Severe pain" for someone recovering from surgery versus someone with a bad headache would likely be different, even though they may both say it's a "10" on a 10-point scale. These distortions are not due to self-serving biases or impression management; rather, they are due to different standards of reference accessed when producing a symptom report (Cacioppo et al., 1989). Social rewards or punishments also play a role in what symptoms someone is willing to disclose. Despite these possible distortions, Cacioppo et al. argue that symptom reports are useful to pursue, and they provide question formats which can minimize the variation in these cognitive and social frames of reference. They further suggest that understanding a major group of determinants of psychophysiological comparison processes can improve the utility of symptom reports in diagnosis and treatment of disease.

Given the individual and social factors that influence symptom reporting, what are the effects of seeking information when someone is experiencing unusual physiological sensations? Sanders (1982) reviews several studies that suggest lay references play a large role in diagnoses, treatments, and referrals. Persons experiencing early signs of head and neck cancer discussed their symptoms with nonprofessionals 62% of the time, and in over half of these instances those opinions became their guide to action (Miller, 1973). Ninety per cent of cardiac patients (Davis & Eichorn, 1963) reported asking others for opinions of physician-prescribed treatment regimens (this percentage was an affirmative response to a specific question) and just over half (52%) said that these lay opinions were more influential than the physician's. Potential cardiac victims were twice as likely to participate in a preventive physical activity program if their spouse had a positive opinion of the program than if it was negative or neutral (Heinzelmann & Bagley, 1970). These studies suggest that the social aspects of illness are an important influence on individuals' illness behavior.

Jemmott, Ditto and Croyle (1986) showed that comparison information from an immediately available reference group could significantly affect threat appraisal. Participants were tested for TAA enzyme deficiency and were told they were one of a group of five subjects being tested. Subjects were given positive or negative test results and one of two types of comparison information. Some participants were told that one of the five tested positive, whereas others were told that four of the five tested positive. The risk factor was appraised as a more serious threat to health when only one of the five were described as testing positive (see also Ditto & Jemmott, 1989). Survey data suggest that perceived prevalence is correlated with threat appraisals of real disorders, as well (Jemmott, Croyle, & Ditto, 1988).

A recent study by Croyle and Hunt (1991) provided further experimental data concerning the effects of social influence on health threats. They manipulated a comparison other's appraisal of a health threat as well as the other's diagnostic status. Half of the subjects were tested with a confederate who openly minimized the deficiency's seriousness after the test results were communicated. The other subjects were tested with a confederate who made no comment following the test. Similarity was manipulated by having the confederate have either a positive (similar) or negative (dissimilar) TAA test result. The subject always received a positive test result.

Croyle and Hunt found that subjects' concern was significantly reduced when the confederate made a minimizing comment. This comment also had the effect of increasing avoidance of a second, more definitive TAA enzyme test. Thus, social communication provided a measure of emotional control, encouraging subjects to minimize their concern, but it also exacerbated immediate avoidance. Nevertheless, the subject's long-term action plans for dealing with the threat itself were unaffected by the comparison person's appraisal. Seven health behavior intention items were completed by subjects. These were influenced not by what the confederate said, but by the confederate's diagnostic status. When the confederate tested negative, subjects reported more preventive health behavior intentions. A mediational analysis showed that intentions were mediated by mental representations of the prevalence of the disorder. Subjects exposed to a confederate who tested negative perceived the disorder as relatively rare. These beliefs concerning prevalence determined behavioral intentions; a perception of the disorder as rare led to greater intentions to modify behavior.

CONCLUSION

Research on illness cognition has come a long way in the past two decades. The study of illness cognition has benefited from the integration, application, and extension of research from numerous subfields of psychology. The illness experience is a rich domain within which the interplay of many psychological forces can be fruitfully examined. Cognitive, affective, somatic, and sensory processes all play important roles in a system that is critical to adaptation and survival.

Basic research concerning illness cognition has already begun to bear clinical fruit. Illness schemata instruments have been developed for use with patient populations (Lacroix, 1991). Research on commonsense beliefs regarding symptoms has been applied to blood glucose monitoring among diabetics (Gonder-Frederick & Cox, 1991). Attribution-related assessment and interventions have been utilized for a number of different health problems (Lewis & Daltroy, 1990; Murdock & Altmaier, 1991; Murray, 1990). Important insights concerning hypertension medication compliance and adaptation to chemotherapy have already been achieved (Leventhal, Nerenz & Steele, 1984). No doubt the 1990s will see numerous additional extensions of illness cognition research into clinical domains.

As the fields of health promotion and behavioral medicine continue their rapid growth, it will become increasingly important that basic research in health psychology keeps pace. The study of illness cognition will complement a longer line of health behavior research as well as continued efforts on the part of medical sociologists and anthropologists. Large empirical gaps remain, including the integration of work on health-related memory and that concerning cognitive appraisal (Croyle & Loftus, in press). We believe that the application of recent work on implicit memory and memory–emotion processes (e.g. Christianson, in press; Schacter, 1992) to illness cognition is a high priority. No doubt new methods will be necessary to fulfill the promise of early efforts and theories. We look forward to additional creative efforts of the sort described in this chapter. Our patients deserve nothing less.

ACKNOWLEDGMENTS

The first author would like to acknowledge the support of grant MH 43097 from the National Institute of Mental Health. We thank Deborah Wiebe, Marybeth Hart, and two reviewers for helpful comments on a draft of the manuscript.

REFERENCES

Affleck, G. & Tennen, H. (1991). Social comparison and coping with major medical problems. In J. Suls and T. A. Wills (Eds), *Social Comparison: Contemporary Theory and Research*. Hillsdale, NJ: Lawrence Erlbaum.

Affleck, G., Tennen, H., Croog, S. & Levine, S. (1987). Causal attribution, perceived control, and recovery from a heart attack. *Journal of Social and Clinical Psychology*, 5, 356–364.

Alexander, J. F. & Parsons, B. V. (1982). *Functional Family Therapy: Principles and Procedures*. Carmel, CA: Brooks/Cole.

Batson, C. D., Duncan, B. D., Ackerman, P., Buckley, T. & Birch, K. (1981). Is empathic motivation a source of altruistic motivation? *Journal of Personality and Social Psychology*. 40, 290–302.

Baumann, L. J. & Keller, M. L. (1991). Responses to threat information: Implications for screening. *Image: Journal of Nursing Scholarship*, 23, 13–18.

Baumann, L., Cameron, L. D., Zimmerman, R. & Leventhal, H. (1989). Illness representations and matching labels with symptoms. *Health Psychology*, 8, 449–469.

Becker, M. H. (Ed) (1974). The health belief model and personal health behavior. *Health Education Monographs*, 2, 324–508.

Bishop, G. D. (1991). Understanding the understanding of illness: In J. A. Skelton & R. T. Croyle (Eds), *Mental Representation in Health and Illness* (pp. 32–59). New York: Springer-Verlag.

Bishop, G. D. & Converse, S. A. (1986). Illness representations: A prototype approach. *Health Psychology*, 5, 95–114.

Brewin, C. R. (1984). Perceived controllability of life-events and willingness to prescribe psychotropic drugs. *British Journal of Social Psychology*, 23, 285–287.

Cacioppo, J. T., Andersen, B. L., Turnquist, D. C. & Tassinary, L. G. (1989). Psychophysiological comparison theory: On the experience, description, and assessment of signs and symptoms. *Patient Education and Counseling*, 13, 257–270.

Cantor, N. & Mischel, W. (1977). Traits as prototypes. Effects on recognition memory. *Journal of Personality and Social Psychology*, 35, 38–48.

Chrisman, N. J. & Kleinman, A. (1983). Popular health care, social networks, and cultural meanings: The orientation of medical anthropology. In D. Mechanic (Ed), *Handbook of Health, Health Care, and the Health Professions* (pp. 569–590). New York: Free Press.

Christianson, S. (in press). *The Handbook of Emotion and Memory*. Hillsdale, NJ: Erlbaum.

Cioffi, D. (1991). Beyond attentional strategies: A cognitive-perceptual model of somatic interpretation. *Psychological Bulletin*, 109, 25–41.

Croyle, R. T. (1992). Appraisal of health threats: Cognition, motivation, and social comparison. *Cognitive Therapy and Research*, 16, 165–182.

Croyle, R. T. (1990). Biased appraisal of high blood pressure. *Preventive Medicine*, 19, 40–44.

Croyle, R. T. & Ditto, P. H. (1990). Illness cognition and behavior: An experimental approach. *Journal of Behavioral Medicine*, 13, 31–52.

Croyle, R. T. & Jemmott, J. B. III (1991). Psychological reactions to risk factor testing. In J. A. Skelton & R. T. Croyle (Eds), *Mental Representation in Health and Illness* (pp. 85–107). New York: Springer-Verlag.

Croyle, R. T. & Loftus, E. F. (in press). Recollection in the kingdom of AIDS. In D. G. Ostrow & R. Kessler (Eds), *AIDS Mental Health Survey Research Methodology*. New York: Plenum.

Croyle, R. T., Sun, Y. & Louie, D. H. (1992). Coping with health threat: Moderators of the psychological minimization of cholesterol test results. Unpublished manuscript, University of Utah.

Croyle, R. T. & Hunt, J. R. (1991). Coping with health threat: Social influence processes in reactions to medical test results. *Journal of Personality and Social Psychology*, 60, 382–389.

Croyle, R. T. & Sande, G. N. (1988). Denial and confirmatory search: Paradoxical consequences of medical diagnosis. *Journal of Applied Social Psychology*, 18, 473–490.

Davis, M. S. & Eichorn, R. L. (1963). Compliance with medical regimens: A panel study. *Journal of Health and Human Behavior*, 4, 240–249.

Ditto, P. H. & Jemmott, J. B. III (1989). From rarity to evaluative extremity. Effects of prevalence information on evaluations of positive and negative characteristics. *Journal of Personality and Social Psychology*, 57, 16–26.

Ditto, P. H., Jemmott, J. B. III & Darley, J. M. (1988). Appraising the threat of illness: A mental representational approach. *Health Psychology*, 7, 183–201.

Farmer, P. & Good, B. J. (1991). Illness representations in medical anthropology: A critical reivew and a case study of AIDS in Haiti. In J. A. Skelton & R. T. Croyle (Eds), *Mental Representation in Health and Illness* (pp. 132–162). New York: Springer-Verlag.

Festinger, L. (1954). A theory of social comparison processes. *Human Relations*, 7, 117–140.

Gonder-Frederick, L. & Cox, D. J. (1991). Symptom perception, symptom beliefs, and blood glucose discrimination in the self-treatment of insulin-dependent diabetes. In J. A. Skelton & R. T. Croyle (Eds), *Mental Representation in Health and Illness* (pp. 220–246). New York: Springer-Verlag.

Heinzelmann, F. & Bagley, R. (1970). Responses to physical activity programs and their effects on health behavior. *Public Health Reports*, 85, 905–911.

Holmes, T. H. & Rahe, R. H. (1967). The Social Readjustment Rating Scale. *Journal of Psychosomatic Research*, 11, 213–218.

Janis, I. L. (1958). *Psychological Stress*. New York: Wiley.

Jemmott, J. B. III, Croyle, R. T. & Ditto, P. H. (1988). Commonsense epidemiology: Self-based judgments from laypersons and physicians. *Health Psychology*, 7, 55–73.

Jemmott, J. B. III, Ditto, P. H. & Croyle, R. T. (1986). Judging health status: Effects of perceived prevalence and personal relevance. *Journal of Personality and Social Psychology*, 50, 899–905.

Jenkins, C. D. (1966). Group differences in perception: A study of community beliefs and feelings about tuberculosis. *American Journal of Sociology*, 71, 417–429.

Jenkins, C. D. & Zyzanski, S. J. (1968). Dimensions of belief and feeling concerning three diseases, poliomyelitis, cancer, and mental illness: A factor analytic study. *Behavioral Science*, 13, 372–381.

Kasl, S. V. & Cobb, S. (1966). Health behavior, illness behavior and sick role behavior. *Archives of Environmental Health*, 12, 246–266.

Kiecolt-Glaser, J. K. & Williams, D. A. (1987). Self-blame, compliance, and distress among burn patients. *Journal of Personality and Social Psychology*, 53, 187–193.

Kim, J. & Mueller, C. W. (1978). *Factor Analysis: Statistical Methods and Practical Issues*. Sage University Paper series on Quantitative Applications in the Social Sciences, 07-014. Beverly Hills, CA: Sage Publications.

Lacroix, J. M. (1991). Assessing illness schemata in patient popultions. In J. A. Skelton & R. T. Croyle (Eds), *Mental Representation in Health and Illness* (pp. 193–219). New York: Springer-Verlag.

Lang, P., Cuthbert, B. & Melamed, B. (1986). Cognition, emotion, and illness. In S. McHugh and T. M. Vallis (Eds), *Illness Behavior: A Multidiscipline Model*. New York: Plenum Press.

Lau, R. R., Bernard, T. M. & Hartman, K. A. (1989). Further explorations of common sense representations of common illnesses. *Health Psychology*, 8, 195–219.

Lau, R. R. & Hartman, K. A. (1983). Common sense representations of common illnesses. *Health Psychology*, 2, 167–185.

Leventhal, H. (1970). Findings and theory in the study of fear communications. *Advances in Experimental Social Psychology*, 5, 119–186.

Leventhal, H. (1975). The consequences of depersonalization during illness and treatment: An information processing model. In J. Howard & A. Strauss (Eds), *Humanizing Health Care* (pp. 119–161). New York: Wiley.

Leventhal, H. (1986). Symptom reporting: A focus on process. In S. McHugh and T. M. Vallis (Eds), *Illness Behavior: A Multidisciplinary Model*. New York: Plenum Press.

Leventhal, H. & Diefenbach, M. (1991). The active side of illness cognition. In J. A. Skelton & R. T. Croyle (Eds), *Mental Representation in Health and Illness* (pp. 247–272). New York: Springer-Verlag.

Leventhal, H., Jones, S. & Trembly, G. (1966). Sex differences in attitude and behavior change under conditions of fear and specific instructions. *Journal of Experimental Social Psychology*, **2**, 387–399.

Leventhal, H., Meyer, D. & Nerenz, D. (1980). The common sense representation of illness danger. In S. Rachman (Ed), *Contributions to Medical Psychology* (Vol. 2, pp. 7–30). Oxford: Pergamon Press.

Leventhal, H. & Nerenz, D. R. (1985). The assessment of illness cognition. In P. Karoly (Ed), *Measurement Strategies in Health Psychology*. New York: John Wiley.

Leventhal, H., Nerenz, D. R. & Steele, D. J. (1984). Illness representations and coping with health threats. In A. Baum, S. E. Taylor & J. E. Singer (Eds), *Handbook of Psychology and Health* (Vol. 4, pp. 219–252). Hillsdale, NJ: Erlbaum.

Leventhal, H., Watts, J. C. & Pagano, F. (1967). Effects of fear and instructions on how to cope with danger. *Journal of Personality and Social Psychology*, **6**, 313–321.

Lewis, F. M. & Daltroy, L. H. (1990). How causal explanations influence health behavior: Attribution theory. In K. Glanz, F. M. Lewis & B. K. Rimer (Eds), *Health Behavior and Health Education: Theory, Research, and Practice* (pp. 92–114). San Francisco, CA: Jossey-Bass.

Linn, M. N., Linn, B. S. & Stein, S. R. (1982). Beliefs about causes of cancer in cancer patients. *Social Science and Medicine*, **16**, 835–839.

Lowery, B. J. & Jacobsen, B. S. (1984). Attributional analysis of chronic illness outcomes. *Nursing Research*, 82–88.

Marks, G. & Miller, N. (1987). Ten years of research on the false consensus effect: An empirical and theoretical view. *Psychological Bulletin*, **102**, 72–90.

Mechanic, D. (1978). *Medical Sociology* (2nd edn). New York: Free Press.

Melzack, R. (1971). Phantom limb pain. *Anesthesiology*, **35**, 409–419.

Meyer, D., Leventhal, H. & Gutmann, M. (1985). Commonsense models of illness: The example of hypertension. *Health Psychology*, **4**, 115–135.

Miller, M. H. (1973). Seeking advice for cancer symptoms. *American Journal of Public Health*, **63**, 955–961.

Mumma, C. & McCorkle, R. (1982). Causal attrtibution and life-threatening disease. *International Journal of Psychiatry in Medicine*, **12**, 311–319.

Murdock, N. L. & Altmaier, E. M. (1991). Attribution-based treatments. In C. R. Snyder & D. R. Forsythe (Eds), *Handbook of Social and Clinical Psychology* (pp. 563–578). New York: Pergamon.

Murray, M. (1990). Lay representations of illness. In P. Bennett, J. Weinman & P. Spurgeon (Eds), *Current Developments in Health Psychology* (pp. 63–92). New York: Harwood.

Pennebaker, J. (1982). *The Psychology of Physical Symptoms*. New York: Springer-Verlag.

Pennebaker, J. W. (1988). Confiding traumatic experiences and health. In S. Fisher & J. Reason (Eds), *Handbook of Life Stress, Cognition, and Health*. London: John Wiley.

Reed, S. D., Harver, A. & Katkin, E. S. (1991). Interoception. In J. T. Cacioppo & L. G. Tassinary (Eds), *Principles of Psychophysiology: Physical, Social, and Inferential Elements*. New York: Cambridge University Press.

Rosch, E. H. (1978). Principles of categorization. In E. Rosch & B. B. Lloyd (Eds), *Cognition and Categorization*. Hillsdale, NJ: Erlbaum.

Rosenstock, I. M. (1990). The Health Belief Model: Explaining health behavior through expectancies. In K. Glanz, F. M. Lewis & B. K. Rimer (Eds), *Health Behavior and Health Education: Theory, Research, and Practice* (pp. 39–62). San Francisco, CA: Jossey-Bass.

Ross, L., Greene, D. & House, P. (1977). The "false consensus effect": An egocentric bias in social perception and attribution processes. *Journal of Experimental Social Psychology*, **13**, 279–301.

Sanders, G. S. (1982). Social comparison and perceptions of health and illness. In G. S. Sanders & J. Suls (Eds), *Social Psychology of Health and Illness*, p. 129–157. Hillsdale, NJ: Erlbaum.

Schachter, S. & Singer, J. (1962). Cognitive, social, and physiological determinants of emotional state. *Psychological Review*, 69, 379–399.

Schacter, D. L. (1992). Understanding implicit memory: A cognitive neuroscience approach. *American Psychologist*, 47, 559–569.

Schiffman, S. S., Reynolds, M. L. & Young, F. W. (1981). *Introduction to Multidimensional Scaling: Theory, Methods, and Applications*. New York: Academic Press.

Sharrock, R., Day, A., Qazi, F. & Brewin, C. (1990). Explanations by professional care staff, optimism and helping behavior: an application of attribution theory. *Psychological Medicine*, 20, 849–855.

Skelton, J. A. (1991). Laypersons' judgments of patient credibility and the study of illness representations. In J. A. Skelton & R. T. Croyle (Eds), *Mental Representation in Health and Illness* (pp. 108–131). New York: Springer-Verlag.

Skelton, J. A. & Croyle, R. T. (1991a). Metal representation, health, and illness: An introduction. In J. A. Skelton & R. T. Croyle (Eds), *Mental Representation in Health and Illness* (pp. 1–9). New York: Springer-Verlag.

Skelton, J. A. & Croyle, R. T. (Eds) (1991b). *Mental Representation in Health and Illness*. New York: Springer-Verlag.

SPSS[x] User's Guide (1986). SPSS Inc., 444 North Michigan Avenue, Chicago, Illinois.

Taylor, S. E. (1983). Adjustment to threatening events: A theory of cognitive adaptation. *American Psychologist*, 38, 1161–1173.

Taylor, S. E., Lichtman, R. R. & Wood, J. V. (1984). Attributions, beliefs about control, and adjustment to breast cancer. *Journal of Personality and Social Psychology*, 46, 489–502.

Thompson, S. C. (1991). The search for meaning following a stroke. *Basic and Applied Social Psychology*, 12, 81–96.

Turk, D. C., Rudy, T. E. & Salovey, P. (1986). Implicit models of illness. *Journal of Behavioral Medicine*, 9, 453–474.

Turnquist, D. C., Harvey, J. H. & Andersen, B. L. (1988). Attributions and adjustment to life threatening illness. *British Journal of Clinical Psychology*, 27, 55–65.

Weiner, B. (1980). A cognitive (attribution)—emotion—action model of motivated behavior: An analysis of judgements of help-giving. *Journal of Personality and Social Psychology*, 39, 186–200.

Wills, T. A. (1981). Downward comparison principles in social psychology. *Psychological Bulletin*, 90, 381–397.

Wong, P. T. P. & Weiner, B. (1981). When people ask 'Why' questions, and the heuristics of attributional research. *Journal of Personality and Social Psychology*, 40, 650–663.

Zeigarnik, B. (1927). Das Bahahlten erfedigter und unerledigter Handlungen. *Psychologoie Forshung*, 9, 1–85. Translated and condensed as "On finished and unfinished tasks" in W. D. Ellis (Ed), *A Source Book of Gestalt Psychology*. New York: Harcourt, Brace & World, 1938.

Part II

HEALTH BEHAVIOUR
AND HEALTH PROMOTION

3 Mood Effects of Exercise Versus Sports Games: Findings and Implications for Well-being and Health

ANDREA ABELE
*Institute of Psychology, University of Erlangen/Nürnberg, Bismarckstraße 1,
D-8520 Erlangen, Germany*

WALTER BREHM
*Institute of Physical Education, University of Bayreuth, Universitätstraße 30,
D-8580 Bayreuth, Germany*

INTRODUCTION

Life in western industrial societies can be characterized by a steady decrease of physical stress and a steady increase of psychical stress in coping with one's daily affairs. The death risk number one today is cardiovascular diseases, which—among others—are caused by a lack in physical, and an overweight in psychical, stress (Powell et al., 1987). The beneficial physiological effects of regular physical exercise on endurance, vigor and flexibility are well documented (for example Hollmann, 1986, Weineck, 1988). They are not only known to specialists in the fields of medicine and physical education, but are by and large also acknowledged by the general public: surveys show that up to 90% of the respondents assume positive health consequences of regular physical exercise (Abele & Brehm, 1990a, 1990b, 1990c, Mrazek, 1984, Wankel, 1988). Physical exercise is one of the most important chances for the prevention of illnesses (Brehm & Pahmeier, 1991).

The possible beneficial psychical effects of exercise and sports are not fully understood yet. We will concentrate here on acute mood effects. We will review findings on mood changes after different types of physical activity, and we will ask how these acute mood changes may contribute to a person's general sense of well-being. Besides a pragmatic concentration on one of the exercise and well-being topics (for reviews see Morgan & Goldstone, 1987, Sachs, 1984), there are two major reasons for focussing on mood:

International Review of Health Psychology. Volume 2. Edited by S. Maes, H. Leventhal and M. Johnston
© 1993 John Wiley & Sons Ltd

1. The first reason is related to the so called "paradox of health" (Barsky, 1988), which says that even though health care is continuously improving in western societies, more and more people are dissatisfied with their health, are depressive and in bad mood. Mood enhancing treatments are asked for. A side aspect of such mood enhancing treatments is a more positive experiencing of one's health (see Abele & Hermer, 1993). Physical exercise could be one such mood enhancing— and health perception enhancing—treatment.

2. The second reason is related to the promotion of exercise behavior and adherence to exercise. The experience of positive mood changes during or immediately after exercise is one of the most important determinants of exercise adherence (Brehm & Pahmeier, 1990, Dishman, Sallis & Orenstein, 1985; Wankel, 1985, 1988). People who do not experience such mood changes have a high risk of dropping out. Positive psychical effects of physical exercise are thus a precondition of positive physiological effects.

The review will be confined on field studies with adult persons of average health, who do exercise as a leisure activity. Studies with top-athletes, or studies with members of specific treatment or rehabilitation groups are excluded (for reviews see Morgan & Goldstone, 1987, Schwenkmezger, 1985). Experimental studies with treadmill- or bicycle-ergometer-training are also excluded. These two approaches to the study of exercise effects are comparable with respect to the aspect of physical work load, but are hardly comparable with respect to other aspects of exercise, for example required skills, environmental factors, commitment, motives for performing the activity, etc. Whereas from a methodological point of view experimental studies have a clear advantage (random assignment of subjects to conditions, controllability of the situation), they are untypical and not representative of actual exercise behavior. It may well be that the psychological effects of these two types of physical activity are quite different (c.f. Morgan & Goldstone, 1987).

THEORETICAL ASSUMPTIONS: ACUTE MOOD, GENERAL SENSE OF WELL-BEING, AND DIFFERENT TYPES OF PHYSICAL ACTIVITIES

Subjective well-being can be defined by state-, trait-, and process aspects (Becker, 1991). Mood is the state aspect of subjective well- or unwell-being. It is less intense than an emotion or affect, not directed towards a specific object, but rather an evaluative tuning of a person's actual experiencing (Abele, 1991, Isen, 1984, Morris, 1989). Mood can be differentiated on two dimensions, the evaluative dimension (good/pleasant versus bad/unpleasant), and the activation dimension (active versus passive). Different moods can be arranged on a circumflex constructed by these two orthogonal dimensions (Abele & Brehm, 1986a, Russell, 1980, Watson & Tellegen, 1985). The trait aspect of subjective well-being is its median level over time, i.e. the most frequent mood state experienced by a person. The process aspect is the variability of mood states over time. It has been found that people tend to equalize their state level of mood to a relatively stable trait level, and that this process may be best described by a dynamical equilibrium model (Abele & Becker, 1991, Headey & Wearing, 1989, Schwenkmezger, 1991).

Two functions are necessary in order to maintain a person's median well-being level: equilibration and disequilibration. Equilibration is the restoration of the median level, for example if a person tries to cope with negative feelings or if an elated mood gradually changes into its average level. Disequilibration, in contrast, is concerned with disturbing the median well-being level. Such a disturbance gets necessary if there are no variations from the median level for a longer time period. Berlyne (1960; see also Heckhausen, 1978) has been one of the first authors who argued that stability in a person's life conditions does not automatically mean maintenance of a certain well-being level, but that stability—and thus stagnation—rather leads to an impairment of well-being: if nothing novel happens, and if everything is highly predictable, a person gets bored, and possibly depressed in the long run.

It is assumed here that physical activities like exercise and sports can have both equilibrating and disequilibrating effects upon a person's actual mood. And it is further assumed that different kinds of physical activities may have differential mood effects. We are specifically concerned with exercise (fitness and endurance training) versus sports games (Other types of physical activities are the acquisition and training of sports skills or the completion of outdoor activities like skiing or surfing.):

1. Activities like noncompetitive fitness- and endurance training, swimming, running, calisthenics, or aerobic exercise are assumed to have mainly equilibrating effects. These equilibrating effects should result in both tension reduction (activation dimension of mood) and elation (evaluative dimension of mood).

2. Competitive sports related activities like soccer, volleyball, or tennis, in contrast, should have disequilibrating effects. Playful activities and games in general are a possibility for disequilibrating a person's present mood level, they are a "quest for excitement in an unexciting society" (Elias & Dunning, 1986). Their main function for the actor is to experience a "tension circle" of increased tension at the beginning, and reduced tension at the end of a game (Grupe, 1982, Heckhausen, 1978, Sutton-Smith, 1973). Competitive sports games, specifically, should also lead to a tension circle of an increase of tension at the beginning and a decrease at the end of the activity (activation dimension of mood). This tension circle should be independent of the outcome, ie, winning or losing. The evaluative dimension of mood, however, is assumed to be directly linked to the outcome, i.e. elation after success and depression after failure.

Summarizing, we assume that exercise and sports have acute effects on a person's mood. Fitness and endurance training activities should have mainly equilibrating effects of tension reduction and well-being enhancement; competitive sports games should mainly have disequilibratring effects of tension circles and—dependent on the result—joy or sadness. Both effects, equilibration and disequilibration, are assumed to be beneficial for a person's general sense of well-being.

STUDIES ON FITNESS AND ENDURANCE TRAINING: THE EQUILIBRATING EFFECT

In the early phase of pertinent research endeavors the respective studies were mainly interview- and self-report-studies without standardized measures: the huge increase of running and jogging activities during the seventies led among other things to research concerned with the "feel-better-phenomenon" and the "runner's high". With respect to the feel-better-phenomenon studies in different countries consistently showed that up to three quarters of the regular runners reported to feel better after their run than before it (Dishman, 1984). The runner's high was defined as a euphoric state in the course of running. Interview studies found, that between 9% and 77% of the runners reported respective experiences (Sachs, 1984). Later approaches are characterized by the use of standardized measurement instruments, as well as by a broader scope of types of activities studied.

Table 3.1 gives an overview over 15 studies which were concerned with pre-/ post-activity mood changes in different kinds of fitness and endurance training activities, like calisthenics, aerobic exercise, running/jogging, dancing or swimming. All studies' subjects had voluntarily selected their activity, and in seven of the studies control conditions were also included (either no exercise or another activity). The design was always a pre-activity, post-activity repeated measures design with a standardized mood self-report instrument. In two of the studies (Berger & Owen 1988, Weinberg, Jackson & Kolodny, 1988) skills acquisition classes (Berger & Owen: fencing; Weinberg et al.: racquetball, tennis) were included in the design. They are omitted in the following table, but discussed later.

In the English speaking studies mainly the Profile of Mood Scales (POMS, McNair, Lorr & Droppleman, 1971) was administered. The POMS consists of six scales: tension/anxiety (nine items, highest loadings "tense", and "nervous"), depression/dejection (15 items, "unhappy", "worthless"), anger/ hostility (12 items, "angry", "ready to fight"), vigor/activation (eight items, "full of pep", "alert"), fatigue/inertia (seven items, "fatigued", "exhausted"), and confusion/bewilderment (seven items, "forgetful", "unable to concentrate"). There is usually a five-point response format, and the instruction is either a trait-oriented, general one, or a state oriented "right now" instruction. The German studies mainly used the BFS (Befindlichkeitsskalen, –mood scales–, Abele & Brehm, 1986a), which was constructed according to the above cited two-dimensional circumflex notion of mood. Every quadrant of this circumflex is operationalized by two scales consisting of five items each. The positive high activation quadrant is operationalized by an activation scale ("active", "full of energy"), and an elation scale ("happy", "pleasant"); the positive low activation quadrant contains a calmness scale ("calm", "relaxed"), and a contemplativeness scale ("dreamy", "full of thought"). The negative high activation quadrant entails an excitation scale ("excited", "tense"), and an anger scale ("angry", "grouchy"), the negative low activation quadrant is operationalized by a fatigue scale ("fatigued", "lazy"), and a depression scale ("sad", "depressed"). The instructions for these scales were always to report the "right now" state (five-point response mode). The POMS and BFS depression, anger, vigor/activation, and fatigue scales are by and large comparable between both measures. The POMS tension/anxiety and the BFS excitation scales have an overlap with respect to tension, but not anxiety. The POMS confusion/bewilderment scale has no equivalent in the BFS, and the BFS elation, calmness and contemplativeness scales have no equivalent in the POMS.

The English and American studies were mainly concerned with tension reduction. Their general hypothesis was that aerobic exercise leads to the so called "iceberg profile" found with top athletes (Morgan, 1980): the iceberg profile is characterized by elevated vigor, and low levels of anxiety, depression, confusion, fatigue and anger. Due to the mood scales utilized it was not possible in these studies to analyze possible mood enhancements, i.e. increases in elation, and calmness.

The German studies using the BFS were concerned with both above mentioned possible effects (see Abele & Brehm, forthcoming, for a review). Their general hypothesis was that aerobic exercise leads to tension reduction (decreases in anger and excitation, increase in calmness), to activation (increase in activation, decrease in fatigue) and to positive feelings (increase in elation, decrease in depression). The BFS contemplativeness scale was thought of as a control scale: its value should change with every activity, i.e. it should be exercise-unspecific.

As can be seen from Table 3.1 all studies reveal positive mood changes after excerise.

Mood enhancement and relaxation

The greatest changes occurred with respect to enhanced elation/pleasantness/positive affect (Abele & Brehm, 1984, 1985, 1989; Abele, Brehm & Gall, 1987; Abele, Brehm & Schmelz, 1989; Christen, 1986; Lichtman & Poser, 1983; McIntyre, Watson & Cunningham, 1990; Nowlis & Greenberg, 1979), reduced excitation/tension (Abele & Brehm, 1984, 1985, 1989; Abele, Brehm & Schmelz, 1989; Abele, Brehm & Rahlmeyer, 1991; Berger & Owen, 1983, 1988; Christen, 1986; Dyer & Crouch, 1988; Lichtman & Poser, 1983; Weinberg et al., 1988) and increased calmness and relaxation (Abele & Brehm, 1984, 1985, 1989; Abele, Brehm & Gall, 1987; Abele, Brehm & Rahlmeyer, 1991; Droste et al., 1989). Depression and anger were reduced, except if the initial level was already very low (Abele & Brehm, 1984; Abele, Brehm & Gall, 1987; Abele,

Table 3.1. Effects of fitness activities like running, swimming, aerobic exercise, etc. on mood

Study	Subjects	Treatment	Measures	Results
Abele & Brehm, 1984, 1986	N = 186 male and female students	60 and 90 min duration classes in: (a) jazz-dance (b) fitness training (c) control condition seminar	Pre- and post-activity repeated measures; 8 BFS scales	No differences between jazz-dance and fitness training classes; Exercise: significant increases in activation, elation, and calmness; decreases in excitation, anger, depression, fatigue, and contemplativeness; people with more negative initial mood experienced stronger changes; Control condition: overall higher level of excitation; significant decrease in contemplativeness
Abele & Brehm, 1985	N = 67 men and women (age 19–52)	Several 60 and 90 min duration fitness trainings	Pre- and post-activity repeated 8 BFS scales	Significant increases in activation, elation, and calmness; significant decreases in excitation, anger, depression, and contemplativeness; no change in fatigue
Abele & Brehm, 1989	N = 30 to 40 male and female participants age 18–45	Experimental variation of four types of fitness training: high versus low intensity of work load by music versus no music	Repeated pre- and post-activity measures in all four types; 8 BFS scales	Significant increases in activation, elation, and calmness; significant decreases in excitation, anger, depression, and contemplativeness; no change in fatigue; no differential effects of the four types of fitness trainings
Abele, Brehm & Gall, 1987	N = 27 male and female regular swimmers age 24–64	Three swimming units (duration between 12 and 45 min); differentiation of swimmers in high versus low intensity groups (increase of heart beats per minute above or below the median 80% increase)	Repeated pre- and post-activity measures in all three units; 8 BFS scales	Mood change by exercise intensity interaction: above median intensity swimmers: higher overall excitation and lower calmness; increases in elation and calmness, decreases in fatigue and contemplativeness; no change in excitation and activation; due to very low initial levels; no change in anger and depression

			below median intensity swimmers: increases in activation, elation, and calmness; decreases in fatigue, and contemplativeness; no changes in excitation, anger, and depression
Abele, Brehm & Rahlmeyer, 1991	$N = 103$ male and female visitors of fitness studios; age range 17–63	Individual training sessions	Repeated pre- and post-activity measures; 8 BFS scales	Significant increases in activation, calmness and elation; decreases in anger, excitement, fatigue, depression and contemplativeness
Abele, Brehm & Schmelz, 1989	$N = 107$ male and female joggers age range 18–64	An individual jogging unit	Repeated pre- and post-activity measures; 8 BFS	Overall increases in elation and calmness, decreases in excitation, anger, depression, and contemplativeness; Activation increases in persons, who do not other exercise than jogging, but no increases in persons, who practice other sports; activation increases further dependent on the social situation: more increase, if jogging alone; Fatigue decreases in advanced joggers, but not in beginning joggers
Berger & Owen, 1983	$N = 100$ male and female students age range 17–50	Swimming classes for beginners versus advanced swimmers (40 min.) Control condition (seminar, 50 min)	Repeated pre- and post-activity measures; 6 POMS scales	No pretest differences between swimmers and control condition; Control condition: no mood changes; Swimmers: Increased vigor, decreased tension, depression, anger, and confusion; no change in fatigue; No differences in mood changes between beginning and advanced swimmers

(continued overleaf)

Table 3.1. (*continued*)

Study	Subjects	Treatment	Measures	Results
Berger & Owen, 1988[1]	N = 170 male and female students; no information on age	Measures in different class types: (a) body conditioning (40 min) (b) swimming (40 min) (c) yoga (80 min) (d) lectures	6 POMS scales ("right now" instruction), pre- and post-activity measures	Pretest differences: Swimmers were highest in vigor, body conditioning and lecture classes lowest, no other differences; Swimmers: reported unusually positive states both before and after exercise, no changes; Body conditioners: higher fatigue after exercise, no other changes; Yoga: decreases in tension, depression, fatigue, anger, and confusion, no changes in vigor; Lecture classes: No changes in one control lecture class, decreases in depression, anger, fatigue, and confusion in the other lecture class
Christen, 1986[1]	N = 64 male and female participants	guided running: experienced versus unexperienced runners; control condition (no treatment)	repeated pre- and postactivity measures (EWL, Jahnke & Debus, 1978)	Increases in well-being, decreases in excitability, and anxiety in the exercise groups, no changes in the control condition; Stronger positive mood changes in unexperienced than in experienced joggers
Droste, Klass & Richterling, 1989	N = 62 male and female students mean age 22	Relaxation and stretching training: 15 min duration	repeated pre- and postactivity measures; 5 BFS scales	Significant increases in activation and calmness, significant decreases in anger, excitement, and fatigue
Dyer & Crouch 1988	N = 70 men and women age range 17 to 26	Measures in four classes: (a) Runners (40 min) (b) Aerobic dancers (60 min) (c) Weight lifters (50 min) (d) Control seminar	6 POMS scales ("right now" instruction), repeated measures: —3 hours before	Within groups comparisons 3 hours before versus 10 min after the activity: Runners: Decrease in tension and Aerobic dancers: Decrease in depression, anger, fatigue, and confusion, increase in vigor;

Study	Sample	Design	Measures	Results
		—10 min before —10 min after —3 hours after		pression, anger, and confusion, increase in vigor; Seminar: Increase in vigor, decrease in fatigue; Between groups comparisons: Runners versus aerobic dancers: No differences; Weight lifters more fatigue than runners; Control seminar more depressed, confused, and less vigor than runners
Lichtman & Poser, 1983[1]	N = 64 male and female participants, mean age 26	45 min jogging and fitness training: control condition (hobby course)	repeated pre- and postactivity measures; 6 POMS scales, 14 MACL scales (Nowlis, 1965)	Significant differences between both groups at the pretest-, and at the posttest level: The exercise group was significantly less sad, angry, depressed, and engaged in thought than the hobby course group; The pretest-posttest difference in the hobby group was only significant with respect to decreased tension and depression; The exercise group increased in pleasantness, and decreased in fatigue, depression, tension/anxiety, and anger/hostility
McIntyre, Watson & Cunningham, 1990	N = 18 males and female students mean age 21	Mood measures at four different occasions: baseline, exercise, social interaction, test stress	PANAS scales (Watson, Clark & Tellegen, 1988)	Significant increases of positive affect during social interaction and exercise, no change during test stress; Significant increases of negative affect during test stress, no change during social interaction, and exercise.
Nowlis & Greenberg,	N = 18 male and female	a 12,5 miles run	MACL, STAI (Spielberger,	Significant increase in elation; marginally significant increase in activation, and

(continued overlead)

Table 3.1. (*continued*)

Study	Subjects	Treatment	Measures	Results
1978	joggers age range 17–55		Gorsuch & Lushene, 1970)	decrease in sadness; no change in relaxation, anxiety, and depression (MACL); no change in state anxiety, marginally significant decrease in trait anxiety (STAI)
Weinberg, Jackson & Kolodny, 1988	N = 183 students no information on sex or age	Measures in different class types (always 30 min, exercise at 60% max.) (a) swimming (b) jogging (c) control test (d) massage	6 POMS scales ("right now" instruction); state anxiety (STAI); high activation (tension and anxiety) and general activation (calmness and relaxation) (Thayer, 1967); pre- and post-activity measures	Massage: Decrease in state anxiety, high activation, tension, depression, anger, fatigue, and confusion; increase in general activation; Jogging: decrease in tension, depression, anger, increase in general activation and vigor; Swimming: increase in general activation; Control test condition: no change Pretest differences: lower state anxiety in massage and swimming groups; higher tension, depression, and anger in jogging group

¹This study reported a number of further measures, which are unimportant in the present context

Brehm & Rahlmeyer, 1991; Berger & Owen, 1988; Dyer & Crouch, 1988; negative affect: McIntyre et al., 1990; Weinberg et al., 1988).

Activation

Activation and vigor were often (Abele & Brehm, 1984, 1985, 1989; Abele, Brehm & Gall, 1987, low intensity swimmers; Abele, Brehm & Rahlmeyer, 1991; Abele, Brehm & Schmelz, 1989, persons who do no other sports than running; Berger & Owen, 1983; Droste et al., 1989; Dyer & Crouch, 1988; Nowlis & Greenberg, 1979; Weinberg et al., 1988, jogging and swimming), but not always enhanced (no changes: Abele, Brehm & Gall, 1987, high intensity swimmers; Abele, Brehm & Schmelz, 1989, frequent exercisers; Berger & Owen, 1988, swimmers and body conditioners; Lichtman & Poser, 1983, swimmers; Berger & Owen, 1986. In a replication study of their 1983 work Berger & Owen (1986) did not find any mood alterations in swimmers. They assume that the uncontrollably high air temperature on the day of testing occulted any mood benefits that might have occurred). Fatigue/inertia scores remained stable in six cases (Abele & Brehm, 1985, 1989; Abele, Brehm & Schmelz, 1989; beginning runners, Berger & Owen, 1983; Dyer & Crouch, 1988, weight lifters; Weinberg et al., 1988), were reduced in seven cases (Abele & Brehm, 1984; Abele, Brehm & Gall, 1987; Abele, Brehm & Schmelz, 1989, advanced runners; Abele, Brehm & Rahlmeyer, 1991; Droste et al., 1989; Dyer & Crouch, 1988, aerobic dancers; Lichtman & Poser, 1983), and increased in two cases after exercise (Berger & Owen, 1988, body conditioners; Dyer & Crouch, 1988, runners).

Contemplativeness

Contemplativeness was reduced, and confusion/bewilderment was not influenced by exercise.

Figure 3.1 shows the average exerciser's post-exercise mood profile as it was found in the present authors' studies (averaged over swimming, Abele, Brehm & Gall, 1987, running, Abele, Brehm & Schmelz, 1989, and fitness training, Abele & Brehm, 1985; Abele, Brehm & Rachlmeyer, 1991). It has the shape of an "Iceberg-profile", but it's highest peak is not in vigor/activation, but rather in calmness and elation.

Sex and age differences

In none of the studies were there any differences in mood changes between male and female participants. If the sample's age range allowed to study age differences, then older people tended to show greater mood enhancement after exercise than younger people (Abele & Brehm, 1985, 1989; Abele, Brehm & Schmelz, 1989; Abele, Brehm & Rahlmeyer, 1991). This finding is mainly due to

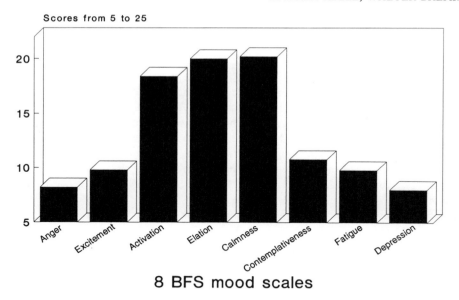

Figure 3.1   Average mood profile after fitness and endurance training (swimming, running, calisthenics).

the pretest already very high mood level of younger people and the pretest lower level of older people.

Initial mood level

The initial mood level was generally an important determinant of mood changes (Abele & Brehm, 1986; Abele, Brehm & Schmelz, 1989; Abele, Brehm & Rahlmeyer, 1991; Berger & Owen, 1988; Christen, 1986). People with an initially rather bad mood experienced a greater "feel-better phenomenon" than people with an initially already very positive mood. Since people with an initially already very positive mood did by and large not change into a more negative direction afterwards, this finding cannot be interpreted by a method-ological regression artifact only, but it demonstrates the beneficial influence of exercise also in the realm of more negative feelings.

Perceived exertion

Both exercisers who experienced their activity as low exerting, and exercisers who experienced their activity as highly exerting showed lower positive mood changes than participants who experienced their activity as medium exerting (Abele & Brehm, 1989; Abele, Brehm & Schmelz, 1989; see also Gondola & Tuckman, 1983). These data converge with experimental findings, which also revealed that medium intensity work load is most suitable for mood enhancement (Morgan, 1987, Steptoe & Bolton, 1988, Steptoe & Cox, 1988).

Experience

The data on mood changes in beginning versus advanced exercisers are ambiguous: Berger & Owen (1983) found no differences between classes of beginning versus advanced swimmers; Christen (1986) compared runners, who had just started this activity with experienced runners and found more positive changes in beginning than in advanced runners. Abele, Brehm & Schmelz (1989) in contrast found more positive changes (decrease in fatigue, increase in elation) in advanced (more than one year's practice) than in beginning runners (less than one year's practice).

Comparison between different types of fitness activities

The comparison between different types of exercise activities shows that aerobic dancing (Dyer & Crouch, 1988), jazz-dancing (Abele & Brehm, 1984, 1986), running/jogging (Abele, Brehm & Schmelz, 1989; Christen, 1986; Dyer & Crouch, 1988; Lichtman & Poser, 1983; Nowlis & Greenberg, 1979; Weinberg et al., 1988) and other fitness-related activities (Abele & Brehm, 1985, 1989; Abele, Brehm & Rahlmeyer, 1991; Droste et al., 1989; Dyer & Crouch, 1988; Lichtman & Poser, 1983) have similar mood effects. Swimming seems to be a less reliable mood inducer than other forms of endurance training (Abele, Brehm & Gall, 1987; Berger & Owen, 1988; Weinberg et al., 1988). The data on body-conditioning (no change, possibly due to a very high work load) and weight-lifting (positive changes) have to be replicated in order to be interpretable.

Control group comparisons

The control group comparisons either revealed no changes in the control conditions (seminar: Abele & Brehm, 1984, Berger & Owen, 1983; no exercise control group: Christen, 1986, Weinberg et al., 1988), only minor positive changes (hobby course: Lichtman & Poser, 1983; lecture class: Berger & Owen, 1988), or even negative changes (Dyer & Crouch, 1988). The comparison with relaxation related activities like yoga (Berger & Owen, 1988) and massage (Weinberg et al., 1988) showed similar effects with respect to tension reduction.

Summary

Summarizing, exercise of the type of fitness and/or endurance training consistently produces a "feel better phenomenon". The "iceberg profile" of tension reduction, i.e. decrease in anger, depression, excitation, fatigue, and confusion, increase in vigor, could frequently be observed in these studies. It is, however, only one element of the feel-better-phenomenon. The other element is mood enhancement (increase in elation, decrease in anger and depression), relaxation (increase in calmness), and mild activation (sometimes increase in activation, decrease in fatigue). These effects are independent of the person's sex and they are greatest for persons with an initially rather bad mood level. The mood effects of different types of fitness and endurance training are similar. The control group comparisons reveal that no-activity control groups and seminar control groups show much smaller, sometimes even negative mood changes compared with the exercise groups; relaxation control conditions, however, have similar mood effects. The findings thus support the above notion of an equilibrating effect of noncompetitive aerobic exercise, fitness and endurance training.

STUDIES ON COMPETITIVE SPORTS GAMES: THE DISEQUILIBRATING EFFECT

Sports games, for example playing tennis, volleyball, or soccer are in several aspects different from the above discussed fitness and endurance training activities: first, they require "open skills", i.e. skills which have to be continuously adapted to the respective situation. Open skills require more conscious cognitive monitoring than closed skills, for example running or swimming. A tuning out of the environment, and a free floating concentration upon the own person, as it has been described as a concomitant of the runner's high (Glasser, 1976), is impossible during performing open skills. Second, sports games are competitive social interactions, and competitive social interactions also require an exact monitoring of the environment. Third, these types of activity require varying degrees of work load, which means that the intensity of work load sometimes is above and sometimes below the "optimal" medium "aerobic" level. Finally, a competitive sports game always produces winners and losers, and success or failure have a definite influence on a person's sense of well-being. Accordingly, Berger & Owen (1988) have assumed that these types of activity are less suited for tension reduction than aerobic activities. There is, however, only very little evidence until now on the effects of activities like tennis, squash, volleyball, or soccer on a person's well-being.

Several studies within our own research group have been specifically concerned with this issue (Abele, Brehm & Klauschke, 1991; Abele, Brehm & Grothues, 1988; Abele, Brehm & Hässlein, 1988; Abele, Brehm & Stute, 1988). In contrast to Berger & Owen (1988) we assumed that the completion of sports games also leads to "tension reduction". This tension reduction, however, is intrinsically related to the activity itself, and is not "imported" from other areas of life. As was argued above, sport games should have a disequilibrating effect on a person's mood by leading to an "anticipatory mood effect" of increased tension and excitation before the game, and a sharp decrease of these mood aspects at its end. This tension circle should be independent of the game's result. The mood's elation component, in contrast, should be mainly dependent on the game's result, i.e. increase in positive feelings after a won and increase in negative feelings after a lost game.

We have analysed mood changes in volleyball (Abele, Brehm & Grothues, 1988), soccer (Abele, Brehm & Stute, 1988), and tennis players (Abele, Brehm & Hässlein, 1988; Abele, Brehm & Klauschke, 1991) before versus after their game. In three of these studies we have additionally compared mood changes during a competition with those during a training session in a within subjects repeated measures design. We assumed that the respective training sessions have no overall mood effects, since the benefits of physical activity are overlapped by repetitive and exhausting sequences of skill acquisition and training. With respect to the tension circle hypothesis we assumed that there should be pretest differences of higher excitation before a game than before a training session, but that there should be no posttest differences after the game versus after the training. Table 3.2 shows the main results.

Tension circle

In accord with the "tension-circle" hypothesis there was a decrease in excitation and activation from the beginning towards the end of the match, and this decrease was independent of the competitions' results and also independent of the type of sports (volleyball, soccer, tennis).

Joy and sadness after success and failure

Also in accord with the above assumption winners felt increased elation (all studies), and calmness (tennis and soccer), whereas losers felt increased anger, and depression (all studies), increased fatigue (three out of four studies), decreased elation (three out of four studies) and calmness (volleyball and soccer) after the game.

Figure 3.2 shows the average mood change profile after either a won or a lost volleyball, soccer, or tennis match. The change scores were corrected for the scale range and pretest mood level using a formula cited by Nitsch (1976, p. 87). Positive differences are computed by $((y_i - x_i)(y_i - a_1))/(a_2 - a_1)^2$; negative differences are computed by $((y_i - x_i)(a_2 - y_i))/(a_2 - a_1)^2$; a_1 is the minimal scale value, a_2 is the maximal scale value, x_i is the pre-test score, y_i is the post-test score.

Effects of training sessions

The training pre-test/post-test differences were much smaller than the competition pre-test/post-test changes. The soccer and volleyball trainings

Table 3.2. Effects of sports games like soccer, tennis and volleyball on mood

Study	Subjects	Activity	Treatment	Results
Abele, Brehm & Grothues, 1988	N = 105 male volleyball players age range 17–38	(a) volleyball training (b) volleyball competion	8 BFS scales, repeated measures before and after both activities	Competition: General decrease in activation, and in excitation, no change in contemplativeness; game won: significant increase in elation; game lost: significant decrease in elation and calmness, significant increase in anger, fatigue, and depression; Training: significant decrease in activation, elation and calmness, significant increase in anger, fatigue and depression, no change in excitation and contemplativeness; Comparison between training and competition: Pretest differences: higher activation, excitement, and lower fatigue before the game than before the training; Posttest differences: no differences in excitation; lower activation after training than after game; lost game—training similarities in fatigue and calmness; won game—training similarities in contemplativeness; training values intermediate between lost and won game; elation, anger, and depression; Changes: greater changes after competition than after training

Abele, Brehm & Hässlein, 1988	$N = 84$ male and female tennis players age range 14–57	tennis competition	8 BFS scales, repeated measures before and after the activity	General decrease in activation and excitation, no change in contemplativeness; match won: increase in elation and calmness, no change in anger, depression, and fatigue; match lost: increase in anger, depression, fatigue, and calmness; no change in elation
Abele, Brehn & Klauschke, 1991	$N = 40$ male and female tennis players: age range 15–65	(a) tennis training (b) tennis competition	8 BFS scales, repeated measures before and after both activities	Competition: General decrease in activation and excitation, increase in fatigue, no changes in calmness and contemplativeness; game won: increase in elation, no change in anger and depression; game lost: decrease in elation, increase in anger and depression Training: decrease in contemplativeness, no further changes Comparison between competition and training: Pretest differences: higher excitation and lower calmness before competition than before training Posttest differences: no differences in excitation and contemplativeness; lost game—training: higher depression, fatigue, anger and lower activation, elation and calmness after the lost game than after the training; Won game—training: higher elation after won game than after training Changes: greater changes after competition than after training

(continued overleaf)

Table 3.2. (*continued*)

Study	Subjects	Activity	Treatment	Results
Abele, Brehn & Stute, 1988	N = 201 male soccer players age range 17–40	(a) soccer training (b) soccer competition	8 BFS scales, repeated measures before and after both activities	Competition: General decrease in activation and excitation; game won: increase in elation and calmness, decrease in contemplativeness, no change in anger, fatigue and depression; game lost: increase in anger, fatigue, depression, decrease in elation and calmness, no change in contemplativeness; balanced result: besides decrease in activation and excitation no further changes; Training: no mood changes; Comparison between training and competition: Pretest differences: higher activation, and excitement, and lower fatigue before competition than before training; Posttest differences: training means similar to players with balanced results; Changes: greater changes after competition than after training

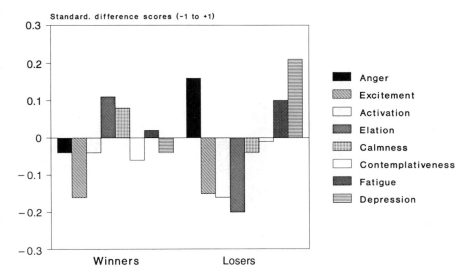

Figure 3.2 Average mood changes after a won versus a lost sports game (volleyball, soccer, tennis.)

revealed a "feel-tired phenomenon" of decreases in activation and calmness, and of increases in fatigue. The tennis trainings only resulted in contemplativeness reductions after the training session.

Competition–training comparison

The within subjects training versus competition comparison of pre-and post-activity excitation scores show preactivity, but no post-activity differences in all three studies. Figure 3.3 graphically depicts these findings.

Further differences between training and competition pre-/post-activity mood scores existed with respect to higher activation (soccer, volleyball) and lower-fatigue (soccer, volleyball) and calmness (soccer, volleyball, tennis) before the competition than before the training. In the volleyball study the post-test training versus competition scores did not differ with respect to contemplativeness, excitation, and calmness, whereas the other scores were more positive with respect to a won match than with respect to a training situation than with respect to a lost match. In the soccer study the post-test training and competition scores differed in all eight mood scales: the post-test training scores were more positive than the post-test lost match and balanced result scores, but more negative than the won match scores. In the tennis study there were again no training versus competition post-test differences in excitation and contemplativeness; a success led to higher elation scores than the

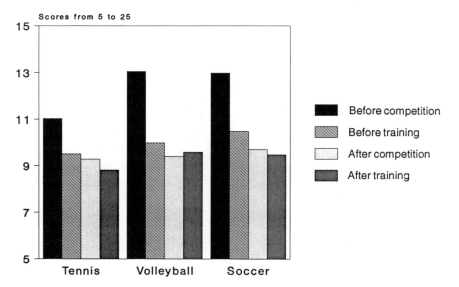

Figure 3.3 Training versus competition, pre- versus post-activity excitation scores (tennis, volleyball, soccer).

training situation; a failure led to higher depression, fatigue, and anger scores, and to lower elation and calmness scores than the training situation.

Sex and age differences

Both female and male tennis players experienced the above described tension circle, but it was sharper in female than in male tennis players. There were again only small differences between different age groups.

Initial mood level

Since the initial mood level of the soccer, volleyball, and tennis players was already influenced by their forthcoming activities, it was not analysed with respect to its influence on the post-test mood changes.

Perceived exertion

Perceived intensity of exertion was measured in the volleyball and soccer studies. In both studies perceived exertion was uncorrelated to mood changes in the training situation. In the competition situation perceived exertion was correlated with the game's result, i.e. higher perceived exertion after a lost than after a won game. After a success the perceived exertion scores were positively correlated to mood changes, i.e. more positive mood changes with high perceived exertion. After a failure, in contrast, perceived exertion was negatively correlated to mood, i.e. the higher the perceived exertion the more negative was a person's mood.

Experience

In all studies the players' skill level was measured by self-ratings and was correlated to the mood changes. There were only very small mood change differences dependent on this skill level: in one tennis study (Abele, Brehm & Hässlein, 1988) a higher skill level led to a smaller tension circle than a lower skill level. In the volleyball study a higher skill level was correlated with a greater increase in calmness, and in the soccer study there were no differences dependent on the players' skill level. However, in the training situations both the volleyball players and the soccer players experienced more positive mood changes, if their skill level was high than if it was low.

Comparison between different types of games

Without being conclusive the present data suggests that the disequilibrating effects of sports games are similar between different types of sports games, i.e. volleyball, soccer, and tennis. Further studies have to support this notion with respect to other sports games.

Other findings on mood effects of sports games (skills acquisition classes)

Berger & Owen (1988) studied fencing classes and found increases in vigor (no other changes). Weinberg et al. (1988) studied racquetball and tennis classes, and found higher general activation levels in these two classes than in the other classes; there were no pre-test post-test mood changes in the racquetball classes, and only one change in the tennis class (decrease in fatigue). Comparable to the above training session findings this data suggests that the mood effects of acquiring and training sports games skills are smaller than those of competitions, and also smaller than those of fitness and endurance training.

Summary

Summarizing, these studies suggest two distinctive mood effects of performing sports games. The first effect is concerned with the tension and activation dimension of mood, and can be described as a "tension circle" of an increased activation and excitation as an anticipatory mood change before the game, and a sharp decrease of activation and excitation at its end. This tension circle is independent of the game's result. And it also seems to be independent of the type of game. The second effect is concerned with the evaluative dimension of mood, and is the usual, i.e. sports unspecific phenomenon of joy after success and sadness after failure. The mood effects of sports games were independent of the participants' sex and age. The effects of perceived exertion and of the person's skill level have to be studied further. The mood effects of respective skills training and acquisition sessions seem to be much smaller than those of actually competing within this activity. And they also seem to be smaller than the effects of fitness- and endurance training activities. These results thus support the above notion of a disequilibrating effect of competitive sports games, which is mainly due to the anticipatory tension experienced before a competitive sports game.

CONCLUSIONS

Methodological questions

It may be argued that these findings are equivocal: there were no random assignments of subjects to procedures, and it is therefore not clear whether the findings reflect treatment- or selection-effects (see Folkins & Sime, 1981, Schwenkmezger, 1985, for a discussion of methodological issues). Since it is extremely difficult in field studies to randomly assign subjects to different exercise or sports games conditions (required skills, motivational aspects, etc.), the validity of the results has to be mainly assessed by convergent findings. As Tables 3.1 and 3.2 show there are many convergences in the findings discussed. However, more work has to be done to disentangle the effects of (self-) selection and treatment.

It may further be argued that the acute mood effects may also be found with other activities than exercise and sports. The above control group comparisons showed that the mood effects of fitness and endurance training were larger and also more positive than the effects of no-activity control conditions, or of seminar control conditions. The within subjects comparisons of competition and training sessions in sports games showed that the respective effects were different. However, the effects of relaxation control conditions (yoga, massage, see Table 3.1) were similar to those of fitness and endurance training. At present, we may conclude that there are specific mood effects of different kinds of physical activities; but that these mood effects may also be reached with some other activities. In his research on state anxiety Morgan (1987) has similarly argued. He assumed that every activity leading to an interruption of ongoing thought processes and to "time out" may have positive mood effects; the beneficial influence of exercise may just be longer.

What kind of physical activity leads to what kind of mood change?

With respect to the above theoretical assumptions on equilibrating and disequilibrating effects of different types of physical activities the present review suggests the following:

1. Fitness and endurance training activities lead to a general feel-better-phenomenon, which can be described as mood enhancement, tension reduction, relaxation, and mild activation. Fitness and endurance training has an equilibrating effect on a person's mood. Stress, tension, and negative feelings experienced in other areas of the exerciser's life can be reduced and altered. This type of exercise therefore can be recommended as a stress management technique (see also Sutherland & Cooper, 1990, Tucker, 1990). It is best achieved with running, calisthenics, and/or dancing, whereas swimming is not always suited for these mood effects.

2. The performance of competitive sport games, in contrast, leads to the experience of a tension circle, of thrill, of quick alterations in excitation and activation, and—dependent on the game's result—to the experience of either happiness or anger and depression. Sports games have a disequilibrating effect on a person's mood. In contrast to the tension reduction experienced in aerobic exercise the tension circle in sports games is intrinsically related to the activity itself, i.e. the pre-game heightened tension as due to the forthcoming competition, and the post-game lowered excitation and activation as due to the termination of the competition. Sports games may be less suited to repair a person's (bad) mood resulting from other activities. They are, however, suited for mood enhancement in the sense of excitation and thrill. The more unexciting and monotonous other aspects of a person's life, the more mood enhancing such a thrill experience should be.

3. Skills acquisition and training is the "necessary evil" for being able to perform sports games and other competitive activities. Even though these volleyball, tennis, soccer, and racquetball trainings are in several aspects comparable to fitness and endurance training activities (running, calisthenics, stretching, etc.), their acute mood effects are different, and by and large relatively weak. It may well be that the actor's interpretation of the situation is crucial. Is the activity a means for itself or is it a means for another ends? Does it lead to a tuning out of the environment or to its sharp monitoring? Is it voluntary or not? etc.

Exercise, sports games, well-being and health

It has been suggested above that both equilibration · and disequilibration processes are helpful for a person's general sense of well-being, and the review of the above empirical studies has supported the assumption that exercise has more equilibrating effects, whereas competitive sports games have more disequilibrating effects. It therefore seems clear that health psychology as related to physical activity cannot be concerned with exercise alone, but that it has also to be concerned with the beneficial effects of competitive sports games as an independent contribution to a person's well-being and health.

Future research perspectives

In the present authors' opinion four topics especially deserve further attention: the construction and evaluation of exercise programs under the perspective of well-being and mental health; the operationalization and measurement of the dependent variable; the differential perspective; and the theoretical integration of the exercise and mood findings into general frameworks of health psychology and into theories of subjective well-being.

Construction and evaluation of exercise programs under the specific perspective of well-being and mental health

One important topic deserving further attention is the construction and evaluation of exercise programs, which are especially designed for improving the participants' mood and psychological well-being. "Health" related exercise must be pleasant in order to be healthy both because psychological well-being is central to health, and because joy and pleasantness are important determinants of exercise adherence. This topic deserves an interdisciplinary approach (see Brehm & Pahmeier, 1991, for a discussion).

Operationalization and measurement of the dependent variable

Findings on exercise induced mood effects are confined to the measures taken. The dependent measures taken in exercise and mood studies have to be oriented at general mood conceptualizations, in order to give a full representation of the respective effects. The POMS, for example, has no operationalization of the positive activation and relaxation quadrants of mood.

The differential perspective

Throughout this paper it has been argued that exercise must be experienced as pleasant and satisfying in order to be healthy. These parameters, however, are highly subjective, and an exercise, which is pleasant to one person need not be pleasant to another person. We still know very little about possible relationships between differential personality factors and preferences for certain types of exercise. From an applied point of view, i.e. in order to give concrete advice, this question is of high importance. Another aspect of a differential perspective is the research into relationships between "life-styles" and mood alterations through exercise. From the above discussion of the tension circle in sports games one could, for example, conclude that this type of activity is less suited for persons generally experiencing high levels of stress and excitement. One could, in contrast, also assume that the experience of a joyful tension circle is advantageous especially for persons who otherwise experience more or less stressful tension circles.

Theoretical integration of the exercise, sports games and mood findings into general frameworks of health psychology and into theories of subjective well-being

The exercise and mood literature has resulted in important and also convergent findings, but it is by and large still in a pretheoretical stage. Theoretical accounts from health psychology and from the well-being literature can help to integrate them, and they can also help to design further theory based studies. The concepts of equilibrating and disequilibrating functions of exercise and sports advanced here and their integration into more general notions of well-being may be steps in this direction.

ACKNOWLEDGMENTS

Support for the here reported research by the Universities of Bielefeld and Erlangen is gratefully acknowledged.

REFERENCES

Abele, A. (1991). Auswirkungen von Wohlbefinden. Oder: Kann gute Laune schaden? In A. Abele & P. Becker (Eds), *Wohlbefinden. Theorie, Empirie und Diagnostik* (pp. 297–325). Weinheim: Juventa.

Abele, A. & Becker, P. (1991) (Eds). *Wohlbefinden. Theorie, Empirie, Diagnostik.* Weinheim: Juventa.

Abele, A. & Brehm, W. (1984). Befindlichkeitsveränderungen im Sport. Hypothesen, Modellbildung und empirische Befunde. *Sportwissenschaft*, 14, 252–275.

Abele, A. & Brehm, W. (1985). Einstellungen zum Sport, Präferenzen für das eigene Sporttreiben und Befindlichkeitsveränderungen nach sportlicher Aktivität. *Psychologie in Erziehung und Unterricht*, 32, 263–270.

Abele, A. & Brehm, W. (1986a). Zur Konzeptualisierung und Messung von Befindlichkeit. Die Entwicklung der Befindlichkeitsskalen (BFS). *Diagnostica.* 32, 209–228.

Abele, A. & Brehm, W. (1986b). Befindlichkeitsveränderungen im Sport II. Zur Bedingungsanalyse von Handlungssituationen im Sport. *Sportwissenschaft*, 16, 288–302.

Abele, A. & Brehm, W. (1988). Sportpsychologie. In Frey, D., Hoyos, C., Stahlberg, D. (Eds). *Angewandte Psychologie. Ein Lehrbuch* (pp. 540–560). München, Weinheim: Psychologie Verlagsunion, 540–560.

Abele, A. & Brehm, W. (1989). Changes in the state of being in physical education through the variation of work load and rhythm. *International Journal of Physical Education*, XXVI, 11–18.

Abele, A. & Brehm, W. (1990a). Sportliche Aktivität als gesundheitsbezogenes Handeln. In R. Schwarzer (Eds), *Gesundheitspsychologie* (pp. 131–150). Göttingen: Hogrefe.

Abele, A. & Brehm, W. (1990b). Gesundheit als Anreiz für freizeitsportliche Aktivitäten im Erwachsenenalter? In H. Lutter & A. Thomas (Eds) *Der Beitrag der Sportpsychologie zur Zielbestimmung einer modernen Erziehung und Ausbildung im Sport* (pp. 193–208). Köln: BPS Verlag.

Abele, A. & Brehm, W. (1990c). Wer ist der typische Fitness-Sportler? *Spektrum der Sportwissenschaft*, 2, 4–32.

Abele, A. & Brehm, W. (forthcoming). *Sport und Wohlbefinden*. Ausleichs- und Anregungseffekte sportlicher Aktivität.

Abele, A., Brehm, W. & Gall, T. (1987). *Befindlichkeitsveränderungen im Sport. Zum möglichen Stellenwert körperlicher Belastung am Beispiel Schwimmen*. Universität Bielefeld: Abteilung Sportwissenschaft.

Abele, A., Brehm, W. & Gall, T. (1991). Wohlbefinden und sportliche Aktivierung. In: Abele, A. & Becker, P. (Eds) *Wohlbefinden. Theorie–Empirie–Diagnostik*. (pp. 279–296). Weinheim: Juventa.

Abele, A., Brehm, W. & Grothues, P. (1988). *Befindlichkeitsveränderungen beim Volleyball in Wettkampf und Training*. Bielefeld: Abteilung Sportwissenschaft.

Abele, A., Brehm, W. & Hässlein, C. (1988). *Befindlichkeitsveränderungen beim Tennis in Abhängigkeit vom Spielausgang*. Universiät Erlangen: Institut für Psychologie.

Abele, A., Brehm, W. & Klauschke, A. (1991). *Befindlichkeitsveränderungen beim Tennis in Wettkampf und Training*. Universität Bielefeld: Abteilung Sportwissenschaft.

Abele, A., Brehm, W. & Rahlmeyer, D. (1991). *Befindlichkeitsveränderungen beim Fitnesstraining im Studio*. Universität Bielefeld: Abteilung Sportwissenschaft.

Abele, A., Brehm, W. & Schmelz, C. (1989). *Befindlichkeitsveränderungen beim Laufen*. Universität Bielefeld: Abteilung Sportwissenschaft.

Abele, A., Brehm, W. & Stute, A. (1988). *Befindlichkeitsveränderungen beim Fußball in Wettkampf und Training*. Universität Bielefeld: Abteilung Sportwissenschaft.

Abele, A. & Hermer, P. (in press) Mood effects on health related judgements: Negativity bias of negative mood and positivity bias of positive mood? *European Journal of Social Psychology*.

Barsky, A. J. (1988). The paradox of health. *The New England Journal of Medicine*, **318**, 414–418.

Becker, P. (1991). Theoretische Grundlagen. In: Abele, A. & Becker, P. (Eds) *Wohlbefinden. Theorie–Empirie–Diagnostik*. (pp. 13–49). Weinheim: Juventa.

Berger, B. G. & Owen, D. R. (1983). Mood alteration with swimming. *Psychosomatic Medicine*, **45**, 425–433.

Berger, B. G. & Owen, D. R. (1986). Mood alterations with swimming: A re-evaluation. In L. Van der Velden & J. Humphrey (Eds), *Current selected research in the psychology and sociology of sport. Vol. 1 (pp. 97–113)*. New York: AMS Press.

Berger, B. G. & Owen, D. R. (1988). Stress reduction and mood enhancement in four exercise moods: swimming, body conditioning, hatha yoga, and fencing. *Research Quarterly for Exercise and Sport*, **59**, 148–159.

Berlyne, D. E. (1960). *Conflict, Arousal and Curiosity*. New York: McGraw-Hill.

Brehm, W. & Pahmeier, I. (1990). Aussteigen oder dabeibleiben? Bruchstellen einer Breitensportkarriere und Bedingungen eines Ausstiegs. *Spectrum der Sportwissenschaften*, **2**, 33–56.

Brehm, W. & Pahmeier, I. (1991). *Gesundheitsförderung durch sportliche Aktivierung als gemeinsame Aufgabe von Ärzten, Krankenkassen und Sportvereinen*. Universität Bielefeld: Abteilung Sportwissenschaft, Projektabschulßbericht.

Christen, J. (1986). *Ausdauertraining und psychisches Befinden*. Zürich: Technische Hochschule.

Dishman, R. (1984). Motivation and exercise adherence. In J. Silva & R. Weinberg (Eds) *Psychological Foundations of Sport* (pp. 420–434). Champaign: Human Kinetics Publ.

Dishman, R., Sallis, J. & Orenstein, D. (1985). The determinants of physical activity and exercise. *Public Health Reports*, **100**, 158–171.

Droste, I., Klass, M. & Richterling, G. (1989). Psychoregulative Erholung über ein bewegungsorientiertes Entspannungsprogramm. Eine Evaluationsstudie. *Sporttherapie in Theorie und Praxis*, **2**, 3–7.

Dyer, J. B. & Crouch, J. G. (1988). Effects of running and other activities on moods. *Perceptual and Motor Skills*, **67**, 43–50.

Elias, N. & Dunning, E. (1986). *Quest for Excitement. Sport and Leisure in the Civilizing Process*. Oxford: 1986.

Folkins, C. & Sime, W. (1981). Physical fitness training and mental health. *American Psychologist*, **36**, 373–389.

Glasser, W. (1976). *Positive Addiction*. New York: Harper & Row.

Gondola, J. & Tuckman, B. (1983). Extent of training and mood enhancement in women runners. *Perceptual and Motor Skills*, **57**, 333–334.

Grupe, O. (1982). *Bewegung, Spiel und Leistung im Sport*. Hofmann: Schorndorf.

Headey, B. & Wearing, A. (1989). Personality, life events, and subjective well-being: Toward a dynamic equilibrium model. *Journal of Personality and Social Psychology*, **57**, 731–739.

Heckhausen, H. (1978). Entwurf einer Psychologie des Spielens. In A. Flitner (Ed), *Das Kinderspiel*. (pp. 133–149). München.

Hollmann, W. (Ed) (1986). *Zentrale Themen der Sportmedizin*. Berlin: Springer.

Isen, A. (1984). Toward understanding the role of affect in cognition. In R. Wyer & T. Srull (Ed). *Handbook of Social Cognition. Vol. I* (pp. 174–236). Hillsdale, NJ: Erlbaum.

Lichtman, S. & Poser, E. (1983). The effects of exercise on mood and cognitive functioning. *Journal of Psychosomatic Research*, **27**, 43–52.

McIntyre, C., Watson, D. & Cunningham, A. (1990). The effects of social interaction, exercise, and test stress on positive and negative affect. *Bulletin of the Psychonomic Society*, **28**, 141–143.

McNair, D. M., Lorr, M. & Droppleman, L. F. (1971). *Manual for the Profile of Mood States*. San Diego: Educational and Industrial Testing Service.

Morgan, W. P. (1980). Test of champions: The iceberg profile. *Psychology Today*, **21**, 92–99.

Morgan, W. P. (1987). Reduction of State Anxiety Following Acute Physical Activity. In: W. Morgan & S. Goldston (Eds), *Exercise and Mental Health* (pp. 105–111). Washington: Hemisphere Publishing Corporation.

Morgan, W. & Goldstone, S. (Eds) (1987). *Exercise and Mental Health*. Washington: Hemisphere Publishing Corporation.

Morris, W. N. (1989). *Mood. The frame of mind*. New York: Springer.

Mrazek, J. (1984). Körper-Fragebogen. Die Verkörperung des Selbsts, Ergebnisse der Psychologie heute Umfrage. *Psychologie heute*, **2**, 50–58.

Nitsch, J. (1976). Die Eigenzustandsskala. In: J. Nitsch & I. Udris (Eds), *Beanspruchung im Sport* (pp. 81–102). Bad Homburg: Limpert.

Nowlis, D. P. & Greenberg, N. (1979). Empirical Description of Effects of Exercise and Mood. *Perceptual and Motor Skills*, **49**, 1001–1002.

Powell, K. E., Thompson, P. D., Caspersen, K. J., Kendric, J. S. (1987). Physical activity and the incidence of coronary heart disease. *Annual Review of Public Health*, **8**, 253–288.

Russell, J. (1980). A circumflex model of affect. *Journal of Personality and Social Psychology*, **39**, 1161–1178.

Sachs, M. L. (1984). Psychological well-being and vigorous physical activity. In J. M. Silva & R. S. Weinberg (Hg). *Psychological Foundations of Sport*. Champaign: Human Kinetics Publ., 435–444.

Schwenkmezger, P. (1985). Welche Bedeutung kommt dem Ausdauertraining in der Depressionstherapie zu? *Sportwissenschaft*, **15**, 117–135.

Schwenkmezger, P. (1991). Wohlbefinden und Persönlichkeit. In: A. Abele und P. Becker (Eds), *Wohlbefinden. Theorie–Empirie–Diagnostik* (pp. 119–137). Weinheim: Juventa.

Steptoe, A. & Bolton, J. (1988). The short term influence of high and low intensity physical exercise on mood. *Psychology and Health*, 2, 91–106.

Steptoe, A. & Cox, S. (1988). The acute effects of aerobic exercise on mood: a controlled study. *Health Psychology*, 7, 329–340.

Strack, F., Argyle, M. & Schwartz, N. (1991). *Subjective Well-Being. An Interdisciplinary Perspective*. Oxford: Pergamon Press.

Sutherland, W. J. & Cooper, E. L. (1990). Exercise and stress-management: Fit employees–healthy organisations? *International Journal of Sport Psychology*, 21, 202–217.

Sutton-Smith, B. (1973). Games—The socialization of conflict. *Sportwissenschaft*, 3, 41–46.

Tucker, L. A. (1990). Physical fitness and psychological distress. *International Journal of Sport Psychology*, 21, 185–201.

Wankel, L. M. (1985). Personal and situational factors affecting exercise involvement: the importance of enjoyment. *Research Quarterly for Exercise and Sport*, 56, 275–282.

Wankel, L. M. (1988). Exercise Adherence and Leisure Activity. In R. Dishman (Ed), *Exercise Adherence. Its Impact on Public Health*. Champaign: Human Kineitcs Publ., 369–396.

Watson, D. & Tellegen, A. (1985). Toward a consensual structure of mood. *Psychological Bulletin*, 98, 219–235.

Weinberg, R., Jackson, A. & Kolodny, K. (1988). The relationship of Massage and Exercise to Mood Enhancement. *The Sport Psychologist*, 2, 202–211.

Weineck, J. (1988). *Sportbiologie*. Erlangen: Perimed.

4 The Alameda Study—25 Years Later

CHARLOTTE A. SCHOENBORN
Centers for Disease Control, National Center for Health Statistics,
6525 Belcrest Road, Room 850, Hyattsville, Maryland 20782, USA

INTRODUCTION AND BACKGROUND

In the nineteenth and early twentieth centuries the health status of a population was measured in terms of mortality rates and incidence of communicable diseases. During the first part of the twentieth century, it was recognized that disease incidence and death rates did not provide a complete picture of the health status of a population (Berkman & Breslow, 1983). New epidemiologic techniques were developed to measure health in the more general sense, using information from the subject rather than from clinical or vital records. More emphasis was placed on the prevalence of chronic conditions and associated disability as opposed to incidence of acute conditions, and studies were conducted in community rather than institutional settings.

Inspired by community-based epidemiologic morbidity surveys, the California State Department of Public Health started a chronic disease program in the late 1940s in order to measure the nature and extent of chronic conditions in California (Berkman & Breslow, 1983). A tumor registry was established under this program. A pilot morbidity survey was conducted in San Jose, California, and after its successful completion, a statewide household interview morbidity survey was undertaken during 1954–55 (Berkman & Breslow, 1983).

At this point, the California investigators began focusing on two broad issues:
1. conceptualization and measurement of health consistent with the World Health Organization's definition (that is, a state of physical, social, and mental well-being); and
2. assessment of the relationship between health and certain ways of living, including personal habits and familial, cultural, economic, social, and environmental factors.

In 1959, with funds from the National Institutes of Health, the Human Population Laboratory (HPL) of the California State Health Department was established with three long-range objectives:

International Review of Health Psychology. Volume 2. Edited by S. Maes, H. Leventhal and M. Johnston
© 1993 John Wiley & Sons Ltd

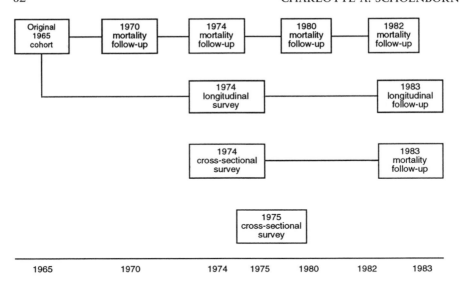

Figure 4.1   The Alameda Study (1965–83).

1. to assess the level of health (including physical, mental, and social) of Alameda County, California residents;
2. to ascertain whether particular levels in one dimension of health tend to be associated with comparable levels in other dimensions; and
3. to determine the association between various ways of living and selected demographic characteristics and health status.

With these as the goals, a multidisciplinary research team was assembled and began work developing a study which would quantify health in a community, based on the World Health Organization's definition of health (Berkman & Breslow, 1983). In each of the three categories of health (physical, social, and mental), a variety of items were employed which measured not only the absence of disease or impairment but the presence of health. This study, entitled "Health and Ways of Living" was fielded in Alameda County, California in 1965 and has come to be known as "The Alameda Study."

The Alameda Study has had a major impact on research related to the study of health—its meaning and its predictors. Data were collected on a probability sample of adults in the county aged 20 years and over. Self-administered, mail questionnaires were completed by 6928 adults, which constituted 86% of the enumerated sample. The original 1965 cohort has been studied for 25 years with two follow-up surveys and numerous mortality follow-ups linking health and other data on deceased respondents with their death records. Studies have been fielded to replicate some of the key findings of the Alameda study. These studies have included national and state-level surveys, local community surveys, and studies of special populations.

This chapter will review concept measurement and findings of the original study and its follow-up components, as well as those of many of its successors. The articles and other publications included in this review, although not comprehensive, constitute a representative selection of the work on the Alameda Survey and its successors. Omissions of work related to the Alameda or related studies were due to either lack of availability or to time and space constraints of this review.

This review proceeds in chronological order, beginning with the original 1965 cross-sectional study and continuing through the 1982 mortality follow-up of the 1974 cohort (Figure 4.1). Because the Alameda Study was designed to measure health in a global sense (a state of physical, mental, and social well-being), resulting in a wide range of issues being examined at the various stages of the survey, it was felt that chronological approach would best allow the reader to understand the nature and scope of this important longitudinal study. Other studies that have been stimulated by the findings from the Alameda study are included as examples of the far-reaching effects that this study has had on the research community and the progress of public health.

THE ORIGINAL ALAMEDA STUDY

For the original Alameda Study, indices were constructed to operationalize the World Health Organization definition of health—physical, mental, and social well-being. Lifestyle factors such as health habits and personal health care thought to influence health also were measured. A description of these health status and related indicators and a brief discussion of selected findings follows.

Health status

Physical health. The indicator of physical health status developed for the Alameda Study was designed to measure a spectrum of health ranging from severely disabled to healthy with a high energy level. The categories were established largely on *a priori* grounds (Belloc, Breslow & Hochstim, 1971) but subsequent methodological research showed the questionnaire items to be valid and highly reliable in a probability sample of Alameda County residents (Hochstim & Renne, 1971; Meltzer & Hochstim, 1970).

The categories of the physical health spectrum and the proportion of persons classified in each category in the Alameda sample were as follows (Belloc, Breslow & Hochstim, 1971):

1. Severely disabled—trouble with activities of daily living (ADLs) such as feeding and dressing, or unable to work for six months or longer (7%);
2. Somewhat disabled—no trouble with ADLs and able to work but had some other work or other limitation for six months or longer (8%);

3. Not disabled but had two or more impairments or chronic conditions in the past 12 months (9%);
4. Not disabled but had one chronic condition or impairment in past 12 months (19%);
5. Not disabled, no chronic condition or impairment but had one or more symptoms in past 12 months (28%);
6. Not disabled, no chronic conditions or impairments, no symptoms, but low to medium energy level (23%); and
7. Not disabled, no chronic conditions or impairments, no symptoms, and a high energy level (6%).

Throughout this chapter, the term "health status" will refer to health measured in terms of this continuum unless otherwise specified.

Initial analyses, examining sociodemographic differentials in physical health status revealed that men, younger persons, and persons with higher incomes were generally in better health than women, older adults and those with inadequate incomes (Belloc, Breslow & Hochstim, 1971). The employed were healthier than persons who were out of work or retired; separated persons were less healthy than persons in other marital status categories. Blacks and whites were about equally healthy in terms of this physical health spectrum, and Chinese and Japanese persons were healthier.

Mental health.   Five indices of psychological health status were contained in the 1965 survey:
1. a 19-item index of "ego-resiliency";
2. a 20-item index of "neurotic traits";
3. a nine-item index of "anomie";
4. an nine-item index measuring positive and negative feelings; and
5. a nine-item index related to satisfaction with social roles (Berkman & Breslow, 1983).

A factor analysis of these items resulted in seven factors:
1. personal uncertainty;
2. anomie, normlessness;
3. life satisfaction;
4. social insecurity;
5. perfectionism;
6. negative feelings; and
7. isolation-depression.

Berkman (1971) constructed an index of psychological well-being using the eight positive and negative feelings. The positive feelings were feeling:
1. on top of the world;
2. particularly excited or interested in something, and
3. pleased about having accomplished something.

The negative feelings were feeling:
1. very lonely or remote from other people;

2. depressed or very unhappy;
3. bored;
4. so restless you couldn't sit long in a chair; and
5. vaguely uneasy about something without knowing why.

As with physical health, sociodemographic variations in mental health status were found (Berkman, 1971). Worse than average mental health was found among the young and the very old, and as well as persons with inadequate income. Ethnic origin, education, occupation, employment status, and marital status were all moderately associated with the index of psychological well-being. Men and women, however, did not differ significantly in terms of mental health status.

Social health. In the Alameda Study, social health was conceptualized in terms of the degree to which individuals were functioning members of their community (Renne, 1974). This measure of social health was designed specifically for Alameda County, California but probably is generalizable to any large urban American setting. The social health index consisted of four parts:

1. an employability index composed of occupation, education, and job stability measured in terms of number of jobs held in the past 10 years;
2. a six-item index of marital satisfaction;
3. a sociability index consisting of number of close friends and relatives and frequency of contact with them; and
4. an indicator of degree of community involvement consisting of church attendance, political activities, and/or membership in labor unions, professional associations, recreational groups or similar organizations.

In the Alameda Study population, older adults tended to score higher on the social health index than younger adults (Renne, 1974). Married men and women did not differ significantly although among unmarried people, women scored much higher than men. Social health also was strongly and positively associated with family income. Differences in social health scores between blacks and whites varied for the different components of social health. Whites tended to be more satisfied with their marriages and to be more highly employable, but blacks tended to score higher in terms of sociability and community involvement. The result was that the overall social health differences between the two groups were quite small. Ethnic differences between whites and other groups such as Chinese, Japanese, and Mexican-Americans, were found only for women, with white women consistently better off than women in the other ethnic groups. No significant ethnic differences were found for men.

Interrelationships: physical, mental, and social health

Physical, mental, and social health were found to be interrelated in the Alameda Study. Mental and physical health were found to be correlated, even after controlling for sex, age, and income adequacy (Berkman, 1971). Social health was found to be associated with physical health, both in terms of an index of physical functioning described earlier and in terms of subjectively-rated health status, and with mental health (Renne, 1974). Renne stuggested that subjective assessments of physical health probably reflect an overall state of mind which both affects and is affected by social health. The association between social and mental health probably reflects a process of mutual reinforcement: people who are emotionally well are more able to engage in healthy social relationships; and people who are socially healthy (that is, have happy marriages, are involved in organized social groups, and are assured of gainful employment) are better able to enjoy emotional well-being (Renne, 1974).

Health habits

Selected health habits or behaviors were included in the Alameda Study based on researcher's hypotheses that these could be related to long-term health outcomes (Belloc & Breslow, 1972). The health habits were: hours of sleep, eating breakfast, snacking, physical activity, alcohol consumption, cigarette smoking, and weight for height. Weight for height, while not strictly a behavior, was included as an indicator that a person was eating more than necessary to maintain desirable weight.

Cross-sectional analyses of the relationship between seven health habits and health status revealed that persons who slept seven–eight hours a night, ate breakfast daily, avoided snacks, maintained desirable weight for height, participated in leisure time physical activities, drank fewer than five alcoholic beverages at a time, and had never smoked cigarettes, were healthier than persons who did not follow these health practices (Belloc & Breslow, 1972). Although a few of the habits were correlated (female smokers were more likely to maintain desirable weight and people who ate breakfast were more likely to be nonsmokers), no common factor seemed to be underlying the association between health habits and health status. The effects of positive health behaviors were additive, however, with individuals reporting more of the seven good habits having better health status than persons reporting fewer of them. These relationships were independent of economic status.

Summary

The Alameda Study thus established a framework for the study of health which includes all aspects of personal well-being. Recognizing that personal well-being depends on considerably more than absence of disease, the Alameda group set out to establish indicators that would allow the assessment of physical, mental, and social well-being in a general population. Early results suggested that the various aspects of health were interrelated and that important differences existed among various population subgroups. Further, the Alameda Study introduced the concept that individual personal health behaviors may influence health status and provided initial evidence to support this hypothesis. Having done this, the course was set to investigate the nature of these interrelationships over time and document the long-term health consequences of personal health habits.

1970 MORTALITY FOLLOW-UP: FIVE AND A HALF YEARS LATER

In 1970, a mortality follow-up of the 1965 cohort was carried out using death records registered in the state of California (Belloc, 1973). Respondents who had moved out of state and subsequently died were missed using this procedure and anyone for whom a death certificate was not located at the end of 1970 was considered to be alive. The mortality rates from this follow-up may have been somewhat understated for this reason.

Findings

Age- and sex-specific mortality rates, as well as age-adjusted rates, were calculated for persons having each of the seven health habits. All seven behaviors were found to predict lower mortality (Belloc, 1973). The habits and behaviors associated with lower mortality rates at the five and a half year follow-up were the same as those associated with better physical health status in cross-sectional analysis of the 1965 cohort: sleeping seven–eight hours; eating breakfast almost every day; rarely or occasionally eating snacks; often or sometimes engaging in active sports or swimming or often gardening or exercising; drinking fewer than five alcoholic beverages at one time; never having smoked cigarettes; and maintaining desirable weight (5% underweight to 20% overweight for men and 10% overweight or less (including underweight) for women).

Alameda County respondent were classified according to whether they had "good" habits or "bad" habits and life tables were calculated according to total number of good health habits (Belloc, 1973). The life expectancy (average number of years of life remaining) of men aged 45 years was 21.6 years for men with zero–three good practices compared with 33.1 years for men with six–seven good practices—a difference of 11 years. The relationship between good health practices and reduced mortality rates was found to be independent of income and baseline health status.

In another analysis based on the 1970 mortality follow-up, Berkman (1975) found that people who said that they stayed indoors or in bed due to illness during the year preceding the 1965 survey had lower five-year mortality rates than people who reported no such disability days. Berkman concluded that some indulgence in the sick role (staying home and/or in bed when ill) may actually be healthier than continuing with one's daily activities and may represent not so much morbidity or disability but appropriate health care. He cautioned, however, that many factors other than days spent in bed may be responsible for the reduced mortality and require further study.

1974 MORTALITY FOLLOW-UP: NINE AND A HALF YEARS LATER

At the beginning of 1974, a second mortality follow-up was undertaken in conjunction with a follow-up mail survey of the original cohort. For persons who could not be located for the mail survey, death records were searched for the state of California and, if none was found, for the person's state of birth (Breslow & Enstrom, 1980). Unlike the 1970 mortality follow-up, all deaths known to have occurred outside California, including those occurring in states other than the person's state of birth, were included in this study. Of the original 6928 respondents, death certificates were located for 717 decedents through the end of 1974. Anyone for whom a death certificate was not located was presumed to be alive. In this phase of the study, baseline physical health status, social network ties, health habits, gender, and poverty were examined as possible predictors of mortality. These analyses were in keeping with the one of the two original Alameda Study missions—that is, assessment of the relationship between health and certain ways of living, including personal habits and familial, cultural, economic, social, and environmental factors.

Findings

Physical health status and mortality

The relationship between perceived health status as reported by the respondent in 1965 and vital status nine and a half years later was examined using data from the 1974 mortality follow-up (Kaplan & Camacho, 1983). This study included the entire 1965 cohort of 6928 men and women aged 20–94 years. The authors examined mortality differentials between persons who rated their health as excellent or good in 1965 versus those who rated their health as fair or poor. Persons who rated their health as poor in 1965 had nearly two-fold increased risk of death over the follow-up period, compared with persons who rated their health as excellent, even after the effects of other significant covariables such as physical health status, health practices, social networks, psychological state, sex, and age were eliminated. Mortality rates of persons who rated their health as *either* fair or poor also were significantly higher than mortality rates for persons who rated their health as *either* excellent or good. The authors cautioned that, although their study found that self-perceived health was associated with subsequent mortality outcomes independently of other social and psychological variables, this does not mean that these other variables are unimportant for survival. In fact, Kaplan & Camacho (1983) noted that persons who had poor perceived health were also more likely to engage in harmful behaviors such as smoking and drinking alcohol and more likely to be socially isolated, and that the individuals who possessed all of these characteristics were at an almost eight-fold increased risk of death during the nine-year follow-up period.

A related study examined self-reports of various symptoms and conditions such as high blood pressure, heart trouble, shortness of breath, chest pain, and swollen ankles as predictors of ischemic heart disease. Using data for persons who were aged 35–94 years in 1965, Kaplan & Kotler (1985) found that men who reported high blood pressure, heart trouble, and shortness of breath and women who reported heart trouble, swollen ankles, and chest pain were more likely to have died from ischemic heart disease by 1974. The same findings were obtained for death from all causes. The authors concluded that the strength and consistency of the relationships between these self-reports and subsequent mortality indicates that such reports are valid indicators of underlying disease states.

Social networks and mortality

Using the original 1965 measure of social health as a foundation, Berkman (1977) developed a social network index based on the nine-year mortality experience of Alameda County respondents. The index consisted of:
1. marital status;
2. number and frequency of contact with close friends and relatives;
3. church membership; and
4. membership in informal and formal group associations, with intimate social contacts weighted more heavily than church affiliations and group memberships.

Each of the four social network characteristics (marital status, close friends and relatives, church membership, and group associations) were examined in terms of their relationship to mortality nine and a half years after the baseline Alameda survey (Berkman & Syme, 1979). The analysis was limited to persons 30–69 years of age at the time of the baseline survey because of the expected low mortality in the under 30 year age group and the expected high mortality among those 70 years and over.

Marital status was found to predict mortality among men, with married men significantly less likely to die than single, divorced or widowed men. Degree of marital satisfaction predicted mortality only for men aged 30–59 years. For women, neither marital status nor marital satisfaction predicted mortality in the nine and a half years between the original survey and the 1974 follow-up. In fact, among women over 50 years of age, those who were more satisfied with their marriages had higher mortality rates than those who were less satisfied.

The second component of the social network index consisted of the number of close friends and relatives and the frequency of contact with them each month. Although individually the items did not predict mortality, when the number of friends and relatives were combined, mortality rates were higher for those with few or no friends or relatives. Absence of *both* friends and relatives resulted in the greatest increase in mortality risk for both men and women but the differential was considerably greater for women.

The less intimate forms of social contact—church and other group memberships—also were found to be associated with mortality outcomes, although not as strongly as the more intimate social ties. Church membership was related to increased probability of survival among both men and women while other formal and informal group memberships were significantly only for women.

Combining the four social network components into one index revealed that the presence of some network features can compensate for the absence of others. For example, people who were not married but had many close friends and relatives had mortality rates comparable to people who were married but had few contacts with close friends and relatives. The relationship between social network ties and mortality was found to be independent of physical health at the time of the 1965 survey, year of death, socioeconomic status, race, level of urbanization, geographic mobility, occupational mobility, level of urbanization, utilization of preventive services, and a variety of psychological factors.

Health habits and mortality

Findings from the 1965 Alameda County Survey revealed an association between health habits and health status but, because of the cross-sectional nature of the data, the direction of causality could not be established. Findings from the 1970 mortality follow-up suggested that poor health habits were a causal agent but since the data were collected only five and a half years after the initial survey, it was still possible that mortality differentials were due to respondents having poor heath habits (sleeping and eating poorly, being underweight, etc.) because they were already sick in 1965. By the time of the 1974 follow-up, any effects of initial ill health on mortality outcomes should have been erased. Yet, nine and a half years after the initial interview, the relationship between good health habits and survival remained, thereby supporting the hypothesis that health habits are causally related to mortality outcomes (Breslow & Enstrom, 1980).

A multivariate analysis of health-related practices showed that four of the original seven Alameda habits (never smoking, physical activity, low alcohol consumption, and sleeping seven–eight hours) were independently related to mortality outcomes (Wingard, Berkman & Brand, 1982). This was true even after adjustment for the other health habits, sociodemographic characteristics, social health status, and original health status. Maintaining desirable body weight showed a slight but non-significant association with mortality. The final two habits of the original seven, breakfast and snacking, were found to be unrelated to mortality after multivariate adjustment.

Wingard & Berkman (1983) used the nine and a half year mortality data to explore in more depth mortality risks associated with sleeping habits. They found that persons sleeping six hours or less or nine hours or more a night had death rates 1.3 times that of persons who slept seven–eight hours a night. This difference was statistically significant even after controlling for differences in age, sex, health status, and other social and behavioral characteristics. When specific causes of death were examined, persons who slept seven–eight hours a night had lower death rates from ischemic heart disease, cancer, and stroke.

Gender and mortality

One of the longstanding and unexplained mysteries in health research is the mortality differentials between men and women. The Alameda Study allowed examination of the popular hypothesis that women live longer than men because men engage in more behaviors detrimental to health. Sex differences in mortality rates after nine and a half years were examined, controlling for 16 demographic and behavioral factors contained in the Alameda survey (Wingard, 1982). Even after controlling for these 16 factors, mortality differentials remained. The authors concluded that examination of the interaction of biologic and behavioral risk factors may more fully explain the sex differential in mortality.

Poverty status and mortality

Haan, Kaplan & Camacho (1987) examined the mortality experience of 1811 adults aged 35 and over who, in 1965, were residents of poverty and non-poverty areas of the largest city in Alameda County, Oakland. Approximately 41% of Oakland's 1965 population lived in the Census tracts designated as poverty areas. In this study, the mortality rates of residents of federally designated Oakland poverty areas were compared with mortality rates of Oakland residents who lived outside the poverty areas. Consistent with earlier studies, this analysis showed that mortality rates in the poverty areas were higher than in the non-poverty areas, even after adjusting for age, sex, race, baseline physical health status, low income, lack of medical care, unemployment, education, health practices, social isolation, psychological uncertainty, and depression. The authors concluded that the association between socioeconomic conditions and mortality was independent of individual-level risk factors and suggested that the search for a causal link between poverty and disease should include the many social and environmental demands (such as high crime rates, poor housing, lack of transportation, and greater exposure to environmental contaminants) placed upon residents of poverty areas.

Summary

Findings from the 1974 Alameda Study mortality follow-up demonstrated that mortality outcomes could be predicted from information obtained in a population-based epidemiologic survey. Physical health status and symptoms of disease, social networks, personal health habits, poverty status, and gender were all found to be predictors of survival nine and a half years after the initial Alameda survey.

1974 FOLLOW-UP QUESTIONNAIRE SURVEY

In 1974, a survey was undertaken to re-contact the original 1965 cohort, with essentially the same questionnaire, to assess their current health practices and health status (Breslow & Enstrom, 1980). Of the 6246 presumed survivors, 5974 were located and 5722 of these received a questionnaire. A total of 4864 questionnaires were completed and returned, constituting a response rate of 78% of presumed survivors and 85% of questionnaire recipients. Although 1974 non-respondents were similar to respondents in terms of age, sex, income, and other sociodemographic characteristics, both non-respondents and decedents had somewhat fewer good health practices than did respondents.

Findings

Changes in health practices over time

Total number of good health practices were found to be quite stable between the two time points (Breslow & Enstrom, 1980). That is, people who had low health practice scores (zero–three good health practices) in 1965 usually had low scores in 1974; people who had high scores (six–seven good practices) in 1965 were likely to have high scores in 1974. Although no data were available for the intervening nine years, the assumption is that the habits remained fairly constant across this time period.

In terms of specific health practices, differences in the distributions between the two surveys were consistent with changes that occurred in the United States as a whole. There was a tendency toward greater prevalence of both overweight and underweight and toward reductions in prevalence of cigarette smoking. Other habits remained stable except for a slight tendency away from eating breakfast every day.

Lazarus et al. (1989) used the longitudinal Alameda data to examine the possible effect of baseline smoking and body mass on physical activity levels nine years later. They found that declines in leisure time physical activity were greater among current smokers than among persons who had never smoked. Persons who had had the greatest exposure to cigarette smoke in terms of number of pack-years, showed the largest declines in physical activity over the follow-up period. An association between body mass index and subsequent physical activity was also found, although men and women differed in some respects. Leaner women registered increases in physical activity while heavier women showed declines in activity over the follow-up period. Among men, initially there appeared to be no relationship between body mass index and subsequent physical activity. When age-specific changes were examined, however, younger, leaner men were found to have increased their activity while older, leaner men decreased their activity compared with men the same age of average weight. The authors concluded that levels of one risk factor can result in changes in other risk factors over time. Therefore, high risk behaviors such as smoking can have both direct health effects stemming from the behavior itself (such as lung cancer) and indirect health effects which result from health changes caused by the related health behavior.

Health practices and subsequent health status

The relationship between health practices and health status was initially investigated using the 1965 cross-sectional data (Belloc & Breslow, 1972). Although evidence was found of an association between good health practices and favorable health status, it was recognized that causal inferences could not be made due to the cross-sectional nature of the data: poor health habits (e.g. poor sleeping habits, underweight, and lack of physical activity) can cause poor health status but poor health status also can cause poor health habits. Mortality studies provided evidence that certain habits were causally linked to survival (Belloc, 1973) but the 1974 follow-up survey was the first to provide clear evidence that health habits do influence subsequent health status (Breslow & Enstrom, 1980).

Wiley & Camacho (1980) looked at changes in health status between 1965 and 1974, among white adults who were 20–69 years of age in 1965. The analysis was limited to whites to control for known correlations among race, lifestyle, and health status (Camacho & Wiley, 1983). Persons 70 years of age and over were excluded because it was felt that health in old age reflects not so much the effects of recent behaviors, but rather the cumulative effect of a lifetime of behaviors.

The outcome variable for this analysis was based on the seven-point health status index developed for the 1965 survey, with some adjustments. The values of the 1965 health status categories ranged from one for persons with severe disability to seven for persons with no symptoms and a high energy level, with equal intervals between scores. Recognizing that the intervals between the health status scores were not actually equivalent, Wiley and Camacho re-scaled the 1965 values for the 1974 analysis, based on the nine-year survival of persons in each level of health. The age-standardized survival rates ranged from 77.0 per 100 for the severely disabled to 93.2 per 100 for persons with no symptoms and a high energy level. The outcome variable for this study consisted of the difference between the actual 1974 health status score and the score expected on the basis of age, sex, and 1965 health status and therefore was a relative rather than an absolute measure of health.

Controlling for the effects of age, sex, and initial health status, five of the seven Alameda health habits reported in 1965 were found to be associated with health status in 1974. The two behaviors shown not to be related to subsequent health status were breakfast and snacking. The other five behaviors were related but not always in precisely the same way as in earlier studies of the Alameda population. Specific results follow.

Smoking. In cross-sectional analyses of the relationship between health habits and health status, persons who had never smoked clearly had more favorable health status than did persons who had ever smoked, including both current and former smokers (Belloc & Breslow, 1972). In the longitudinal analysis, although persons who were nonsmokers in 1965 had better health in 1974 than did persons who were smoking in 1965, the group with the most favorable adjusted health status scores at follow-up were those who had been smokers but who had quit smoking by the time of the 1965 survey. This finding can be attributed to differences in measurement between the cross-sectional analysis and the longitudinal one. The 1974 health status score reflects the difference between expected and actual health status rather than a measure of absolute level of health.

Alcohol consumption. Findings concerning the relationship between alcohol consumption and health status varied between the cross-sectional and longitudinal studies. Cross-sectionally, consuming fewer than five drinks at one sitting was found to be associated with better health (Belloc & Breslow, 1972). Longitudinally, moderate alcohol consumption at baseline, defined as between 17 and 45 drinks per month, was associated with the most favorable health outcomes at follow-up. Both heavy alcohol consumption and absention were found to be related to poorer health outcomes.

Physical activity. As with the cross-sectional and mortality studies, longitudinal results showed that persons who engaged in physical activities in 1965 were in better health in 1974. This analysis was limited to respondents who were not disabled in 1965 in order to reduce the possibility that lack of physical activity at the time of the original study was due to ill health. The most striking difference in health outcomes was between persons who reported no physical activity and those who reported even a little.

Sleep and body weight. The final two behaviors that were associated with long-term health outcomes were sleep and desirable body weight. The findings for sleep were the same as in earlier analyses: persons who slept seven–eight hours in 1965 had better health in 1974 than did persons who slept more or less (Wiley & Camacho, 1980). The findings for weight differed somewhat from the cross-sectional and mortality results. In the cross-sectional analyses (Belloc & Breslow, 1972) and mortality studies (Belloc, 1973; Breslow & Enstrom, 1980), both overweight and underweight were associated with unfavorable outcomes.

In the 1974 longitudinal survey, only persons who had been extremely overweight in 1965 (30% or more) had clearly poorer health outcomes than persons who had been of more moderate weight. When people with any chronic conditions were excluded from the analysis, underweight did not prove to be a risk factor for subsequent poor health.

The epidemiology of depression

A study by Kaplan and colleagues, using data from the 1965 study and the 1974 follow-up questionnaire, examined the relationship between four classes of variables—sociodemographic characteristics which they termed "status attributes"; personal resources (i.e. psychologic states, coping, social support, and health behaviors), life stress, and physical health—and depression (Kaplan et al., 1987). Findings revealed a strong association between physical health status in 1965 and subsequent symptoms of depression. The study also found that social isolation as measured in the initial survey was a strong predictor of depression at follow-up. Although stressful life events initially appeared to be associated with subsequent depression, this was no longer the case when adjustment was made for all other variables. Health practices and sociodemographic characteristics, with the exception of education, were found to be unrelated to depressive symptoms nine and a half years after the baseline survey.

Summary

Stability and changes in health habits over time were important issues addressed by the 1974 follow-up mail survey. Both stability of health habits within individuals (people tend to maintain the same habits over time) and changes in the prevalence of some health practices in the general population (e.g. reduction in smoking prevalence) were important research questions that were answered with this study. The study of predictors of depression underscored the interrelatedness of the three dimensions of health—physical, mental, and social—as set out in the original Alameda Study.

1974 and 1975 CROSS-SECTIONAL ALAMEDA SURVEYS

Simultaneously with the 1974 longitudinal survey, an independent sample was drawn to be representative of the Alameda County population at that time. The "new" 1974 survey had 3119 respondents. This component of the Alameda Study allowed comparisons of the 1974 findings for the original cohort with those for the 1974 general population. The 1974 survey, while similar to the original Alameda study, contained an expanded set of items on medical care and a question on ethnic identity.

In 1975, using the same questionnaire and survey procedures as the 1974 cross-sectional survey, an independent probability sample was selected from the five Alameda County census tracts having the largest concentrations of Spanish surname residents. The sample size was considerably smaller than other Alameda surveys: only 657 questionnaires were completed, representing a 70% response rate. Of these survey respondents, 39% classified themselves as Mexican American or Chicano and 53% as Anglo.

Data from these two surveys were used to examine racial and ethnic differences in mental and physical health and health behaviors. One study, comparing symptoms of depression among blacks and whites, found no differences after controlling for sociodemographic factors (Roberts, Stevenson & Breslow, 1981). Combining data from the 1974 and 1975 cross-sectional surveys, Roberts & Lee (1980) compared health practices of Mexican Americans with those of the whites and blacks. Overall, Mexican Americans were found to have fewer good health practices, although they did have lower smoking rates than the general population. This study confirmed the original Alameda survey finding that health practices are related to health status, independent of sociodemographic factors and it demonstrated that the relationship holds for all three ethnic groups.

NINE-YEAR MORTALITY FOLLOW-UP OF 1965 AND 1974 COHORTS

Two studies examined mortality data for the 1965 and 1974 cohorts simultaneously in order to explore reasons for declines in ischemic heart disease mortality observed in recent years (Kaplan et al., 1988; Cohn, Kaplan & Cohen, 1988). The first study found that there was a 45% decline in the nine-year odds of ischemic heart disease mortality between the two cohorts, after adjusting for age, sex, race, and baseline heart disease conditions and symptoms (Kaplan et al., 1988). The changes could not be explained by differences in risk factors such as smoking status, physical activity, alcohol consumption, body mass index, social network participation, or by differences in education, occupation, utilization of preventive services, availability of a regular physician, health insurance coverage, or number of physician visits in the past twelve months. Further analyses of these data suggested that early detection and treatment of ischemic heart disease contributed to the declines in mortality observed in Alameda County (Cohn, Kaplan & Cohen, 1988).

1980 MORTALITY FOLLOW-UP: 15 YEARS LATER

In 1980, a 15-year mortality follow-up was conducted, using the same methods employed in the 1970 and 1974 mortality follow-up surveys. Data from this 15-year mortality follow-up was used to test the hypothesis that alcohol consumption and mortality are associated in a U-shaped or J-shaped fashion—that is, that light or moderate alcohol intake is associated with lower mortality than either abstention or heavy drinking (Camacho, Kaplan &

Cohen, 1987). Earlier, Wiley & Camacho (1980) had found in longitudinal analyses that favorable health status was associated with moderate consumption of alcohol, with both abstainers and heavy drinkers showing poorer health outcomes. Mortality data from the 15-year follow-up were not consistent with these findings.

Using multiple logistic models, the mortality experience of light drinkers (1–30 drinks per month) was compared with that of abstainers, moderate drinkers (31–60 drinks per month), heavy drinkers (61–90 drinks per month), and very heavy drinkers (91 drinks or more per month). The abstainer category contained both lifetime abstainers and former drinkers, which is a significant limitation of this study.

The hypothesis of a U- or J-shaped curve was not supported in this study, even after adjusting for 12 covariates found to be associated with alcohol consumption (age, sex, race, overall physical health, perceived health, income, education, smoking habits, exercise, an index of social contacts, depression, and personal uncertainty). No significant increase in risk was found for abstainers of either sex for either all-cause mortality or ischemic heart disease mortality. The only significant finding was that of a positive association between very heavy drinking and death from all causes for men. Heavy drinking was not associated with increased all-cause mortality for women or with ischemic heart disease mortality for either sex.

Although there was no overall significant association between alcohol consumption and risk of death in this study, the results were nevertheless suggestive of a curvilinear relationship. The authors concluded that more careful measurement of alcohol consumption and drinking history is needed along with analysis of the interactions between alcohol consumption and factors such as age, sex, other health habits, socioeconomic status, and living environment. Based on their findings, they cautioned public health officials to reserve judgment concerning the protective effects of moderate alcohol consumption that have been suggested by other studies.

1982 MORTALITY FOLLOW-UP: 17 YEARS LATER

In 1982, yet another death record check of the 1965 cohort was conducted using the California Death Registry as well as extensive in-state and out-of-state tracing procedures (Arellano et al., 1984; Belloc & Arellano, 1973; Berkman & Breslow, 1983; Kaplan et al., 1987). At this point, the focus of the Alameda research shifted somewhat from its previous concentration primarily on the younger age groups to increased concern with the importance of health risk behaviors among the elderly.

Health habits and the elderly

An analysis by Kaplan and colleagues (Kaplan et al., 1987) found that among persons who were at least 60 years old at baseline, smoking, physical activity, and regular breakfast eating habits were strong predictors of mortality outcomes 17 years later. There was also an association between body weight at baseline and 17-year mortality, although it was somewhat weaker. The remaining three habits (alcohol consumption, snacking, and sleep), were not significantly associated with 17-year survival among older persons. These increased risks were independent of age, race, socioeconomic status, other behavioral risk factors, and baseline physical health status.

Social support and the elderly

Another study based on the 1982 data looked at the importance of social network ties as predictors of mortality among the elderly (Seeman et al., 1987). This study included examination of mortality rates for persons who were 38–94 years at baseline. Earlier analyses, based on the 1974 mortality follow-up, found that social network ties were associated with nine-year mortality among persons less than 70 years of age (Berkman & Syme, 1979). The 1982 data showed that social ties were significant predictors of survival among those aged 70 and older as well. Comparisons of the relative importance of the different types of social ties across age groups revealed that marital status was of primary importance among those less than 60 years old at baseline whereas contacts with close friends and relatives were most important among persons 60 years and older.

Multiple role responsibilities

Kotler & Wingard (1989) studied the effects of multiple role responsibilities on 17-year mortality, using data from the 1982 follow-up. They examined the effect of occupational, marital, and parental roles on the mortality experience of 3700 men and women who were 35–64 years of age in 1965. The authors reported that women with the largest number of social roles—employed, married women with children present in the home—had the lowest mortality risk and women with the fewest roles—unemployed, unmarried women with no child in the home—had a greatly increased risk of mortality, suggesting that multiple social roles are at least not harmful to women's health. Neither the number of children nor their presence in the home affected the mortality rates of men.

1983 MORTALITY FOLLOW-UP OF THE 1974 COHORT

Enstrom and colleagues reported on a 10-year mortality follow-up of the 1974 cross-sectional survey of 3119 adults (Enstrom, Kanim & Breslow, 1986). Using the same methods employed for the earlier Alameda mortality follow-up studies, 276 deaths were identified. The authors were investigating the potential association between intake of vitamin C and subsequent mortality outcomes.

No association was found. However, their study did reconfirm, with an independently drawn sample, the association between the original seven Alameda habits (never smoking cigarettes, regular physical activity, moderate or no use of alcohol, seven–eight hours of sleep, maintaining proper weight, eating breakfast regularly, and not eating between meals) and subsequent mortality. Never smoking and engaging in physical activity were the two most important predictors of reduced mortality, with never smoking the most important single practice.

Mortality follow-up studies: a summary

The original framework for the Alameda study—measuring physical, mental, and social health over time and assessing the relationship between health and certain ways of living, including personal habits, and familial, cultural, economic, social, and environmental factors—continued to guide the analytic focus of this project into the 1980s. Mortality studies of the elderly and Hispanic subgroups and examination of the effects of multiple role responsibilities are examples of the way in which the Alameda Study has addressed contemporary research questions within the original analytic framework. Use of the Alameda mortality data to explore possible explanations for declines in ischemic heart disease is an example of the way in which this rich data source has been called upon to answer questions of current public health interest which were not part of the original study mission.

REPLICATIONS AND PARTIAL REPLICATIONS OF THE ALAMEDA COUNTY STUDY

The Alameda Study, particularly the findings related to health habits and to a lesser extent those concerning social support, stimulated tremendous interest throughout the United States. The idea that people could actually influence the course of their future health was very appealing both to health professionals and to lay individuals. Shortly after the 1973 publication of initial mortality findings, plans were underway to obtain national prevalence estimates of the original seven Alameda health habits. The first national estimates were obtained in the 1977 National Health Interview Survey (NHIS). Subsequent years of the NHIS provided updated estimates and trend data on the Alameda habits. Two studies, one national and one at state-level were designed specifically to replicate the Alameda Study, including measurement of health habits, and physical, mental, and social health. A number of community studies and studies of special populations provide examples of the breadth and depth of the influence the Alameda Study has had on the study of health and its predictors. The following sections will describe some studies that have been stimulated either directly or indirectly by the Alameda Study.

NATIONAL STUDIES

National Health Interview Survey

Background and methods

The National Health Interview Survey (NHIS) is an ongoing national household interview sample survey of the non-institutionalized population of the United States. The NHIS is a survey conducted by the National Center for Health Statistics, Centers for Disease Control, an agency of the US Department of Health and Human Services.

The NHIS has two parts: a basic health and demographic questionnaire that remains the same from year to year, and special topic questionnaires that address topics of current public health concern and change each year. The survey follows a multistage probability design with interviews conducted continuously throughout the year. The basic health and demographic questionnaire collects information for the full NHIS sample (usually 120 000 people) and the special topic is administered to a subset of these respondents (usually one adult per family).

A number of indicators of physical health status are included in the basic health and demographic questionnaire each year. Among these are: limitation of activity due to chronic conditions, restricted activity days such as days spent in bed or at home due to illness, and perceived health status. Indicators of health care utilization, similar to those included in the 1974 Alameda Survey, are also part of the ongoing NHIS. These include physician visits, hospitalizations, and hospital days. The basic health and demographic component of the NHIS does not contain measures of mental or social health, although these topics are covered occasionally in the special topic questionnaires.

The 1977 National Health Interview Survey

In 1977, the NHIS special topic covered the Alameda Study's seven health habits. The basic health and demographic questionnaire was administered to approximately 111 000 people of all ages and the questions on health practices were administered to about 23 000 adults aged 20 years and over (Howie & Drury, 1978). The response rate for the full survey was about 97% and for the subsample about 91%.

Questionnaire content. The 1977 NHIS questions on the seven Alameda health habits differed somewhat from the Alameda Study but six of the seven measures were fairly good approximations of the Alameda concepts. The exception was the NHIS question on physical activity which asked about the respondent's perception of his or her physical activity relative to other persons the same age; the Alameda measure asked about participation in specific physical activities and sports. The NHIS questions have been published (Howie

& Drury, 1978).

One of the primary goals of the 1977 National Health Interview Survey section on the Alameda habits was to produce national prevalence estimates of the practices which Alameda investigators had concluded were significantly related to favorable health status and reduced mortality. The 1977 NHIS effort to replicate the Alameda study was limited to the area of health habits and health status; the survey did not contain any information on social or mental health. The NHIS health status indicators included limitation of activity due to chronic conditions and self-perceived health status. These offer the potential to test the Alameda County findings concerning the relationship between health habits and health status with a nationally representative sample, although no such analyses have been published to date.

Findings. US national prevalence estimates for the Alameda habits were produced from the 1977 NHIS, as were estimates for various population subgroups (Schoenborn & Danchik, 1980). Overall, about two-thirds of U.S. adults reported getting seven–eight hours of sleep each night, 58% ate breakfast every day, 35% said they never ate between meals, 29% had consumed five drinks or more at one sitting in the past year (a variation of the Alameda definition of a poor habit), 36% were current smokers, 15% were 30% or more above desirable body weight, and 37% said they were more physically active than other persons the same age.

Another study based on data from the 1977 NHIS examined the relationship between the seven Alameda habits and health care utilization (Wetzler & Cruess, 1985). The authors classified persons according to whether they had "good" or "bad" habits, based on the Alameda definitions, and examined the associations between these habits and three measures of health care utilization: number of doctor visits in past 12 months, number of short-stay hospital days in the past 12 months, and number of dental visits in the past two weeks (multiplied by 26 to get an annual estimate). This study found that persons who slept seven–eight hours a night had significantly fewer doctor visits and hospital days than persons who slept more or less, and persons who were more active or at least as active as other persons their own age had significantly fewer doctor visits than persons who reported being less active than their peers. There was a strong consistent relationship between total number of good health practices and number of doctor visits and hospital days. The only significant finding for dental visits was that persons who had never smoked reported fewer visits than either current or former smokers. Total number of good health practices was not associated with dental visits.

The 1983 National Health Interview Survey

In 1983, the special topic section of the National Health Interview once again included the seven Alameda health habits, this time as part of a larger questionnaire designed to measure alcohol consumption practices of the US population (Division of Health Interview Statistics, 1986). With the exception of the alcohol questions, which were considerably more detailed, the health practice questions were very similar to those included in the 1977 NHIS.

US prevalence estimates for the Alameda habits for 1983 have been published (Schoenborn & Cohen, 1986). Comparisons with the 1977 findings revealed that, rather than showing improvements over time as might be expected in view of the increasing national interest in health promotion in the early 1980s, four of the seven practices (sleep, physical activity, overweight, and alcohol consumption) showed a significant change for the worse. Smoking was the only habit to register an improvement, declining from a prevalence of 36% in 1977 to 32% in 1983.

The 1985 National Health Interview Survey

In 1985, the special topic for the National Health Interview Survey, entitled the NHIS of Health Promotion and Disease Prevention (HPDP), was designed to provide data for tracking the Nation's progress toward the 1990 Prevention Objectives (Schoenborn, 1988). The Prevention Objectives, published in 1980, included 226 objectives in 15 priority areas (Office of Disease Prevention and Health Promotion, 1980). Their development, to some extent, was stimulated by the findings of the Alameda County and other studies from the 1960s and 1970s that documented the benefits of certain health-related behaviors.

Questionnaire content. NHIS-HPDP topics included general health habits, high blood pressure, stress, exercise, smoking, alcohol consumption, dental knowledge and care, occupational health, smoking and pregnancy, child health safety, and injury control. Among the approximately 200 questions on this survey, several were devoted to the Alameda health habits, most of them measured similarly to the original study. The questions on physical activity more closely approximated the Alameda conceptualization of exercise than did earlier NHIS surveys, asking detailed questions about specific types of exercise. The NHIS-HPDP measure went further still, however, and asked about the frequency and duration of the exercise and the perceived increase in heart rate experienced while exercising.

The NHIS-HPDP contained a few questions on stress which could serve as proxy measures of mental health status, although no specific mental health indicators were included. Similarly, social health as conceptualized in the Alameda County study was not included in this survey. The NHIS-HPDP did contain information which will allow mortality follow-up of respondents through the National Death Index but no such follow-up has been carried out to date.

Findings. Prevalence estimates for 1985 for breakfast eating, snacking, sleeping, alcohol consumption, smoking, exercise, and body weight among

U.S. men and women aged 18 years and over have been published (Schoenborn, 1986). A summary indicator of total number of "good" health practices, as defined in the Alameda County study, was also presented. For US men and women combined, the prevalence estimates for the Alameda habits in 1985 were as follows: 55% of adults ate breakfast daily, 28% never ate snacks, 66% slept seven–eight hours a night, 6% drank five or more drinks at a time, 30% smoked cigarettes, 28% said they were more physically active than others the same age and 13% were 30% or more above desirable body weight. In determining desirable weight, the 1983 Metropolitan Life Insurance Company standards for weight were used rather than the 1960 standards (Metroplitan Life Insurance Company, 1960, 1983) used in analysis of the 1977 and 1983 data. Because of this change, the results for body weight cannot be compared with those cited earlier.

Data from the 1985 NHIS of Health Promotion and Disease Prevention substantiate the Alameda finding that health behaviors vary among the various sociodemographic subgroups. In general, persons in the more socially and economically advantaged subgroups are more likely to engage in healthy practices (Schoenborn, 1988). Although the Alameda study found that the seven practices investigated were independently associated with health status and mortality, questions concerning the interrelationships among the various behaviors remain. Using data from the 1985 NHIS, a study of the relationship between smoking and the other six Alameda behaviors shed some light on the issue (Schoenborn & Benson, 1988). This study found that smokers tended to drink more heavily, get less sleep, skip breakfast, and not exercise compared with nonsmokers. In contrast, smokers also were more likely to maintain desirable body weight and to avoid snacks.

National Survey of Personal Health Practices and Consequences

Background

In 1979, the National Center for Health Statistics fielded a national telephone survey entitled the "National Survey of Personal Health Practices and Consequences" (NSPHPC) which was designed to replicate the Alameda County survey on a nationally representative sample of US adults (Wilson & Elinson, 1981). The NSPHPC was designed to collect data on the extent and distribution of positive health practices, their stability over time, and their relationships to morbidity and mortality.

Methods

The NSPHPC was a two-wave panel survey in which sample persons were interviewed in the Spring of 1979 and then again one year later. The sampling plan was a three-stage stratified cluster design, using random digit dialing.

Self-response was required for all items. The survey was administered by telephone to a sample of US adults 20–64 years of age. The response rate was about 81% with a total of 3025 completed interviews.

Questionnaire content

NSPHPC questionnaire items were designed to measure many of the same concepts as those contained in the Alameda Study, including six of the seven health practices (snacking was omitted), health status, use of health services, psychological well-being, social support, critical life events, and sociodemographic characteristics. The survey also obtained information needed to track respondents through the National Death Index (National Center for Health Statistics, 1981) to assess their long-term mortality experience.

To the extent possible, every effort was made to produce measures of physical, mental and social health that approximated those contained in the Alameda Study. The questions on health status combined to form a five-point index (rather than the Alameda's seven) but with conceptually similar categories measuring a spectrum of health from disabled to very healthy. Most of the social health items covered in the Alameda Study were also contained in the NSPHPC, including employment stability, involvement of social and community groups, contacts with close friends and relatives, and marital satisfaction. The mental health component was perhaps the least complete in terms of replicating the Alameda Study although the NSPHPC contained several questions related to mental health. These included general well-being (i.e. feeling loved, downhearted and blue, lonely, and cheerful), feeling like one was having or going to have a nervous breakdown, and having any severe personal, emotional, behavioral, or mental problems. The health habit measures were very similar to the Alameda County Survey although there were some differences. The complete questionnaire has been published (Danchik, Schoenborn & Elinson, 1981).

Sex, age, and education-specific findings for many health-related factors have been reported (Danchik, Schoenborn & Elinson, 1981) as have sex-specific distributions on most of the variables contained in the survey (Schoenborn, Danchik & Elinson, 1981; Eisenstadt & Schoenborn, 1982). This survey included not only variables from the Alameda study but a number of other behaviors thought to reflect a general health promotion orientation such as use of seatbelts, limiting consumption of red meat, vitamin usage, and tooth brushing. The highly detailed, descriptive nature of the reports from this survey do not lend themselves to summarization here.

Gottleib & Green (1984) conducted a multivariate analysis of NSPHPC data, looking at the relationships among social structure, stress, social support, life-style health behavior, and health status. This study, like the Alameda Study, found a relationship between age, education, and income on health practices and health status. Stress, measured in terms of experiencing nine significant life events, was found to be associated with unfavorable sleep and smoking patterns in women and with smoking and heavier alcohol consumption, as well as increased physical activity in men. Social network ties were found to be associated with health status although the relationship appeared to be mediated through health practices. A positive association between the social network index and health practices was observed. In contrast to the Alameda findings, this study failed to find an association between health practices and health status for men.

STATE-LEVEL STUDIES

A state-wide telephone survey conducted in Michigan in 1978 came close to replicating the health practices component of the Alameda study (Brock, Haefner & Noble, 1988). In the Michigan study, 3259 adult residents were interviewed by telephone. When the Michigan and Alameda County populations were compared, the relationships between the seven Alameda health habits and health status were found to be quite similar.

Since 1981, Behavioral Risk Factor Surveillance System (BRFSS) has been used to collect state-level data on the prevalence of personal health practices and behaviors including cigarette smoking, alcohol use, weight control, and physical activity (Remington et al., 1988). The BRFSS uses a telephone interview method of data collection. The samples are selected using a multistage cluster design procedure based on the Waksberg method. The BRFSS is a collaborative effort of the Federal Centers for Disease Control and state health departments and yields data needed to plan, initiate, and support health promotion and disease prevention programs at the state level. As of 1988, over 40 states were participating in the BRFSS, most collecting data on a monthly basis. Sample sizes and response rates vary substantially by state.

In 1986, the state of Wisconsin fielded a state-level survey entitled the "Wisconsin Health Status Survey". The completed sample consisted of 6872 persons, representing a 67% response rate. This study, while not designed as a replication of the Alameda Study, included many of the same health risk behaviors (Wisconsin Department of Health and Social Services, 1987). Sleep, body weight, exercise, smoking, and alcohol consumption were among the health behaviors, along with measures of health status and disability, health care utilization, and mental health status. Selected findings from this survey were compared with national estimates and estimates from the Behavioral Risk Factor Study conducted in Wisconsin by the Centers for Disease Control.

COMMUNITY STUDIES

National studies that were modeled after the Alameda Study, have been used by a number of investigators as the basis for designing local area studies. One study, entitled the Davis Avenue Community Study, was implemented to assess the need for health promotion programs in the local service area (Morris & Windsor, 1985). This study used the National Survey of Personal Health Practices and Consequences as a model for a study of health behavior among adult, inner-city, predominantly black residents of a particular health service area in Mobile, Alabama, and is one example of the far-reaching impact of the original Alameda work.

A longitudinal, epidemiological study, the Tecumseh Community Health Study, covered many of the same topics as the Alameda County Study, including the seven habits and social support. Metzner, Carman & Howe (1983) carried out a study of the Alameda health habits based on data for 2754 men and women in the third wave of the Tecumseh study, conducted during 1967–1969. The outcome measures in this study were specific diseases—coronary heart disease, hypertension, and chronic bronchitis—and risk factors—blood pressure readings, serum cholesterol, blood glucose, and forced expiratory volume—rather than general health status as was the case in the Alameda Study. Four of the seven habits were found to be associated with one or the other health measures—desirable weight, physical activity, never having smoked cigarettes, and moderate or no alcohol consumption. House, Robbins & Metzner (1982), using data from the same cohort, examined the relationship between social relationships and activities in 1967–1969 and mortality rates 9–12 years later. Using measures that were somewhat different from those used in Alameda County, the authors found that social relationships were important predictors of mortality among men but not women.

The initial emphasis in the study of health behavior, both in Alameda County and in related studies, was on young and middle-aged persons. The shift to studying the older age groups of the Alameda cohorts has been mentioned. In the 1980s, interest in health of the elderly accelerated and more and more studies began looking at ways health behaviors might be important for health and longevity in the oldest age groups (Enstrom & Pauling, 1982; Branch & Jette, 1984; Branch, 1985; Brown & McCreedy, 1986; Lubben, Weiler & Chi, 1989). Because these studies were conducted on very small, local populations, findings cannot easily be generalized to larger populations. However, these studies do point to the far-reaching impact of the original Alameda County research more than a generation after its inception.

STUDIES OF SPECIAL POPULATIONS

A study of runners in North Carolina used questions similar to the Alameda-type questions in the National Health Interview Survey (Macera, Pate & Davis, 1989). Mail questionnaires were completed by 966 runners, representing an estimated 75% response rate. Comparison of findings for runners and the total US population revealed that the two groups were surprisingly similar. In both cases, persons with low incomes and little education were less likely to engage in healthy practices (as defined in the

Alameda study), than were persons in higher socioeconomic categories. Among runners, a presumably very healthy, vigorous group, only about half were found to have five or more good health habits, suggesting the need for further improvements in the adoption of habits known to be associated with reduced morbidity and mortality.

Two studies have compared data from the National Health Interview Survey with health behavior data for military personnel in large-scale military-sponsored surveys. Unlike the Davis Avenue and runners' studies which attempted to replicate the national studies, these surveys used the national surveys as standards of comparison for their particular populations of interest.

In 1977, the US Air Force (USAF) conducted a health survey of a random sample of Air Force personnel, stratified by rank. The survey contained questions on the seven Alameda health habits, dietary attitudes, coronary-prone behavior, and psychological well-being, as well as demographic and job classification information (Wetzler & Cruess, 1985). A total of 6675 question-naires were returned, representing an 81% response rate. Wetzler & Cruess described the personal health practices of US Air Force personnel and compared these to findings for the 1977 US civilian population. The questions on sleep, relative body weight, and cigarette smoking were comparable between the two surveys and most other questions were sufficiently similar to allow comparisons. Overall, USAF personnel tended to get less sleep than their civilian counterparts. They also were more likely to drink alcohol and somewhat more likely to smoke cigarettes and to eat snacks. When age was controlled, breakfast eating habits of Air Force personnel and US civilians did not differ significantly. In terms of body weight, USAF personnel were significantly less likely to be extremely overweight (30% or more above desirable weight) than were civilians. Because of differences in question content between the USAF survey and the 1977 NHIS, physical activity levels of the two populations could not be compared. The 1977 NHIS question on physical activity referred to perceived levels of activity relative to others the same age while the USAF questions asked about frequency of specific types of physical activities, an approach used later in the 1985 NHIS.

A second study involving a military population compared prevalence estimates from 1985 Worldwide Survey of Alcohol and Nonmedical Drug Use Among Military Personnel with findings from the 1985 National Health Interview Survey (Ballweg & Li, 1989). The military survey, sponsored by the US Department of Defense, was administered to a sample of 17 328 military personnel worldwide—92% of them male. Six of the seven Alameda habits were included in this study (snacking was omitted), as were several health status indicators. Mental and social health indicators were not included.

In contrast to the USAF/1977 NHIS comparison, this study was able to include a comparison of military personnel and civilians in terms of their levels of physical activity. This was possible because the 1985 NHIS contained a detailed inventory of physical activity questions not found in the 1977 NHIS. As one might expect based on the nature of the military population, military personnel were more likely to exercise than their civilian counterparts. They were also more likely to be of desirable weight. Civilians, on the other hand, displayed better sleeping and breakfast eating habits. Military persons were more likely to smoke cigarettes while civilians were more likely to have quit smoking. Finally, the military personnel had a higher prevalence of alcohol consumption but were more likely to be light drinkers (one–two drinks a day) than their were civilians. Both USAF Survey/1977 NHIS and the Worldwide Military Survey/1985 NHIS comparisons included discussions of sociodemographic differentials in prevalence estimates for military personnel and civilians.

In the mid-1970s a large-scale social experiment, entitled the Health Insurance Experiment (HIS), was undertaken by the Rand Coroporation of Santa Monica, California (Ware et al., 1980). This study, funded by the federal government, was designed to investigate the effects of different health care financing arrangements on use of personal medical care, quality of care, satisfaction with care, and health status. The study, conducted at six sites throughout the United States, had a sample size of 7708 individuals in 2753 families.

The measures of health status used in this study paralleled those of the Alameda County Study. Like the Alameda Study, Rand researchers conceptualized health in terms of the World Health definition of physical, mental, and social well-being and included both positive and negative indicators (Stewart et al., 1978; Ware et al., 1979; and Donald et al., 1978). The Rand Study also covered the seven Alameda health habits (smoking, overweight, alcohol consumption, exercise, sleep, breakfast, and snacking) (Stewart, Brook & Kane, 1979; Stewart, Brook & Kane, 1980), as well as use of preventive services.

Discussion

The original Alameda Study was designed to measure health according to the World Health Organization's concept of a state of physical, mental, and social well-being and to examine the relationship between health and a variety of other factors, including personal health habits. The Alameda research demonstrated clear interrelationships among physical, mental and social health. However, in the two and half decades since the original study, there has been a disproportionate amount of interest in the health habits content of the original study—perhaps because of the popular appeal of the notion that individuals could affect the course of their own health. The Alameda Study has repeatedly shown that personal health behaviors are associated with physical, mental, and social health. One interpretation of the Alameda findings on health behavior is that a moderate lifestyle is conducive to good health. The seven "favorable" Alameda habits—not smoking, drinking moderately, maintaining desirable weight, exercising, eating breakfast regularly, and avoiding snacks—are suggestive of a philosophy of "moderation in everything".

There is clear biological evidence for the health effects of several of the Alameda habits. The health consequences of smoking are without doubt the best documented. The Surgeon General of the United States estimates that smoking is responsible for 30% of all cancer deaths, including 87% of lung cancer; 21% of deaths from coronary heart disease; 18% of stroke deaths; and 82% of deaths due to chronic obstructive pulmonary disease (US Department of Health and Human Services, 1989). Alcohol has been linked to deaths due to cirrhosis and cancer, as well as accidents, homicides, and suicides (National Center for Health Statistics, 1990; Pollack et al., 1984). Overweight has been linked to a variety of adverse health outcomes including cancer, hypertension, and coronary artery disease (National Institutes of Health, 1985). Exercise has been shown to be associated with reduced risk of coronary heart disease, effective weight control, and improved mental health (Bouchard, 1990; Powell et al., 1989; Powell et al., 1986; Stephens, 1988). Both inadequate and excessive amounts of sleep have been linked to mortality due to heart disease, cancer, stroke, and suicide (Kripke et al., 1979). The scientific evidence for the health consequences of behaviors such as eating breakfast and snacking is less clear but some studies have suggested that changes in the frequency of food consumption may alter metabolism and that large but infrequent meals are associated with overweight (Berkman & Breslow, 1983).

Although there is a substantial amount of biological evidence to explain why most of the Alameda seven health habits should be related to long-term good health and increased survival, such explanations do not tell the whole story. The study of the health effects of personal habits is complicated by the extensive interrelationships among the habits and other factors. Poor health habits have been shown to be associated with unfavorable physical, mental, and social health outcomes. Conversely, physical, mental, or social health may promote or impede a person's ability or desire to participate in health promoting activities. Psychosocial factors such as hostile personality characteristics have been shown to be associated with increased risk of coronary heart and other diseases (Matthews et al., 1977; Dembroski et al., 1978) and recent evidence suggests that this relationship may be mediated through poor health habits engaged in by persons with high hostility scores (Leiker & Hailey, 1988). There is also evidence that the physical health benefits of social support so often noted, may be due, in part, to better health behaviors of people with strong social ties (Cwikel et al., 1988).

Personal health behaviors, found to be independently related to health status and mortality in the Alameda Study have actually been shown in other research to cluster—that is, people who smoke are more likely to drink and not exercise, and it may be the combination that helps determine health outcomes. A number of studies have been devoted to examining possible interrelationships among various behaviors and trying to classify them according to type (e.g. direct versus indirect; avoidant versus protective, active versus passive; awareness versus denial (Langlie, 1977; Langlie, 1979; Tapp & Goldenthal, 1982; Williams & Wechsler, 1972).

Use of preventive health care services is sometimes considered to be a personal health behavior (Langlie, 1977). Use of such services may be greater among persons who also participate in other health promoting or risk reducing activities such as exercise, weight control, or smoking cessation, either because of a clustering of health promoting behaviors or because people who use preventive services are exposed to health education that encourages good health habits.

SUMMARY

Since its inception in 1965, the Alameda Study has had a profound effect on the direction of research in the areas of health status measurement, social support, and health behavior. The Human Population Laboratory, the research group responsible for its development, continues to study the original cohort, reassessing the associations between health behavior and health status, health behavior and mortality, and social support and mortality over time. In general, the original conclusions have held: people who engage in selected healthy behaviors and have strong social networks are healthier and live longer than people who don't. The precise definition of a "healthy behavior" or what constitutes a "strong social network" have not always been the same in all analyses, but the minor variations have not modified the overall conclusions.

Alameda researchers also have used these data to investigate important measurement issues, such as the usefulness of self-reported health status and self-reported symptoms for predicting mortality. The longitudinal nature of the data makes it a particularly rich resource for such investigations.

Findings from the Alameda Study have been used by the research community as the basis for many other studies. The federal government has fielded a number of studies to assess the prevalence of the Alameda habits in the general population. State and local studies have been implemented, using either the original Alameda Study or its national replications as models. Most of these studies have focussed exclusively on health habits or on the relationship between health habits and health status. Several studies have examined the importance of social support in other populations. Only the National Survey of Personal Health Practices and Consequences and the Rand study attempted to operationalize all three components of health status—physical, mental, and social—as was done in the original Alameda Study.

Of the three dimensions of health, mental health has received the least attention during the course of the Alameda Study. Early studies found that mental health was related to both physical and social health in the 1965 cohort and some later work has been done in the area of depression, but, overall, considerably more attention has been given to measuring health habits, physical health status, and social support over time.

THE FUTURE

Studies based on the Alameda survey will continue. In fact, a second follow-up survey has already been conducted but no results have been published to date. This survey, fielded in 1983, was similar to the 1974 survey and will shed further light on the long-term health consequences of health behavior and social support.

In 1990 and 1991, the National Health Interview Survey (NHIS) once again included topics related to the Alameda health habits as well as indicators of physical health status. Data from these surveys will provide updated estimates of the prevalence of these important behaviors in the general US population and permit assessments of changes in these behaviors over time. They also will make it possible to study the associations between the Alameda habits and health status into the 1990s.

In 1965, when the original Alameda Study was undertaken, the concept that personal health behaviors could influence health status was just beginning to receive the attention of the medical and research communities. Today the impact of this pioneering study continues to be felt as medical researchers and health planners search for ways to promote the health and well-being of our nation's people. Many lessons have been learned from the Alameda Study. Many more questions remain. One thing is certain. The study of health cannot be approached piecemeal—mental, physical, and social health all must be considered, in the context of a variety of other social, economic, and personal factors.

REFERENCES

Arellano, M. G., Petersen, G. R., Pettiti, D. B. & Smith, R. E. (1984). The California Automated Mortality Linkage System (CAMLIS). *American Journal of Public Health*, 74, 1324–1330.

Ballweg, J. A. & Li, L. (1989). Comparison of health habits of military personnel with civilian populations. *Public Health Reports*, 104, 498–509.

Belloc, N. B. (1973). Relationship of health practices and mortality. *Preventive Medicine*, 2, 67–81.

Belloc, N. B. & Arellano, M. G. (1973). Computer linkage on a survey population. *Health Services Reports*, 88, 344–350.

Belloc, N. B. & Breslow, L. (1972). Relationship of physical health status and health practices. *Preventive Medicine*, 1, 409–421.

Belloc, N. B., Breslow, L. & Hochstim, J. R. (1971). Measurement of physical health in a general population survey. *American Journal of Epidemiology*, 93, 328–336.

Berkman, P. L. (1971). Measurement of mental health in a general population survey. *American Journal of Epidemiology*, 94, 105–111.

Berkman, P. L. (1975). Survival, and a modicum of indulgence in the sick role. *Medical Care*, 13, 85–94.

Berkman, L. F. (1977). *Social networks, host resistance, and mortality: a follow-up study of Alameda County residents*. Doctoral dissertation. Berkeley, CA: University of California.

Berkman, L. F. & Breslow, L. (1983). *Health and Ways of Living: The Alameda County Study*. New York: Oxford University Press.

Berkman, L. F. & Syme, S. L. (1979). Social networks, host resistance, and mortality: a nine-year follow-up study of Alameda County residents. *American Journal of Epidemiology*, **109**, 186–204.

Bouchard, C., Shephard, R. J., Stephens, T., Sutton, J. R. & McPherson, B. D. (Eds) (1990). *Exercise, Fitness, and Health. A Consensus of Current Knowledge*. Champaign, IL: Human Kinetics Books.

Branch, L. G. (1985). Health practices and incidence disability among the elderly. *American Journal of Public Health*, **75**, 1436–1439.

Branch, L. G. & Jette, A. M. (1984). Personal health practices and mortality among the elderly. *American Journal of Public Health*, **74**, 1126–1129.

Breslow, L. & Enstrom, J. E. (1980). Persistence of health habits and their relationship to mortality. *Preventive Medicine*, **9**, 469–483.

Brock, B., Haefner, D. P. & Noble, D. S. (1988). Alameda County Redux: replication in Michigan. *Preventive Medicine*, **17**, 483–495.

Brown, J. S. & McCreedy, M. (1986). The hale elderly: health behavior and its correlates. *Research in Nursing and Health*, **9**, 317–329.

Camacho, T. C., Kaplan, G. A. & Cohen, R. D. (1987). Alcohol consumption mortality in Alameda County. *Journal of Chronic Disease*, **40**, 229–236.

Camacho, T. C. & Wiley, J. (1983). Health practices, social networks, and changes in physical health. In Berkman, L. F. & Breslow, L. *Health and Ways of Living* (pp. 176–209). New York: Oxford University Press.

Cohn, B. A., Kaplan, G. A. & Cohen, R. D. (1988). Did early detection and treatment contribute to the decline in ischemic heart disease mortality? Prospective evidence from the Alameda County Study. *American Journal of Epidemiology*, **127**, 1143–1154.

Cwikel, J. M. G., Dielman, T. E., Kirscht, J. P. & Israel, B. A. (1988). Mechanisms of psychosocial effects on health: The role of social integration, coping style, and health behavior. *Health Education Quarterly*, **15**, 151–173.

Danchik, K. M., Schoenborn, C. A. & Elinson, J. E. (1981). Highlights from Wave I of the National Survey of Personal Health Practices and Consequences: United States, 1979. *Vital and Health Statistics*. **15** (1). DHHS Publication No. (PHS)81-1162.

Dembroski, T. M., MacDougall, J. M., Shields, J. L., Pettito, J. & Lushene, R. (1978). Components of the Type A coronary-prone behavior pattern and cardiovascular responses to psychomotor challenge. *Journal of Behavioral Medicine*, **1**, 159–176.

Donald, C. A., Ware, J. E., Brook, R. H. & Davies-Avery, A. (1978). *Conceptualization and Measurement of Health in the Health Insurance Study: Volume IV. Social Health*. Prepared under a grant from the US Department of Health, Education, and Welfare. Santa Monica, CA: Rand Corporation.

Division of Health Interview Statistics (1986). Current Estimates from the National Health Interview Survey: United States, 1983. *Vital and Health Statistics*. **10** (154). DHHS Pub. No. 86-1582. Hyattsville, MD: National Center for Health Statistics.

Donald, C. A. & Ware, J. E. (1982). *The Quantification of Social Contacts and Resources*. Prepared under a grant from the US Department of Health and Human Services. Santa Monica, CA. Rand Corporation.

Eisenstadt, R. K. & Schoenborn, C. A. (1982). *Basic data from wave II of the National Survey of Personal Health Practices and Consequences: United States, 1980*. Working Paper No. 13. Hyattsville, MD: National Center for Health Statistics.

Enstrom, J. E., Kanim, L. E. & Breslow, L. (1986). The relationship between Vitamin C intake, general health practices, and mortality in Alameda County, California. *American Journal of Public Health*, **76**, 1124–1130.

Enstrom, J. E. & Pauling, L. (1982). Mortality among health-conscious elderly Californians. *Proceedings of the National Academy of Sciences*, 79, 6023–6027.

Gottlieb, N. H. & Green, L. W. (1984). Life events, social network, life-style, and health: an analysis of the 1979 National Survey of Personal Health Practices and Consequences. *Health Education Quarterly*, 11, 91–105.

Haan, M., Kaplan, G. A. & Camacho, T. (1987). Poverty and health: prospective evidence from the Alameda County Study. *American Journal of Epidemiology*, 125, 989–998.

Hochstim, J. R. & Renne, K. S. (1971). Reliability of response in a sociomedical population study. *Public Opinion Quarterly*, 35, 69–79.

House, J. S., Robbins, C. & Metzner, H. L. (1982). The association of social relationships and activities with mortality: prospective evidence from the Tecumseh Community Health Study. *American Journal of Epidemiology*, 116, 123–140.

Howie, L. J. & Drury, T. F. (1978). Current estimates from the National Health Interview Survey. *Vital and Health Statistics*, 10 (126) DHEW Pub. No. (PHS)78-1554. Hyattsville, MD: National Center for Health Statistics.

Kaplan, G. A. & Camacho, T. (1983). Perceived health and mortality: a nine-year follow-up of the human population laboratory cohort. *American Journal of Epidemiology*, 117, 292–304.

Kaplan, G. A., Cohn, B. A., Cohen, R. D. & Guralnik, J. (1988). The decline in ischemic heart disease mortality: prospective evidence from the Alameda County study. *American Journal of Epidemiology*, 127, 1131–1142.

Kaplan, G. A. & Kotler, P. I. (1985). Self-reports predictive of mortality from ischemic heart disease: a nine-year follow-up of the Human Population Laboratory cohort. *Journal of Chronic Disease*, 38, 195–201.

Kaplan, G. A., Roberts, R. E., Camacho, T. C. & Coyne, J. C. (1987). Psychosocial predictors of depression: prospective evidence from the Human Population Laboratory studies. *American Journal of Epidemiology*, 125, 206–220.

Kaplan, G. A., Seeman, T. E., Cohen, R. D., Knudsen, L. P. & Guralnik, J. (1987). Mortality among the elderly in the Alameda County Study: behavioral and demographic risk factors. *American Journal of Public Health*, 77, 307–312.

Kotler, P. & Wingard, D. L. (1989). The effect of occupational, marital, and parental roles on mortality: The Alameda County Study. *American Journal of Public Health*, 79, 607–611.

Kripke, D. F., Simons, R. N., Garfinkel, L. & Hammond, E. C. (1979). Short and long sleep and sleeping pills: is increased mortality associated? *Archives of General Psychiatry*, 36, 103–116.

Langlie, J. K. (1977). Social networks, health beliefs, and preventive health behavior. *Journal of Health and Social Behavior*, 18, 244–260.

Langlie, J. K. (1979). Interrelationships among preventive health behaviors: a test of competing hypotheses. *Public Health Reports*, 94, 216–225.

Lazarus, N. B., Kaplan, G. A., Cohen, R. D. & Leu, D. J. (1989). Smoking and body mass in the natural history of physical activity: prospective evidence from the Alameda County Study, 1965–1974. *American Journal of Preventive Medicine*, 5, 127–135.

Leiker, M. & Hailey, B. J. (1988). A link between hostility and disease: poor health habits? *Behavioral Medicine*, 14, 129–133.

Lubben, J., Weiler, P. G. & Chi, I. (1989). Health practices and the elderly poor. *American Journal of Public Health*, 79, 731–734.

Macera, C. A., Pate, R. R. & Davis, D. R. (1989). Runners' health habits, 1985—"the Alameda 7" revisited. *Public Health Reports*, 104, 341–349.

Matthews, K. A., Glass, D. C., Rosenman, R. H. & Bortner, R. W. (1977). *Journal of*

Chronic Disease, **30**, 489–498.

Meltzer, J. W. & Hochstim, J. R. (1970). Reliability and validity of survey data on physical health. *Public Health Reports*, **85**, 1075–1086.

Metropolitan Life Insurance Company (1960). Overweight, its prevention and significance. *Statistical Bulletin*, April. New York.

Metropolitan Life Insurance Company (1983). Metropolitan health and weight tables. *Statistical Bulletin*, **64** (1), New York.

Metzner, H. L., Carman, W. J. & House, J. (1983). Health practices, risk factors, and chronic disease in Tecumseh. *Preventive Medicine*, **12**, 491–507.

Morris, J. & Windsor, R. A. (1985). Personal health practices of urban adults in Alabama: Davis Avenue Community Study. *Public Health Reports*, **100**, 531–539.

National Center for Health Statistics (1981). *User's Manual: The National Death Index*. DHHS Pub. No. 81-1148. Hyattsville, MD: NCHS.

National Center for Health Statistics (1990). *Prevention Profile. Health, United States, 1989*. Hyattsville, MD: Public Health Service.

National Institutes of Health (1985). *Health Implications of Obesity*. Consensus Development Conference Statement. 5 (9).

Office of Disease Prevention and Health Promotion (1980). *Promoting Health, Preventing Disease: Objectives for the Nation*. U.S. Public Health Service, Washington.

Pollack, E. S., Nomura, A. M. Y., Heilbrun, L. K., Stemmermann, G. N. & Green, S. B. (1984). Prospective study of alcohol consumption and cancer. *New England Journal of Medicine*, **310**, 617–621.

Powell, K. E., Spain, K. G., Christenson, G. M. & Mollenkamp, M. P. (1986). The status of the 1990 objectives for physical fitness and exercise. *Public Health Reports*, **101**, 15–21.

Powell, K. E., Caspersen, C. J., Koplan, J. P. & Ford, E. S. (1989). Physical activity and chronic diseases. *American Journal of Clinical Nutrition*, **49**, 999–1006.

Remington, P. L., Smith, M. Y., Williamson, D. F., Anda, R. F., Gentry, E. M. & Hogelin, G. C. (1988). Design, characteristics, and usefulness of state-based behavioral risk factor surveillance: 1981–1987. *Public Health Reports*, **103**, 366–375.

Renne, K. S. (1974). Measurement of social health in a general population survey. *Social Science Research*, **3**, 25–44.

Roberts, R. E. & Lee, E. S. (1980). Health practices among Mexican Americans: further evidence from the Human Population Laboratory studies. *Preventive Medicine*, **9**, 675–688.

Roberts, R. E., Stevenson, J. M. & Breslow, L. (1981). Symptoms of depression among blacks and whites in an urban community. *Journal of Nervous and Mental Disease*, **169**, 774–779.

Schoenborn, C. A. (1986). Health habits of U.S. adults, 1985: the "Alameda 7" revisited. *Public Health Reports*, **101**, 571–580.

Schoenborn, C. A. (1988). Health promotion and disease prevention: United States, 1985. *Vital and Health Statistics*. 10 (163). DHHS Pub. No. (PHS) 88-1591. Hyattsville, MD: National Center for Health Statistics.

Schoenborn, C. A. & Benson, V. (1988). Relationships between smoking and other unhealthy habits: United States, 1985. *Advanced Data from Vital and Health Statistics*. No. 154. DHHS Pub. No. (PHS)88-1250. Hyattsville, MD: National Center for Health Statistics.

Schoenborn, C. A. & Cohen, B. H. (1986). Trends in smoking, alochol consumption, and other health practices among U. S. adults, 1977 and 1983. *Advanced Data from Vital and Health Statistics* No. 118. Hyattsville, MD: National Center for Health Statistics.

Schoenborn, C. A. & Danchik, K. M. (1980). Health practices among adults: United States, 1977. *Advanced Data from Vital and Health Statistics*. No. 64. Nov. 4. Hyattsville, MD: National Center for Health Statistics.

Schoenborn, C. A., Danchik, K. M. & Elinson, J. E. (1981). Basic data from Wave I of the National Survey of Personal Health Practices and Consequences: United States, 1979. *Vital and Health Statistics*. Series 15, No. 2. DHHS Publication No. (PHS)81-1163. Hyattsville, MD: National Center for Health Statistics.

Seeman, T. E., Kaplan, G. A., Knudsen, L., Cohen, R. & Guralnik, J. (1987). Social network ties and mortality among the elderly in the Alameda County Study. *American Journal of Epidemiology*, 126, 714–723.

Stephens, T. (1988). Physical activity and mental health in the United States and Canada: evidence from four population surveys. *Preventive Medicine*, 17, 35–47.

Stewart, A. L., Brook, R. H. & Kane, R. L. (1979). *Conceptualization and Measurement of Health Habits for Adults in the Health Insurance Study: Volume I, Smoking*. Prepared under a grant from the US Department of Health Education and Welfare. Santa Monica, CA: Rand Corporation.

Stewart, A. L., Brook, R. H. & Kane, R. L. (1980). *Conceptualization and Measurement of Health Habits for Adults in the Health Insurance Study: Volume II. Overweight*. Prepared under a grant from the US Department of Health Education and Welfare. Santa Monica, CA: Rand Corporation.

Stewart, A. L., Ware, J. E., Brook, R. H. & Davies-Avery, A. (1978). *Conceptualization and Measurement of Health for Adults in the Health Insurance Study: Volume II. Physical Health in Terms of Functioning*. Prepared under a grant from the U.S. Department of Health Education and Welfare. Santa Monica, CA: Rand Corporation.

Tapp, J. T. & Goldenthal, P. (1982). A factor analytic study of health habits. *Preventive Medicine*, 11, 724–728.

US Department of Health and Human Services (1989). *Reducing the Health Consequences of Smoking: 25 Years of Progress. A Report of the Surgeon General*. US Department of Health and Human Services, Public Health Service, Centers for Disease Control, Center for Chronic Disease Prevention and Health Promotion, Office on Smoking and Health. DHHS Publication No. (CDC)89-8411.

Ware, J. E., Brook, R. H., Davies-Avery, A., Williams, K. N., Stewart, A. L., Rogers, W. H., Donald, C. A. & Johnston, S. A. (1980). *Conceptualization and Measurement of Health for Adults in the Health Insurance Study: Volume I, Model of Health and Methodology*. Prepared under a grant from the US Department of Health Education and Welfare. Santa Monica, CA: Rand Corporation.

Ware, J. E., Johnston, S. A., Davies-Avery, A. & Brook, R. H. (1979). *Conceptualization and Measurement of Health for Adults in the Health Insurance Study: Volume III, Mental Health*. Prepared under a grant from the US Department of Health Education and Welfare. Santa Monica, CA: Rand Corporation.

Wetzler, H. P. & Cruess, D. F. (1985). Self-reported physical health practices and health care utilization: findings from the National Health Interview Survey. *American Journal of Public Health*, 75, 1329–1330.

Wetzler, H. P. & Cruess, D. F. (1985). Health practices in United States Air Force personnel compared to United States adult civilians. *Aviation, Space, and Environmental Medicine*, 56, 371–375.

Wiley, J. A. & Camacho, T. C. (1980). Life-style and future health: evidence from the Alameda County Study. *Preventive Medicine*, 9, 1–21.

Williams, A. F. & Wechsler, H. (1972). Interrelationship of preventive actions in health and other areas. *Health Services Reports*, 87, 969–976.

Wilson, R. W. & Elinson, J. (1981). National Survey of Personal Health Practices and

Consequences: Background, conceptual issues, and selected findings. *Public Health Reports*, **96**, 218–225.

Wingard, D. L. (1982). The sex differential in mortality rates. Demographic and behavioral factors. *American Journal of Epidemiology*, **115**, 205–216.

Wingard, D. L. & Berkman, L. F. (1983). Mortality risk associated with sleeping patterns among adults. *Sleep*, **6**, 102–107.

Wingard, D. L., Berkman, L. F. & Brand, R. J. (1982). A multivariate analysis of health-related practices. A nine-year mortality follow-up of the Alameda County Study. *American Journal of Epidemiology*, **116**, 765–775.

Wisconsin Department of Health and Social Services (1987). *Reducing Risks: Behavior and Health in Wisconsin*. Center for Health Statistics. Bureau of Community Health and Prevention, Division of Health.

5 Primary and Secondary Prevention of Cancer: Opportunities for Behavioural Scientists

ROB SANSON-FISHER
NSW Cancer Council Education Research Project Faculty of Medicine, University of Newcastle, Australia

INTRODUCTION

What is cancer?

Cancer is characterized by an excessive and purposeless proliferation of cells. This abnormal growth of cells is called a "neoplasm". The original mass of abnormal cells is called the "primary cancer". These abnormal cells can almost always be categorized histologically according to a specific tissue of origin. For example, melanoma is an abnormal growth of melanocytes in the skin. Colon cancer is an abnormal proliferation of epithelial cells which line the large intestine (Diamandopoulos & Meissner, 1985).

In most instances, cancer endangers health by unchecked growth and spread or, much less commonly, an inappropriate secretion of hormones and other body chemicals. Cancer growth and spread can be localized or systemic. In the former, a primary cancer will continue to invade its organ of origin unchecked, and can extend into neighbouring structures such as viscera, skin and muscle. This localized growth can lead to compromise of the normal function of the organ through pressure effects, obstruction, perforation, and destruction and replacement of the normal, functional cells.

A primary cancer can also spread systemically beyond the organ of origin when tumour cells break off from the primary cancer and travel along lymphatic vessels to be caught in the regional lymph nodes. This is known as lymphatic spread. For example, regional lymph nodes such as those in the groin or arm-pit can become clogged with cancer cells from a primary melanoma on the leg or from primary breast cancer. Tumour cells can also disseminate through the blood-stream to other more distant organs of the body. Optimally,

International Review of Health Psychology. Volume 2. Edited by S. Maes, H. Leventhal and M. Johnston
© 1993 John Wiley & Sons Ltd

these cells are recognized as abnormal by the immune system and destroyed before they attach to distant organs (Miescher & Muller-Eberhard, 1976). If not, the cells invade these organs. These distant colonies or metastases of secondary cancer can cause pain, dysfunction and eventual death. Common sites for the systemic spread of such epithelial metastases include the liver, lung and bone marrow (Montgomery, 1965).

The speed and extent of spread of metastases beyond the primary neoplasm vary both between and within cancer types. For example, cancer of the uterine cervix typically remains local and is unlikely to spread into the lymphatic system or blood stream for several years. In contrast, some types of breast cancer grow slowly and remain localized yet others have early systemic spread via the lymphatics and blood stream. The degree of metastatic spread is a major determinant of prognosis once a diagnosis of cancer is made.

Prevalence

Cancer is a major cause of death throughout the world, although the mortality rates attributable to cancer vary from country to country. There is also considerable variation across countries with regard to the major types of cancer causing death. For example, female breast cancer is rare in much of Asia and Africa but is three to five times more common as a cause of female deaths in developed countries (Muir et al., 1987). Cancer of the liver is three times more common in males of developing countries than elsewhere (Muir et al., 1987). These variations suggest that genetic and environmental factors are important in both the genesis of cancer and the immune system's capacity to seek and destroy abnormal cellular proliferation when still relatively harmless (Doll & Peto, 1981).

Causation of cancer

Unlike the identification of bacteria and viruses as causal agents of infection, scientific research has only rarely been able to identify single, sufficient and necessary causes of cancer. Typically, the scientific evidence used to determine causality in cancer is largely circumstantial, although nonetheless convincing (Doll & Peto, 1981). Laboratory experiments can measure in vitro effects of dietary, chemical and hormonal factors in carcinogenesis. Animal experiments measure these effects in vivo. Epidemiological studies seek to confirm the influence of these factors in populations of humans using increased probabilities of risk to infer a causal association. Examples include the accepted causal association of cigarette smoking and lung cancer based on studies which demonstrate disproportionate numbers of smokers amongst those diagnosed with the disease than would be expected by chance, and the significant reduction over time of the risk of developing lung cancer amongst smokers who have quit (Fielding, 1985). A link between dietary factors and female breast cancer has been supported by studies demonstrating that rates of breast cancer amongst black Americans are similar to those of white Americans rather than black Africans, and the rates amongst immigrant Japanese women reflect those of their adopted countries which are high, not that of their native Japan which is low (Muir et al., 1987).

Given the above association, it is claimed that three quarters of cancer deaths are due to environmental factors, many of which can be modified and potentially controlled (Tomatis, 1990). Reliably established and practicable ways to reduce cancer risk include avoiding tobacco smoke, obesity, excessive exposure to sunlight, alcohol and known occupational and chemical carcinogens (Peto, 1985).

THE ROLE OF BEHAVIOURAL SCIENTISTS IN CANCER CONTROL

Traditionally, behavioural scientists have adopted an individual and curative focus to diseases such as cancer, working with patients who are receiving treatment or who have a terminal disease (Leventhal, 1983; Winett, King & Altman, 1989). However, it can be argued that the most productive task for behavioural scientists in the cancer field is to find ways of modifying relevant health-risk behaviours of whole populations rather than of selected individuals (Green, 1984).

Four main distinctions are evident between the individual and population approaches to cancer control. First, in the population, or public health approach, the unit of analysis is not the individual, but populations which are defined by their geographical location, gender, race, age, occupational status, or health risk behaviours (World Health Organization, 1986). This allows a single intervention to reach a much larger audience and is thus potentially more cost-effective (Farquhar, 1978).

Second, in the individual approach the clinician usually waits for individuals to define themselves, or to be defined by others as ill, and then to seek assistance. This has been termed the "waiting" mode (Rappaport, 1977). The clinicans' task in this role may involve history taking, physical examination, diagnostic tests and, if cancer is diagnosed, treatment through the use of drugs, surgery, and radiotherapy. In contrast, the public health approach is based on a "seeking" mode of service delivery (Rappaport, 1977). This involves identification of the risk characteristics of large populations using epidemiological research methods, and mortality, morbidity and large-scale survey data. Common intervention strategies in the public health approach consist of health education, health promotion, legislative change, community development and environmental change (Green, 1984; Winett, King & Altman, 1989).

Third, in the individual approach, the traditional location for intervention or treatment is the psychologist's or doctor's office, or the hospital (Winett, King & Altman, 1989). In the public health approach the legislature, schools, workplaces, self-help groups; primary care physician's offices, and the broader community all constitute possible sites for intervention (Green, 1984; Redman

& Sanson-Fisher, 1989). The final difference between the two approaches to cancer control are reflected in the types of professionals who are the principal practitioners (Winett, King & Altman, 1989). Currently the dominant professional groups in the individual approach are medical practitioners such as medical oncologists, radiologists and surgeons. In contrast, within the public health approach, the professionals most likely to be involved are behavioural scientists, biostatisticians, epidemiologists, administrators and health planners (Redman & Sanson-Fisher, 1989). The following review will highlight the role of the behavioural scientist in a preventive, population oriented approach to cancer control.

A PREVENTIVE APPROACH TO CANCER CONTROL

There are three main ways to effect cancer control: primary prevention—the reduction of the incidence of the disease; and secondary cancer prevention—the early detection or treatment of the disease. A third level, tertiary prevention, relates to minimizing the impact of established disease. To date, behavioural scientists have largely been involved in tertiary prevention. However, they can greatly contribute to primary prevention by developing ways to discourage behaviours associated with cancer risk, and to secondary prevention by encouraging behaviours associated with early detection and effective care.

PRIMARY PREVENTION

The following section briefly covers some selected cancers where primary changes in health risk behaviour have the potential to prevent the initiation of cancer development, and where behavioural scientists have a population based role in achieving this potential. The literature reviewed considers the prevention of skin cancer by decreasing solar exposure, and the prevention of smoking-related cancers by decreasing the uptake of smoking and increasing the rate of smoking cessation.

Skin cancer

Skin cancer is one of the more common forms of cancer. In the United States of America, half a million new cases of skin cancer are diagnosed each year (American Cancer Society (ACS), 1987), most of which are basal cell and squamous cell carcinomas that are highly treatable and rarely metastasize (ACS, 1987). The more serious type of skin cancer is malignant melanoma which is estimated to account for approximately 74% of all skin cancer deaths in the United States of America (ACS, 1987). The lifetime risk for developing melanoma is 2%, and 70% for the more common skin cancer types such as basal cell and squamous cell carcinomas (ACS, 1987).

The number of cases of malignant melanoma and skin cancer are increasing in many western countries, partly as a consequence of changes in solar exposure habits, and as a possible outcome of atmospheric ozone depletion (McCarthy & Shaw, 1989). Taking into consideration the number of work days lost, the deaths associated with skin cancer, and the cost of preventive measures, Australian annual expenditure related to skin cancer is estimated to approach $400 million (McCarthy & Shaw, 1989).

Prospects for prevention

The major risk factors for melanoma include the presence of moles, sun exposure, a previous history of melanoma or other skin cancers, and a family history of melanoma (Evans et al., 1988). Other risk factors for non-melanocytic skin cancer include advanced age, predominantly outdoor occupations, fair skin colour, and sensitive skin which burns rather than tans (Evans et al., 1988). Given the nature of these risk factors, there is significant potential for the primary prevention of skin cancers through changes in lifestyle factors associated with exposure of the skin to ultraviolet rays. Particular behaviour changes include remaining in a sheltered position during periods of high ultraviolet intensity, and the use of protective measures such as hats, protective clothing, and high sun protection factor sunscreens. It is estimated that approximately 80% of skin cancers can be prevented by primary prevention early in life through such measures (Goldsmith, 1987).

Youth represent a high priority group for primary prevention of skin cancer for several reasons. First, they represent an "at-risk" group, since excessive exposure to the sun between the ages of 10 to 24 years is a strong factor in the development of skin cancers later in life (Holman et al., 1986). Second, it has been estimated that children spend more time outdoors than adults (Wakefield & Bonett, 1990) and receive three times more ultraviolet radiation than adults (Hurwitz, 1988). Third, the benefits of solar protection can be maximized if adopted during childhood and maintained thereafter. Stern, Weinstein, & Kiviranta (1986) have calculated that the use of sunscreens with SPF of 15 or more in the first 18 years of life would reduce the lifetime risk of non-melanocytic skin cancers by around 78%. Fourth, youth are at a stage when habits, attitudes and lifestyles are still malleable (Immarino & Weinberg, 1985), so attempts to modify their health related behaviours may be more effective than attempts with adults, whose behaviour patterns are more entrenched.

Despite the very considerable scope for prevention of skin cancers, a survey of 2029 adolescent school students found that only 30% were protected adequately in circumstances which warranted protection (Cockburn et al., 1989). Given that children spend a significant amount of their time at school, this venue provides a means whereby the great majority of children can be accessed for the implementation of solar protection programmes. Such programmes, developed by behavioural scientists could involve schools implementing organizational changes that minimize the solar exposure of children through the provision of shade, the timetabling of outdoor activities to avoid the high risk period of the day, and the implementation of policies to facilitate the adoption of personal protective behaviours.

Although school-based measures have the potential to significantly improve primary prevention, a recent survey of schools indicates that current practices are less than optimal (Schofield et al., 1991). It was reported that children spent seven–eight hours per week in outdoor activities at school, and that the majority of this time (80–90%) occurred between 11.00 a.m. and 3.00 p.m., the period of peak ultra-violet exposure. While 64% of primary schools in the survey had formulated some form of solar protection policy, such a policy existed in only 39% of secondary schools. Furthermore, the provision of shade was minimal, with only 18% of secondary school playgrounds being shaded at midday. However, the utilization of this shade was quite high, with 64% of students observed using the available shaded area. This suggests a potential demand for more shade within school environments.

The study by Schofield et al. (1991) also found that education about solar protection in both primary and secondary school curricula is minimal. A recent randomized controlled trial has however, provided evidence that such education programmes can be effective in changing the knowledge, attitudes and solar protection behaviours of primary school children (Girgis et al., 1991b). In this study the effectiveness of a comprehensive programme called "Skin Safe", which incorporated some of the principles of co-operative learning by children, was compared with a single didactic lecture and a no intervention control condition. The results indicated that children who participated in the "Skin Safe" programme were almost three times as likely to use a high level of solar protection eight months after the formal intervention compared to either the lecture or control groups.

Outdoor workers constitute another at-risk group for the development of the more common skin cancers due to the high level of ultraviolet exposure their work entails (Marks, Ponsford & Selwood, 1983). The potential benefit of primary prevention efforts directed to this group is demonstrated by research which reports a substantial reduction in the number of solar keratoses presenting in outdoor workers who were able to reduce their exposure to the sun in a 12 month period (Marks, Ponsford & Selwood, 1983). The above data indicate a need for behavioural scientists to develop, implement and evaluate behaviour change programmes that encourage the practice of solar protection in this high risk group. However, many workplace health education pro-grammes have not been systemically evaluated (Orleans & Shipley, 1982). A recent evaluation of a skin screening and education programme indicated a significant 16% increase in solar protection measures employed by an experimental group relative to a control group of outdoor workers. However the intervention involved dermatologist's examining workers skin for solar damage which is unlikely to be a cost-effective mechanism for achieving solar protection (Girgis & Sanson-Fisher, 1991).

Smoking-related cancers

Smoking is a major aetiological factor in many cancers. In adult men, smoking accounts for 90% of carcinoma of the lung/trachea/bronchus; 92% of carcinoma of the lip/oral cavity/pharynx; and 80% of carcinoma of the larynx (U.S. Preventive Services Task Force, 1989). In all, it is estimated that 30% of cancer deaths are directly attributable to smoking (Better Health Commission, 1986).

Smoking initiation

While estimates on the uptake of smoking vary due to methodological issues, data from a number of countries suggest that smoking uptake remains a major health problem for the young. Prevalence studies in industrialized countries show that by the end of adolescence, most people likely to become smokers are already smoking (Morris & Koyama, 1990). The US Surgeon-General's Report on smoking (Department of Health and Human Services, 1989) indicated that for American high school seniors, prevalence of daily cigarette consumption was approximately 18–21%. Among Australian 12 year olds, 5% of both males and females smoke, while in the 16–19 years age group, 20% of the males and 31% of the females smoke (Hill et al., 1990). The greater increase in smoking rates among females was a consistent and disturbing finding in the majority of prevalence studies from the 1950s to the 1980s. The reasons for an increase in uptake in this gender group are not yet fully understood. However, it has been suggested that it may be a consequence of the targeting of females by media advertising and the perception that smoking is a "liberated" habit. Covington and Omelick (1988) have suggested that cigarettes enhance self perceptions of maturity particularly among females.

Prospects for preventing smoking initiation

A considerable body of descriptive research has attempted to explain the psychosocial domains involved in the uptake of smoking. This work is well summarized in the US Surgeon General's Report (Department of Health and Social Services, 1989) which identified two major explanations for smoking uptake, the cognitive decision making, and the personal characteristics, social context approaches. In the cognitive decision making area, knowledge of health effects has been argued to be an influencing factor when adolescents are considering uptake (Friedman, Lichenstein & Biglan, 1985). For example, adolescents who smoke have been found to be less knowledgeable about the negative health consequences of smoking compared to their non-smoking peers (Pederson, Baskerville & Lefcoe, 1981).

It has also been reported that young people often underestimate the addictive nature of smoking (Brecher, 1972) and that teenagers' perceptions of the attractiveness or desirability of smoking may influence whether or not they take up the habit. Charlton's (1984) work suggests that children will be more likely to smoke if they perceive that smoking will help in weight loss while Murray and Perry (1984) note that uptake of smoking among adolescents is often associated with efforts to relieve boredom.

Personal characteristics, such as extraversion (Eysenck et al., 1960) and neuroticism (Cherry & Kierran, 1976, 1978) have consistently been found to be related to smoking status. Low academic goals and performances have also been associated with the smoking status of adolescents (Pirie, Murray & Luepker, 1988), as have behavioural problems including rule breaking in school, delinquency, low levels of responsibility and rebelliousness (Jessor & Jessor, 1977; Mittelmark et al., 1987).

Parental influences, and the pressure of peer groups are important social context factors affecting smoking uptake. Peers appear to act as models who can either encourage or discourage uptake. Various studies report that the majority of adolescents smoke their first cigarette with friends of the same age (Biglan et al., 1983; Needle et al., 1986; Morgan & Grube, 1989). In fact, during the initial act of experimentation almost 90% of people present have been identified as either adolescents' friends, acquaintances or siblings (Friedman, Lichenstein & Biglan, 1985).

These data suggest that preventive behaviourally orientated programmes should be directed at children in the early adolescent stage of development. The most common and best researched of these programmes over the last 25 years have been school-based psychosocial orientated programmes which use social learning theory as their basic structure. Two main types of psychosocial programmes have been developed. The first of these are the social influence programmes which focus on helping students to understand the social pressures involved in making a decision to smoke, and attempt to teach skills to resist these pressures (Flay et al., 1983; Evans et al., 1978).

The second type of psychosocial programmes are the "Life Skills Training" (LST) programmes. These programmes attempt to modify broader life skills and include training designed to increase self-efficacy and social competence. Components of these programmes have included social resistance training, problem solving and decision making, assertiveness training, self-control and self-esteem (Botvin & Wills, 1985).

A recent review using meta-analysis techniques suggested smoking prevention programmes in schools had modest effects (Rundall & Bruvold, 1988). The US Surgeon General (Department of Health and Social Services, 1989) also reports that the potential of school-based programmes is restricted by environmental factors such as the natural history of smoking acquisition, and the need for long term follow-up beyond the initial intervention. In addition, most reported studies were conducted under ideal conditions, which are frequently not achievable in the normal, non-experimental school environment. Furthermore, it is argued that there is also a need for environmental changes to occur in areas which currently support the smoking habit among adolescents, such as modification to media messages, access to cigarettes (Difranza et al., 1987) changes in societal norms and social networks. Hence, behavioural scientists should include components which address all such aspects of a young person's environment in intervention programmes (Morris & Koyama, 1990). The development of such programmes represents a considerable challenge to behavioural scientists.

Smoking cessation

Estimates of the prevalence of tobacco smoking vary across countries. In Australia 30.2% of males and 27.0% of females over the age of 15 were found to be smokers (Hill, White & Gray, 1991). In the United States of America, the rates are approximately the same (US Preventive Services Task Force, 1989). Characteristics of smokers suggest that there is a strong tendency for smoking to be concentrated in men and women who are aged 20–29 years and over, and in the lower socioeconomic classes. The lowest prevalence rates are found among well educated men and women, and in persons with high occupational status (US Preventive Services Task Force, 1989). Smoking-attributed mortality in the United States of America represents 22% of all deaths amongst men and 11% among women (Department of Health and Human Services, 1989). Male smokers are 22 more times at risk of dying from lung cancer than male non-smokers while female smokers are 12 times more at risk than female non-smokers.

Prospects for increasing smoking cessation

Smoking has now been shown to be a causal factor in the development of serious medical problems, including cardiovascular disease, cerebral vascular disease, lung cancer, and chronic obstructive airways disease, as well as tumours of the mouth, larynx, oesophagus, lip and bladder (Centers for Disease Control, 1987; Department of Health and Social Services, 1989). Following the cessation of smoking, the associated health risks diminish substantially in proportion to the period of abstinence, eventually returning to the level of non-smokers for some diseases, such as coronary artery disease, cerebral vascular disease and oral cavity cancers. For example, a smoker who quits before the age of 50 years has half the risk of dying in the next 15 years of a continuing smoker (Department of Health and Human Services, 1989). The same report found that there were demonstrable improvements in mortality even in smokers who quit in the 70–74 years age group.

Smoking is a complex habit which is maintained by psychological, physiological and social factors. While 90% of former smokers report stopping without the use of a special programme (DHHS, 1989), there has been increasing interest in using primary care physicians and the workplace as access points for the implementation of smoking cessation programmes.

Doctors as agents for smoking cessation programmes

There are a number of reasons why doctors can be effective agents for smoking cessation. They see a high proportion of the population in any 12 month period and approximately one-third of these will be smokers (Australian Bureau of Statistics (ABS), 1983). Furthermore, patients view physicians as one of the more desirable sources of health information, with a majority preferring assistance for smoking cessation from a medical practitioner or qualified health professional, rather than self-help approaches (Slama et al., 1989). Doctors themselves perceive an important part of their role as the identification and intervention for modifiable risk factors such as smoking (Dickinson et al., 1989).

Before doctors can play an effective part in smoking cessation interventions, they need to be aware of their patient's current smoking status. An American study of family physicians revealed that doctors had recorded smoking status in only 18% of all their smoking patients (Chu & Day, 1981). Another study involving 56 randomly selected general practitioners found that 56% of smokers were detected, and of these only 22% had received treatment for their smoking (Dickinson et al., 1989). In a study assessing interns performance in detecting health risks in their patients, only 44% of smokers were identified (Gordon, Sanson-Fisher & Saunders, 1988). Such research suggests that doctors are often missing many opportunities for intervention with their smoking patients.

Smoking cessation programmes for use by medical practitioners have taken a number of forms, including simple advice, the use of counselling, follow-up visits, and the prescription of nicotine gum to increase the effectiveness of physicians as agents of smoking cessation. Russell et al. (1983) randomly allocated 1938 general practice patients to three groups; either a non-intervention control group; a booklet and advice for two minutes; or advice, booklet and nicotine gum. Follow-up measures four months and one year following the intervention, utilizing chemical validation of self-report, showed abstinence rates of 4.1% in the advice and booklet group, and 8.8% in the nicotine group. Similar interventions have found essentially the same results (Jamrozik et al., 1984; Russell et al., 1987). Interventions taking more of the physicians' time, for example, between three and eleven minutes, show higher rates of cessation ranging from 6% to 19% at one year (Wilson et al., 1982; Page et al., 1986; Wilson et al., 1988; Slama et al., 1990). In an intensive intervention involving six separate counselling sessions, Richmond and Webster (1985) achieved a remarkable cessation rate of 33% at six months follow-up. However, few doctors were able to implement this programme even after receiving special programmes given the response cost involved in undertaking the intervention (Copeman et al., 1989).

While the quality of the research undertaken in this area varies, it appears that the more time a physician devotes to smoking cessation effort, the greater likelihood there is that the cessation rates obtained will be higher. A meta-analysis of 39 controlled trials in medical practice by Kottke et al. (1988) suggested that success was associated with reinforcement rather than novel or unusual interventions. Reinforcement was considered to involve the number and type of contacts with smokers as well as the range of staff involved. For example, trials that involved professionals such as nurses and psychologists, in addition to physicians, had better results than those involving physicians alone (Kottke et al., 1988).

While the proportion of patients who succeed in quitting and remaining non-smokers after a brief message or warning from the doctor is small, the yield is potentially large. For example, in Australia there are approximately 3.7 million smokers. Approximately 75% of these will visit their practitioner at least once per year (ABS, 1983). If primary care physicians achieved an overall 5% cessation rate, using a simple advice approach, it would yield approximately 140 000 quitters per year. A major question for behavioural scientists is how to develop strategies which will increase the probability that primary care physicians will adopt simple smoking cessation interventions for every day clinical use, so that the proportion of smokers treated will increase. A related issue is that the proportion of heavy smokers detected is likely to increase as the prevalence of smoking declines. The cessation programmes trialled in medical practice to date have been most effective with light smokers (less than 20 cigarettes per day). Consequently another challenge to behavioural scientists will be to develop effective strategies targeted at more addicted smokers.

Workplace smoking cessation programmes

The workplace provides an opportunity to access a broad group of the smoking community, and the opportunity to teach cessation skills through specific individual or group programmes. Target populations which have been difficult to reach with cessation programmes, for example, young males, blue-collar workers and working mothers, can be accessed at their place of employment. This access point also offers implicit benefits and incentives for both the employee and employer alike. For the employee, workplace interventions offer a free or inexpensive, conveniently located programme with in-built social and environmental support systems. Employers stand to benefit economically from improved employee health, increased worker morale and productivity; although these gains may be offset to some extent by the ongoing costs of intervention strategies and programmes. Partly as a result of these reasons, a number of worksite smoking cessation programmes have been conducted during the last decade. However, although the virtues of such interventions have been espoused, the empirical evidence for these claims is less clear. The methodological problems of existing studies and the lack of replication makes evaluation of particular programmes difficult and this provides an opportunity for further behavioural science research.

Three broad types of smoking cessation interventions have been used in worksites. The first involves enforcement of smoking restrictions or bans. Relatively few organizations have attempted to evaluate the impact of this policy on employee smoking habits. Of eleven evaluative studies located in this field, five assessed attitude and compliance rates as the sole outcome measures, while the remaining studies examined the effect of restrictive smoking practice on smoking cessation rates. Of these six, only three found that the policy impacted upon smoking cessation (Andrews, 1983; Hocking et al., 1991); Health & Welfare Canada, 1988). In the latter report, an overall decrease in smoking prevalence of 5% was found amongst employees in the 18 month interim period before and after policy implementation. A similar rate of decrease was found by Hocking et al. (1991) at 18 months follow-up. Andrews (1983) reported a 26% decrease in prevalence as a consequence of a restrictive policy on smoking. However, less than one-third of the quitters attributed their cessation to the workplace policy.

Such findings suggest that restrictive smoking policy can have a significant and positive impact on smoking rates. However, this interpretation needs to be tempered due to a range of methodological limitation existing in most of the studies. In general, these limitations involve the use of small, non-random and self-selected samples, self-report of smoking behaviour and cigarette consumption rates, lack of biochemical validation of smoking status, and often, little monitoring of policy compliance.

Other forms of workplace intervention programmes have been implemented to facilitate individuals stopping smoking. These programmes have included the use of self-help manuals, nicotine chewing gum, nicotine fading and physician advice. Glasgow and Terborg (1988) report that self-help interventions in the workplace generally produce low cessation rates but can be successful in maintaining cessation. Using volunteers in a "Stop Smoking" programme Hallet (1986) found an abstinence rate after one year of 12% compared to a control group rate of 2%. A later study (Hallett & Sutton, 1987), using nicotine chewing gum in combination with videotapes achieved a 16% abstinence rate at one year follow-up compared to a 2% rate among the no intervention control group. These results suggest that workplace programmes using nicotine gum are effective in changing smoking behaviour.

A third form of workplace intervention involving utilization of workplace peer support appears to have provided mixed results. Glasgow, Klesges and O'Neill (1986) found that the addition of a social support component to a nicotine fading programme was not effective in enhancing the maintenance of smoking abstinence. However, multi-faceted interventions have shown some capacity to facilitate cessation. Diguisto (1987) utilized a range of intervention components in a small group of 28 subjects and achieved an abstinence rate of 25% at one year. In a much larger study, Shipley et al. (1988) analysed the outcome of a two year cessation intervention which was part of the Johnson and Johnson "Live for Life" Programme. This intervention involved annual health checks, with physicians providing quit smoking advice, environmental change to support non-smoking, and the repeated availability of quit smoking clinics. Relapse prevention training was offered, as well as family support, relaxation training, and a buddy system. The researchers reported a significantly higher quit rate (22.6%) amongst employees in the multi-faceted programme, compared to smokers at companies that conducted health screen programmes only (17.4%). This study found that the "Live for Life" programme was particularly effective with smokers at high risk of coronary heart disease. However, the study sample was non-representative of all smoking employees since females with higher smoking rates were less likely to volunteer. Despite this, the results of the study are particularly encouraging given the methodological strength of the research design, allowing the conclusion that multi-faceted programmes may be effective in maintaining abstinence as well as eliciting initial smoking cessation.

SECONDARY PREVENTION

The following section addresses the role of behavioural scientists in enhancing the use of tests or measures used to identify (screen) persons who have already developed cancer risk factors, or who have pre-clinical or clinically apparent disease. The objective of such screening is to allow treatment of those identified so as to reduce cancer morbidity and/or mortality.

Criteria for establishing a screening programme

Before considering the data regarding the prevention of particular cancers through screening, it is necessary to briefly review the criteria of what constitutes an appropriate screening programme. These criteria were initially developed by the Canadian Task Force on the Periodic Health Examination (1979) and further refined by the US Preventive Services Task Force (1989). These groups have argued that a screening test should have demonstrable accuracy. It should also have a high sensitivity, that is, the test should identify a high proportion of persons with the condition. A test with poor sensitivity will miss those individuals who have the condition and produce a large proportion of false negative results, that is, true cases will be told incorrectly that they are free of the disease and consequently will be inappropriately reassured. The test should have a high specificity, that is, a high proportion of persons without the condition will correctly be tested as not having the disease. A test with poor specificity will result in a large proportion of healthy people being told they have the condition (false positives) resulting in anxiety and unnecessary further testing. For the sensitivity and specificity of screening tests to be assessed, it is necessary to have an accepted reference or gold standard which provides an accurate distinction between those with and those without the condition. Unfortunately with some forms of cancer there is no clear consensus as to what constitutes a gold standard.

As well as having acceptable levels of sensitivity and specificity, the screening test must also possess reliability, that is, the ability to produce the same result when repeated on the same person with the same condition. Poor reliability might arise as a result of differences in judgment between different individuals or laboratories (inter-observer variation), or by differences within the same individual or laboratory (intra-observer variation).

For screening to be beneficial there is a need for a procedure or treatment to be available which can prevent or delay the natural progression of the cancer once detected. If an individual is told that they have cancer without there being adequate treatment available there is unnecessary pain and the screening procedure provides little benefit. For some cancers, such as cervical, skin, and breast cancers, there now appears to be clear data supporting the argument that early detection will significantly improve the course of the disease. However, in other cancers such as lung and colon, the benefit of early detection appears equivocal (US Preventive Services Task Force, 1989).

When evaluating whether early detection is effective, it is also necessary to consider whether or not an individual has simply been diagnosed at an earlier stage of the disease, thereby appearing to lengthen survival, when in fact it only increases the amount of time for which a patient knows that they have cancer. This phenomena is known as lead-time bias. Another problem of particular relevance for cancer screening is the notion of length-bias. This refers to the tendency to detect a disproportionate number of cases of a slowly progressing disease and to miss those cases of a disease where there is a rapid progression of the condition. In this situation, people with the more aggressive malignancies may be underestimated in the number of cases detected by screening, with those that are detected having a better prognosis, even if the screening itself does not influence outcome. Such a bias may lead to the assumption that screening is more effective than it really is.

The justification for implementing a screening programme must also ensure that the potentially adverse effects of screening do not outweigh its benefits. For example, some screening procedures for colon cancer, such as sigmoidoscopy or colonoscopy, may result in colonic perforation. The number of cases for which this might happen needs to be balanced against the potential increase in life expectancy or quality of life that may occur as a result of early detection. Obviously, screening can also have high psychological as well as physical costs, although this is an area which has been largely under-studied.

The following sections review the potential benefits of screening for cervical, breast and skin cancers and highlight areas where behavioural scientists can make a significant contribution to achieving these benefits.

Cervical cancer

Evidence from historical studies and case control studies supports the effectiveness of regular Papanicolaou (Pap) screening to reduce morbidity and premature mortality amongst women at risk of cervical cancer, that is, women who have ever been sexually active and who have not had the uterine cervix removed by hysterectomy (Eddy, 1990). Pap smears detect epithelial lesions with a high malignant potential which can subsequently be removed by local ablation, cone biopsy or hysterectomy (Channen, 1990). Using data from cervical cancer screening programmes evaluated in the 1960s and 1970s mathematical projections suggest that three-yearly screening will prevent 91% of new cases of cervical cancer: biennial screening will prevent 93% and annual screening, 94% (International Agency for Research on Cancer (IARC) Working Group, 1986). However, Pap screening for women at risk rarely achieves this preventive potential. For example, in America, the number of new cases reported annually exceed 13 000 and approximately 7000 women will die each year (ACS, 1989). In Australia, it is estimated that existing cervical cancer screening is preventing about 46% of the cancers which would be occurring in the absence of any screening. (Australian Institute of Health (AIH) 1991.) In the United Kingdom, the figure is approximately 25% (Parkin, Nguyen-Dinh & Day, 1985). In the majority of cases, women with cervical cancer have never been screened (Fruchter, Boyce & Hunt, 1980; Holman et al., 1981). Amongst the minority who have had a previous Pap smear yet have still developed cancer, false negatives and lack of follow-up of women with known abnormalities can often be cited as reasons for failure of the screening test (Holman et al., 1981; Koss, 1989; Elwood et al., 1984).

Prospects for prevention

While the value of the Pap test is now largely accepted, the screening rate for women at risk remains disturbingly low in many countries. In Australia for example, 62% of women have Pap smears at an interval of every three years, suggesting that a large proportion of at-risk women are not taking advantage of screening services (AIH, 1991). Women who are least likely to be screened include older women, those of lower socio-economic status and those from ethnic minorities. The reasons women are not screened are likely to be the result of a complex range of factors including women's perceptions (Hayward et al., 1988), providers' knowledge (Ballie & Petrie, 1990), attitude and skills, and the acceptability and accessibility of services (Johnston, 1989). Each of these issues provide an opportunity for behavioural scientists to develop and implement interventions designed to increase the rate of Pap smear screening.

Women's perceptions

Women's acceptance of Pap smears as a screening test depend on a number of factors. These include: cultural background; health beliefs; previous Pap smear experience; body image; knowledge and understanding of the purpose of the Pap test, and of its relationship to sexual activity, contraception, and childbirth. It has been suggested that a woman needs to: know that the Pap smear exists as a screening test; have a positive concept of the screening process; believe in its efficacy and its relevance to her; find the idea acceptable; know when and where to have a smear; and find the venue and system acceptable (Hobbs, 1986). A number of studies suggest that the majority of women have heard of the Pap smear and understand that it relates to cancer of the cervix (Schwartz et al., 1989; Shelly & Irwig, Unpublished data). However, a substantial proportion of women appear unclear about the preventive nature of the smear in detecting pre-cancerous lesions (Bowman, 1991). There is also some suggestion that women do not know the recommended screening interval and the requirement for repeated smears over a lifetime (Bowling, 1989). It appears that postmenopausal women often believe that they are no longer at risk, when in fact the data suggests they should maintain their screening habits (Bowling, 1989; Bowman, 1991).

Women also require a range of organizational skills and capacities if they are to have Pap smears. They must locate a suitable provider, make an appointment, often arrange child care or take time off work, organize transport, remember to attend, have the test, and rember to repeat the cycle at a defined time in the future. Many women find it difficult to remember accurately when their last smear was done and so may be unaware that another smear is due. A Canadian study showed that women tend to underestimate the time since their last Pap smear was performed (Walter et al., 1988). A more recent study indicated that pathology records could not be located for almost 50% of women who reported they had a Pap smear within the previous three years (Bowman et al., 1991). Such data indicates a considerable degree of inaccuracy in self-reported screening histories and suggests the need for screening registers, reminder systems, and consistent screening guidelines.

While most medical textbooks advise that a Pap smear is quick, simple, and painless, women's experiences do not seem to coincide with this view. An American study indicated that 38% of women experienced physical discomfort, 20% felt uncomfortable because it was an examination of sexual organs, and 7% cited the physician's attitude and/or gender as a reason for discomfort (Petravage et al., 1979). A Swedish study suggested that 45% of women had feelings of humiliation during pelvic examination (Areskog-Wijma, 1987), while in the United Kingdom, the strongest predictor of non-attendance at a cervical screening clinic was the belief that the procedure would be painful, embarrassing or unpleasant (King, 1987). A community study in Australia indicated that possible barriers to women's utilization of Pap smears may include both knowledge and attitude factors as well as more practical impediments (Bowman, 1991). Fear of cancer, failure to perceive cervical cancer as a preventable disease, lack of knowledge of appropriate screening behaviour, and a lack of acceptable sources of provision were factors in not having regular Pap smears. However, the perception that the experience is unpleasant (53%), and the difficulty remembering to have Pap smears (50%) were identified as the major barriers to screening.

Provider factors

Practitioner belief in the importance of cervical cancer screening has been shown to strongly correlate with its provision by both specialists and family physicians. For instance, a United Kingdom study found that a younger age of primary care physician, a more rural practice, a larger practice size, employment of a practice nurse, a belief in the effectiveness of cervical screening, and a positive view of the time spent on screening were strong predictors of a systematic approach to cervical screening (Havelock et al., 1988). A random survey of primary care physicians in Australia found that almost all practitioners acknowledged the preventive value of Pap smears and perceived themselves to have an important role as providers (Bowman et al., 1990). However, 33% indicated uncertainty about screening criteria and optimal frequency. Provider perceptions of their clinical skills, both in terms of taking a smear and their ability to convince women to have a smear, were also important factors. In this study, 59% of primary care physicians indicated that their difficulty in asking patients about Pap smears acted as a barrier to their provision of screening (Bowman et al., 1990).

A number of strategies have been devised to improve practitioners provision of Pap smears. One recent study involved women over 40 years, who had not had a Pap smear within the previous two years, being offered a smear by a practitioner (Cockburn et al., 1990). Twenty six per cent agreed to a smear during the consultation and a further 23% made an appointment and returned at a later date. Similarly, a study by Ward et al. (1990) examined the acceptability and effectiveness of two interventions designed to encourage opportunistic cervical screening by primary care physicians. In one intervention, a brief strategy was used where the doctor simply mentioned to women who had not had a recent Pap smear that it was important to do so, and that they were prepared to take the smear for them. A more elaborate intervention which addressed the health beliefs of patients produced a slightly (non-significant) greater rate of acceptance, as compared to the simple approach. Importantly, the longer intervention, as well as being no more effective, was also less acceptable to the general practitioners.

One method which has been trialled to systemize the provision of screening by practitioners, and to remind women when their next smear is due, is the use of regular reminder (recall) letters. As an example, a practitioner-based computerized recall system instituted by a Scottish Health Board involving 29 general practitioners resulted in 84% of women between 50–60 years of age being screened (Robertson et al., 1989). In another general practice study, a letter sent to all eligible women aged 16–64 years resulted in a response rate of 90% (Standing & Mercer, 1984). The success of this recruitment drive was attributed to the participation of practice nurses. A third study, using a randomized control design, examined the effectiveness of two methods of call/recall for women in a United Kingdom group practice. Women eligible for a Pap smear were allocated at random to one of three groups. A written invitation to attend the practice for a Pap smear was sent to the first group, 32% of whom attended within one year. In the second group, the medical notes of women were tagged to indicate their need for a Pap smear to the practitioner. Twenty seven per cent of women in this group had a Pap smear during the year of the study. In the control group only 15% of women attended for a Pap smear (Pierce et al., 1989). A recent Australian study found that reminder letters for general practitioners were significantly more effective than two other recruitment strategies when evaluated in a randomized controlled trial (Bowman, 1991). Thirty-seven per cent of women who reported not having had a smear in the previous three years reported that they had a smear within six months after receiving a reminder letter from their practitioner.

Systematic recruitment

In contrast to practioner-based strategies, some countries have instituted national or regional systems whereby all at-risk women receive call/recall letters to attend for screening (Smith, Elkind & Eardley, 1989). For many countries however, there are major problems with establishing accurate and comprehensive lists of all at-risk women to whom such letters should be sent. Voluntary reminder services have often failed to recruit more than a small minority of the targeted population (New South Wales Cancer Council, 1988). In an attempt to overcome such difficulties, a recent randomized controlled trial (Byles et al., 1991) evaluated the effectiveness of two types of letters sent by direct mail to women listed on electoral rolls. In the first group, a simple reminder was sent by the State Cancer Council which provided basic information about Pap smears, a list of local service providers and an invitation to enrol in the Cancer Council's free Pap smear reminder service. In the second intervention group, women received the same letters plus a set of five prompt cards which were designed to assist women to overcome commonly reported barriers to screening: forgetting to make an appointment, feeling uncomfortable about asking for a test, finding the test unpleasant, not knowing enough about Pap smears, and not knowing where to go to have a test. The results indicated that direct-mail strategies can be effective in prompting attendance for cervical cancer screening. Furthermore, the simple reminder was at least as effective as the more elaborate strategy, with both approaches resulting in a 40% increase in attending for screening over the immediate post-intervention quarter.

Breast cancer

In 1989 it was estimated that 142 000 new cases of breast cancer would occur in American women and that 43 000 would die of the disease (US Preventive Services Task Force, 1989). The incidence of breast cancer rises rapidly with age. Figures show that for the United States of America the incidence per

100 000 women at age 30–34 is 24.8 cases, increasing to 106.8 at age 40–44 and increasing further to 188.2 cases per 100 000 at age 50–54 (Vogel et al., 1990). In Australia, the lifetime risk of a woman developing the disease is one in sixteen (AIH, 1990).

The major risk factors for breast cancer are being female, increasing age, a family history of breast cancer and a personal history of benign breast disease. The relative risk for a woman with one first-degree relative with breast cancer is increased two to two and half times (Taplin et al., 1990). Yet it has been estimated that only 11–22% of women with breast cancer have a first-degree relative with breast cancer and only 6–12% of the female population have this risk factor, limiting its usefulness for identifying populations for screening.

Prospects for prevention

Limited opportunities for primary prevention of breast cancer are available given that the known risk factors are generally non-modifiable and occur in only a small proportion of the population who contract the disease. Consequently, the best chance of reducing mortality associated with breast cancer is early detection of the cancerous growth. The three most common screening tests for early breast cancer are breast self-examination (BSE), physical examination by a health care provider and mammography. BSE involves women examinming their own breasts on a regular basis for abnormalities. A meta-analysis conducted by Hill et al. (1988) provides some evidence that BSE can result in earlier detection of breast cancer. Of women with breast cancer who had practised BSE prior to diagnosis, significantly fewer had tumours of greater than 2 cm in diameter and fewer had lymph node involvement compared to those who had not practised BSE. However, there was no evidence that detection at this stage enhanced survival. Furthermore, BSE obviously cannot detect impalpable breast cancer, and has been shown to lead to high biopsy rates for benign breast disease, especially in younger women (AIH, 1990).

The sensitivity and specificity of clinical examination of the breast varies according to the skill and experience of the provider and with the character- istics of the breast being examined. Using manufactured breast models, the sensitivity of nurses in detecting lumps was found to be 65% compared with 55% for untrained women (O'Malley & Fletcher, 1987; Haughey et al., 1984). Detection by physicians was 87% for lumps 1 cm in diameter, a size comparable to that used in the studies involving nurses and women (Fletcher, O'Malley & Bunce, 1985). There are no survival data available from prospective ran- domized trials of clinical breast examination although a number of studies are currently underway. Despite this, clinical examination is still widely recom- mended, particularly for the detection of interval cancers (those that occur between mammographic screening) and in detecting palpable cancers missed by mammography.

X-ray mammography is a potentially effective screening method for reducing breast cancer mortality and morbidity as it can detect cancers as small as 2 cm in diameter which are not palpable at clinical examination. Evidence for the effectiveness of mammographic screening in reducing the risk of death from breast cancer came first from the Health Insurance Plan of New York (HIP) study (Shapiro et al., 1982; Shapiro et al., 1988). Women between 40 and 64 years were randomly allocated to control and screening groups. Women in the experimental group were offered four annual screens comprising physical examination and mammography. The breast cancer mortality rate in this group was found to be 29% lower than in the control group ten years after commencement of the study. Mortality reduction in the experimental group has persisted for 18 years.

A similar reduction in breast cancer mortality was observed in the Swedish "Two Counties" Studies (Tabar et al., 1989). This project screened approximately 78 000 women every 20–36 months and found a significant decrease in breast cancer mortality of 32% among women aged more than 50 years. Studies with somewhat similar findings supporting the role of mammography in reducing breast cancer mortality have been undertaken in Nijmegen (Verbeek et al., 1984; Verbeek, Straatman & Hendriks, 1988); in Utrecht (Collette et al., 1984; Waard et al., 1984); and in Florence (Palli et al., 1986). As a result of these studies, the United Kingdom, Sweden, Finland, Iceland and Australia have embarked upon national breast cancer screening programmes using mammography. Current recommendations indicate women 50 years or over should attend for mammography screening every 1–2 years (US Preventive Services Task Force, 1989).

For mammography to be effective, there has to be adequate training of those interpreting the mammograms to ensure that reliability is maintained. For example, in a study where 100 mammograms were examined, the number of lesions identified as suspicious for cancer by nine radiologists ranged from 10 to 45, suggesting that there is a need to maintain tight control on interpretation (Boyd et al., 1982).

There is also a need to find mechanisms by which women can be encouraged to attend for screening. Studies comparing the characteristics of women who attend for screening to those who do not, have found no consistent association between attendance and demographic characteristics. A review by Vernon, Laville & Jackson (1990) concluded that women at greatest risk due to age and family history were not more likely to attend for screening, thereby suggesting a need to target these groups. Rimer et al. (1989) identified several barriers to mammographic screening following an invitation from a health maintenance organisation: belief that screening was unnecessary in the absence of symptoms; absence of physician recommendation; perceived inconvenience; preferring not to think of it; and worry about radiation. Other studies have identified cost of screening and pain associated with screening as further barriers. The review by Vernon et al. (1990) indicates that physicians are important in determining attendance for screening. Non-attenders were found to be more likely to report that their physician had not recommended mammography. Of women advised to have a mammogram by their physician, only 3% failed to do so.

Primary care physicians have many advantages for encouraging women to attend for mammography screening. They are viewed by patients as credible sources of health information, they see mammographic screening as part of their role and they come into contact with a high proportion of the target age group (Cockburn et al., 1989). For example, in Australia, 82% of women aged between 45–64 will visit their primary practioner in a 12 month period (ABS, 1983). In the United Kingdom, attendance rates of up to 84% have been obtained following a written invitation from the general practitioner to attend for mammographic screening (Williams & Vessey, 1989). In Australia, attendance rates of 28% were obtained when a personalized invitation for mammographic screening was sent from general practitioners (AIH, 1989). It rose to 36% if the letter also contained an appointment time for the screening facility.

An alternative mechanism is that of opportunistic recruitment, that is, practitioners suggest to women that they should attend for mammographic screening when they consult for another health problem. Cockburn et al. (1990b), found that 41% of women attended for screening following such a verbal recommendation by their primary care physician. Similarly, a recent study (Clover et al., in press), compared the effectiveness of two strategies aimed at increasing adherence with mammographic screening recommendations. An intensive patient education approach, based on health belief principles, was compared with a simple recommendation by the general practitioner to have a mammogram. No statistically significant differences in attendance rates were observed between groups. Eighty two per cent of the simple recommendation group and 91% of the patient education group attended for screening. Such findings suggest that mammographic screening can be effectively promoted in general practice without extensive patient education. Scope therefore exists for behavioural scientists to develop and test strategies for recruiting women to participate in mammographic screening, particularly through primary care physicians.

An additional aspect of breast cancer screening which deserves the attention of behavioural scientists concerns the psychological costs to participating women. Approximately 10% of screened women will be recalled for further investigation. Two or three of these will undergo biopsy, however, only one will be found to have cancer. Considerable potential for adverse psychological effects arising from these "false positives" is therefore evident. However, very little research has currently focussed on the psychological impact of mammographic screening and this area remains an import area for behavioural scientists to work in the future.

Skin cancer

It is argued that skin cancers are 100% curable if lesions are detected early, before they have penetrated deeply, and surgically excised (McCarthy & Shaw, 1989). The ten year survival rate of patients in whom thin malignant melanomas are excised is approximately 93%, while the rate for melanomas with a thickness of 4 mm or more is about 30% (Balch & Soong, 1983; Balch et al., 1985). Consequently, there are benefits in the early detection of melanomas through effective screening.

Prospects for prevention

Three methods for screening for melanoma and other skin cancers are available: self-screening, being screened by another person such as a partner, and screening by a health care provider. A survey by Girgis et al. (1991a) using self-report data from approximately 1300 individuals examined the rates of screening by self, others and health care providers. Self-screening or screening by another person on an annual basis was reported by 48% of the sample. Unscreened persons were more likely to be male, of low socioeconomic status, unemployed or too ill to work, and with only basic health insurance cover. Those individuals more at-risk of melanoma were more likely to screen, as were those with a perceived personal susceptibility to developing melanoma.

Girgis et al. (1991a) also reported that while 89% of the sample consulted a doctor in the previous 12 months, only 17% of these said that their skin had been checked by a practitioner. This lack of practitioner screening may partly be attributable to a lack of practitioner training in dermatology. A survey of non-dermatologists indicated that 56% of practitioners thought that their training in the diagnosis of skin lesions was only "fair" while 35% indicated that they had no training at all (Cassileth et al., 1986).

Hennrikus et al. (1991) examined the self-reported delay of individuals seeking advice following their finding of signs suggestive of melanoma. The results indicate that a relatively large proportion of the sample (11.9%) had observed signs of skin cancer in the previous year, such as changes in the colour of the mole, itchiness etc. Of those people reporting such signs, 32% consulted a medical practitioner within the recommended period. This suggests that responses by individuals to the signs of melanoma are less than optimal.

Research indicates that a lack of knowledge about melanoma and its treatment are related to longer periods of delay in seeking advice (Hennrikus et al., 1991; Temoshok et al., 1984a; 1984b; Doherty & Mackie, 1986). For example, Hennrikus et al. (1991) found that almost half the sample reporting signs suggestive of melanoma thought that these were not serious or would clear up, and a further 27% reported that they would "wait and see", that they had no time or that they were too busy to seek advice. Such findings indicate a role for behavioural scientists in the development of more effective intervention strategies which are designed to inform individuals of the need for prompt medical attention.

ACKNOWLEDGMENTS

Thanks to the following friends and colleagues who assisted in critically reading and modifying sections of this report: R. Burton, J. Byles, J. Bowman, K. Clover, A. Girgis, J. Perkins, M. Schofield, R. Walsh, J. Ward and J. Wiggers. Without their constructive help, the chapter would have involved considerably more time and pain.

REFERENCES

American Cancer Society (1987). *Cancer Facts and Figures—1987*. New York: American Cancer Society.

Andrews, J. (1983). Reducing smoking in the hospital: An effective model program. *Chest*, **84**, 206–209.

Areskog-Wijma, B. (1987). The gynaecological examination: Women's experiences and preferences and the role of the gynaecologist. *Journal of Psychosomatic Obstetrics and Gynaecology*, **6**, 59–69.

Australian Bureau of Statistics (1983). *Australian Health Survey 1983*. Canberra: Australian Government Publishing Service.

Australian Institute of Health (1990). *Breast cancer screening in Australia: Future directions*. Canberra: Australian Institute of Health.

Australian Institute of Health (1991). *Cervical cancer screening in Australia: Options for change*. Australian Institute of Health: Prevention program evaluation series No. 2. Canberra: Government Publishing Service.

Bailie, R. & Petrie, K. (1990). Women's attitudes to cervical smear testing. *New Zealand Medical Journal*, **103**, 293–295.

Balch, C. M. & Soong, S. J. (1983). Characteristics of melanoma that predict the risk of metastases. In J. J. Costanzi (Ed), *Malignant melanoma. Cancer treatment and research 9*. Hague: Martinus Nijhoff.

Balch, C. M., Soong, S. J., Shaw, H. M. & Milton, G. W. (1985). An analysis of prognostic factors in 4,000 patients with cutaneous melanoma. In C. M. Balch & G. W. Milton (Eds), *Cutaneous Melanoma: Clinical management and treatment results worldwide* (pp. 321–338). Philadelphia: Lipincott.

Better Health Commission (1986). *Looking Forward to Better Health*. Canberra: Australian Government Publishing Service.

Biener, L., Abrams, D., Follick, M. & Dean, L. (1989). A comparative evaluation of a restrictive smoking policy in a general hospital. *American Journal of Public Health*, **79**, 192–195.

Biglan, A., Severson, H. H., Bavry, J. & McConnell, S. (1983). Social influence and adolescent smoking: A first look behind the barn. *Health Education*, **14**(5), 14–18.

Botvin, G. J. & Wills, T. A. (1985). Personal and social skills training: Cognitive-behavioural approaches to substance abuse prevention. In C. Bell & R. Batjies (Eds), *Prevention research: Deterring drug abuse among children and adolescents* (pp. 8–49) NIDA Research Monograph 63. Washington, DC: US Government Printing Office.

Bowling, A. (1989). Implications of preventive health behaviour for cervical and breast cancer screening programmes: A review. *Family Practice*, **6**, 224–231.

Bowman, J. (1991). Screening for cervical cancer: Barriers and strategies for prevention. Dissertation, University of Newcastle.

Bowman, J., Redman, S., Dickinson, J., Gibberd, R. & Sanson-Fisher, R. (1991). The accuracy of pap smear utilization self-report: A methodological consideration in cervical screening research. *Health Services Research*, **26**, 97–107.

Bowman, J., Redman, S., Reid, A. & Sanson-Fisher, R. (1990). General Practitioners and the provision of Papanicolaou smear-tests: current practice, knowledge and attitudes. *Medical Journal of Australia*, **152**, 178–183.

Boyd, N. F., Wolfson, C., Moskowitz, M., Carlile, T., Petitclerc, M., Ferri, H. A., Fishell, E., Gregoire, A., Kiernan, M., Longley, J. D., Simor, I. S. & Miller, A. B. (1982). Observer variation in the interpretation of xeromammograms. *Journal of the National Cancer Institute*, **68**, 357–363.

Brecher, E. M. (1972). *Licit and Illicit drugs*. Boston: Little, Brown.

Byles, J., Redman, S., Sanson-Fisher, R. W. & Boyle, K. (1991). Unpublished Data. Faculty of Medicine, University of Newcastle, Australia.

Canadian Task Force on the periodic health examination (1979). The periodic health examination. *Canadian Medical Association Journal*, **121**, 1194–1254.

Cassileth, B. R., Clark, W. H., Lusk, E. J., Frederick, B. E., Thompson, J., Walsh, R. N. & Walsh, W. P. (1986). How well do physicians recognise melanoma and other problem lesions? *Journal of the American Academy of Dermatology*, **14**, 555–560.

Centers for Disease Control (1987). Smoking-attributable mortality and years of potential life lost—United States, 1984. *Morbidity and Mortality Weekly Report*, **36**, 693–697.

Channen, W. (1990). The CIN Saga: The biological and clinical significance of cervical intraepithelial neoplasia. *The Australian and New Zealand Journal of Obstetrics and Gynaecology*, **30**, 18–32.

Charlton, A. (1984). Smoking and weight control in teenagers. *Public Health*, **98**, 277–281.

Cherry, N. & Kiernan, K. E. (1976). Personality scores and smoking behaviour: A longitudinal study. *British Journal of Preventive and Social Medicine*, **30**, 123–131.

Cherry, N. & Kiernan, K. E. (1978). A longitudinal study of smoking and personality. In R. E. Thornton (Ed), *Smoking Behavior. Physiological and Psychological Influences*. Edinburgh: Churchill Livingstone.

Chu, F. Z. & Day, R. G. (1981). Smoking recognition by family physicians. *Journal of Family Practice*, **12**, 657–660.

Clover, K., Redman, S., Forbes, J. & Sanson-Fisher, R. W. (in press). A randomised trial of two general practice-based strategies to promote attendance for mammography screening.

Cockburn, J., De Luise, T., Hill, D., Hurley, S., Reading, D. & Russell, I. (1990a). Boosting recruitment to breast screening programmes. *The Medical Journal of Australia*, **152**, 332.

Cockburn, J., Hennrikus, D., Scott, R. & Sanson-Fisher, R. W. (1989). Adolescent use of sun-protection measures. *The Medical Journal of Australia*, **151**, 136–140.

Cockburn, J., Hirst, S., Hill, D. & Marks, R. (1990b). Increasing cervical screening in women over 40: An intervention in general practice. *The Medical Journal of Australia*, **152**, 190–194.

Collette, H. J. A., Day, N. E., Romback, J. J. & Waard, F. de. (1984). Evaluation of screening for breast cancer in a non-randomised study (the DOM project) by means of a case-control study. *Lancet*, **1**, 1224–1226.

Copeman, R. C., Swannell, R. J., Princus, D. F. & Woodhead, K. A. (1989). Utilisation of the smoke screen smoking cessation programme by general practitioners and their patients. *The Medical Journal of Australia*, **151**, 83–87.

Covington, M. V. & Omelick, C. L. (1988). I can resist anything but temptation: Adolescent expectations from smoking cigarettes. *Journal of Applied Social Psychology*, **18**, 203–227.

Department of Health and Human Services (1989). *Reducing the health consequences of smoking: 25 years of progress.* A report of the Surgeon General. Rockville, MD: Department of Health and Human Services (Publication no. DHSS (PHS) 82-50179).

Diamandopoulos, G. & Meissner, W. (1985). Neoplasia. In J. Kissane (Ed), *Anderson's Pathology*, 8th edn. (pp. 514–559). St. Louis: Mosby Co.

Dickinson, J. A., Wiggers, J., Leeder, S. R. & Sanson-Fisher, R. W. (1989). General practitioners' detection of patients' smoking status. *The Medical Journal of Australia*, **150**, 420–426.

Difranza, J. R., Norwood, B. D., Garner, D. W. & Tye, J. B. (1987). Legislative efforts to protect children from tobacco. *Journal of the American Medical Association*, **257**(24), 3387–3389.

Digiusto, E. (1987). A workplace smoking cessation program. A strategy with potential mass application. *Community Health Studies (Supplement)*, **11**, 45S–52S.

Doherty, V. R. & Mackie, R. (1986). Reasons for poor prognosis in British patients with cutaneous malignant melanoma. *British Medical Journal*, **292**, 987–989.

Doll, R. & Peto, R. (1981). *The causes of cancer: Quantitative estimates of avoidance risks of cancer in the US today.* Oxford: Oxford University Press.

Eddy, D. (1990). Screening for cervical cancer. *Annals of Internal Medicine*, **113**, 214–226.

Elwood, J., Cotton, R., Johnson, J. & Jones, G. (1984). Are patients with abnormal cervical smears adequately managed? *British Medical Journal*, **289**, 891–894.

Evans, R. D., Kopf, A. E., Lew, R. A., Rigel, D. S., Bart, R. S., Friedman, R. J. & Rivers, J. K. (1988). Risk factors for the development of malignant melanaoma—I: Review of case control studies. *Journal of Dermatologic Surgery and Oncology*, **14**, 393–408.

Evans, R. I., Rozelle, R. M., Mittelmark, M. B., Hansen, W. B., Bane, A. L. & Harvis, J. (1978). Deterring the onset of smoking in children: Knowledge of immediate physiological effects and coping with peer pressure, media pressure, and parent modelling. *Journal of Applied Social Psychology*, **8**, 126–135.

Eysenck, H. J., Tarrant, M., Woolf, M. & England, L. (1960). Smoking and personality. *British Medical Journal*, **1**, 1456–1460.

Farquhar, J. W. (1978). The community-based model of life-style intervention trials. *American Journal of Epidemiology*, **108**(2), 103–111.

Fielding, J. E. (1985). Smoking: Health effects and control. *New England Journal of Medicine*, **313**, 491–498.

Fielding, J. (1990). Smoking: Health effects and control. *New England Journal of Medicine*, **142**, 190–194.

Flay, B. R., D'Avenas, J. R., Best, J. A., Kersell, M. W. & Ryan, K. B. (1983). Cigarette smoking: Why young people do it and ways of preventing it. In P. McGrath & P. Firestone (Eds), *Paediatric and Adolescent Behavioural Medicine* (pp. 132–183). New York: Springer Publishing.

Fletcher, S. W., O'Malley, M. S. & Bunce, L. A. (1985). Physicians' abilities to detect lumps in silicone breast models. *Journal of the American Medical Association*, **253**, 2224–2228.

Friedman, L. S., Lichenstein, E. & Biglan, A. (1985). Smoking onset among teens: An empirical analysis of initial situations. *Addictive Behaviors*, **10**, 1–13.

Fruchter, R., Boyce, J. & Hunt, M. (1980). Missed opportunities for early diagnosis of cancer of the cervix. *American Journal of Health*, **70**, 418–420.

Girgis, A., Campbell, E. M., Redman, S. & Sanson-Fisher, R. W. (1991a). Screening for melanoma: A community survey of prevalence and predictors. *The Medical Journal of Australia*, **154**, 338–343.

Girgis, A., Sanson-Fisher, R., Tripodi, D. A. & Golding, T. (1991b). *Evaluation of intervention to promote solar protection in primary schools*. Manuscript submitted for publication.

Girgis, A. & Sanson-Fisher, R. (1991). *Evaluation of a workplace interventions to increase the use of solar protection in outdoor workers*. Manuscript submitted for publication.

Glasgow, R., Klesges, R. & O'Neill, H. (1986). Programming social support for smoking modification: An extension and replication. *Additive Behaviors*, **11**, 453–457.

Glasgow, R. & Terborg, J. (1988). Occupational health promotion programs to reduce cardiovascular risk. *Journal of Consulting and Clinical Psychology*, **56**, 365–373.

Goldsmith, M. F. (1987). Pale is better, say skin cancer fighters. *Journal of the American Medical Association*, **257**, 893–894.

Gordon, J. J., Sanson-Fisher, R. W. & Saunders, M. A. (1988). Identification of simulated patients by interns in a casualty setting. *Medical Education*, **22**(6), 533–538.

Green, L. W. (1984). Modifying and developing health behaviors. In L. Breslow, J. A. Fielding & L. B. Lave (Eds), *Annual Review of Public Health*, (Vol. 5, pp. 215–236). Palo Alto, CA: Annual Reviews, Inc.

Hallett, R. (1986). Smoking intervention in the workplace: review and recommendations. *Preventive Medicine*, **15**, 213–231.

Hallett, R. & Sutton, S. (1987). Predicting participation and outcome in four workplace smoking intervention programmes. *Health Education Research*, **2**, 257–266.

Haughey, B. P., Marshall, J. R., Mettlin, C., Nemoto, T., Kroldart, K. & Swanson, M. (1984). Nurses' ability to detect nodules in silicone breast models. *Oncology Nursing Forum*, **1**, 37–42.

Havelock, C., Edwards, R., Cuzick, J. & Chamberlain, J. (1988). The organization of cervical cancer screening in general practice. *Journal of the Royal College of General Practice*, **38**, 207–211.

Hayward, R. A., Shapiro, M. F., Freeman, H. E. & Corey, C. R. (1988). Who gets screened for cervical and breast cancer? Results from a new national survey. *Archives of Internal Medicine*, **148**, 1177–1181.

Health and Welfare Canada (1988). *Smoke in the workplace: An evaluation of smoking restrictions*. Ottawa: Minister of Supply and Services Canada.

Hennrikus, D., Girgis, A., Redman, S. & Sanson-Fisher, R. W. (1991). A community study of delay in presenting to medical practitioners with signs of melanoma. *Archives of Dermatology*, **127**, 356–361.

Hill, D. J., White, V. M. & Gray, N. J. (1991). Australian patterns of tobacco smoking in 1989. *The Medical Journal of Australia*, **154**, 797–801.

Hill, D. J., White, V. M., Jolley, D. & Mapperson, K. (1988). Self examination of the breast: is it beneficial? Meta-analysis of studies investigating breast self examination and extent of disease in patients with breast cancer. *British Medical Journal*, **297**, 271–275.

Hill, D. J., White, V. M., Pain, M. D. & Gardner, G. J. (1990). Tobacco and alcohol use among Australia secondary schoolchildren in 1987. *The Medical Journal of Australia*, **152**, 124–128.

Hobbs, P. (1986). The behavioural aspects of breast and cervical screening. *Radiography*, **52**, 287–290.

Hocking, B., Borland, R., Owen, N. & Kemp, G. (1991). A total ban on workplace smoking is acceptable and effective. *Journal of Occupational Medicine*, **33**, 163–167.

Holman, C. D., Armstrong, B. K., Hennan, P. J., Blackwell, J. B., Cumming, F. J., English, D. R., Holland, S., Kelsall, G. R., Matz, L. R. & Rouse, I. L. (1986). The causes of melanoma: Results from the West Australian Lions Melanoma Project. *Recent Results in Cancer Research*, **102**, 18–37.

Holman, C., McCartney, A., Hyde, K. & Armstrong, B. K. (1981). Cervical cytology histories of 100 women with invasive carcinoma of the cervix. *The Medical Journal of Australia*, **2**, 597–598.

Hurwitz, S. (1988). The sun and sunscreen protection: Recommendations for children. *Journal of Derrmatologic Surgery and Oncology*, **14**, 657–660.

Immarino, N. K. & Weinberg, A. D. (1985). Cancer prevention in schools. *Journal of School Health*, **55**, 86–95.

International Agency for Research on Cancer Working Group (1986). Screening for squamous cell cancer, duration of low risk after negative results of cervical cytology and its implication for screening policies. *British Medical Journal*, **293**, 659–664.

Jamrozik, K., Vessey, M., Fowler, G., Wald, N., Parker, G. & Van Vunakis, H. (1984). Controlled trial of three different antismoking interventions in general practice. *British Medical Journal*, **288**, 1499–1503.

Jessor, R. R. & Jessor, S. C. (1977). *Problem behavior and psychosocial development: A longitudinal study of youth*. New York: Academic Press.

Johnston, K. (1989). *Screening for cervical cancer: A review of the literature*. Health Economics Research Unit. University of Aberdeen.

King, J. (1987). Women's attitudes towards cervical smears. *Update*, 160–168.

Koss, L. (1989). The Papanicolaou test for cervical cancer detection: A triumph and a tragedy. *Journal of the American Medical Association*, **261**, 737–743.

Kottke, T. E., Battista, R. N., DeFriese, G. H. & Brekke, M. L. (1988). Attributes of successful smoking cessation interventions in medical practice: A meta-analysis of 39 controlled trials. *Journal of the American Medical Association*, **259**, 2882–2889.

Leventhal, H. (1983). Behavioral medicine: Psychology in health care. In D. Mechanic (Ed), *Handbook of Health, Health Care, and the Health Professions* (pp. 709–744). New York: Free Press.

McCarthy, W. H. & Shaw, H. M. (1989). Skin cancer in Australia. *The Medical Journal of Australia*, **150**, 469–470.

Marks, R., Ponsford, M. W. & Selwood, T. S. (1983). Non-melonocytic skin cancer and solar keratoses. *International Journal of Dermatology*, **26**, 201–205.

Miescher, P. & Muller-Eberhard, H. (1976). *Testbook of Immunopathology* (2nd edn. Vol. 2). New York: Grune & Stratton.

Mittelmark, M. B., Murray, D. M., Luepker, R. V., Pechacek, T. F., Pirie, P. L. & Pallonen, U. E. (1987). Predicting experimentation with cigarettes: The childhood antecedents of smoking status. *American Journal of Public Health*, **77**, 206–208.

Montgomery, G. (1965). *Textbook of Pathology*. Vol. 1. Edinburgh: Livingstone.

Morgan, M. & Grube, J. W. (1989). Adolescent cigarette smoking: A developmental analysis of influences. *British Journal of Developmental Psychology*, **7**, 179–189.

Morris, C. & Koyama, O. (1990). *A manual on tobacco & young people for the industrialised world*. Geneva: International Union Against Cancer.

Murray, D. M. & Perry, C. L. (1984). *The functional meaning of adolescent drug use*. Paper presented at the 92nd Annual Meeting of the American Psychological Association, Toronto, Canada.

Muir, C., Waterhouse, J., Mack, T., Doll, R., Payne, P. & Davis, W. (Eds) (1987). Cancer Incidence in five continents 5. Lyon: International Agency for Research on Cancer.

Needle, R., McCubbin, H., Wilson, M., Reiner, R., Lazar, A. & Mederer, H. (1986). Interpersonal influences in adolescent drug use—the role of older siblings parents and peers. *The International Journal of the Addictions*, **21**, 739–766.

New South Wales State Cancer Council (1988). *Annual Report*. Sydney: NSW State Cancer Council.

O'Malley, M. S. & Fletcher, S. W. (1987). Screening for breast cancer with breast self examination. *Journal of the American Medical Association*, **257**, 2197–2203.

Orleans, C. S. & Shipley, R. H. (1982). Worksite smoking cessation initiatives: Review and recommendations. *Addictive Behaviors*, **7**, 1–16.

Page, A. R., Walters, D. J., Schlegel, R. P. & Best, J. A. (1986). Smoking cessation in family practice: The effects of advice and nicotine chewing gum prescription. *Addictive Behaviors*, **11**, 443–446.

Palli, D., Del Turco, M. R., Buiatti, E., Carli, S., Ciatto, S., Toscani, L. & Maltoni, G. (1986). A case-control study of the efficacy of a non-randomized breast cancer screening program in Florence (Italy). *International Journal of Cancer*, **38**, 501–4.

Parkin, D., Nguyen-Dinh, S. & Day, N. (1985). The impact of screening on the incidence of cervix cancer in England and Wales. *British Journal of Obstetrics and Gynaecology*, **92**, 150–157.

Pederson, L. L., Baskerville, J. C. & Lefcoe, N. M. (1981). Multivariate prediction of cigarette smoking among children in grades six, seven and eight. *Journal of Drug Education*, **11**, 191.

Peto, R. (1985). The preventability of cancer. In M. Vessey & M. Gray (Eds), *Cancer risks and prevention* (pp. 1–14). Oxford: Oxford Medical Publications.

Petravage, J., Reynolds, L. J., Gardner, H. J. & Reading, J. C. (1979). Attitudes of women toward the gynecologic examination. *Journal of Family Practice*, **9**, 1039–1045.

Pierce, M., Lundy, S., Palanisamy, A., Winning, S. & King, J. (1989). Prospective randomized controlled trial of methods of call and recall for cervical cytology screening. *British Medical Journal*, **299**, 160–162.

Pirie, P. L., Murray, D. M. & Luepker, R. V. (1988). Smoking prevalence in a cohort of adolescents, including absentees, dropouts and transfers. *American Journal of Public Health*, **78**, 176–178.

Rappaport, J. (1977). *Community psychology: Values, research, action*. New York: Holt, Rinehart, & Winston.

Redman, S. & Sanson-Fisher, R. W. (1989). Community Medicine. In N. J. King & A. Remenyi (Eds), *Psychology for Health Social Science Students: An Introduction* (pp. 345–383). Australia: Thomas Nelson.

Richmond, R. L. & Webster, I. W. (1985). A smoking cessation programme for use in general practice. *The Medical Journal of Australia*, **142**, 176–178.

Rimer, B. K., Keintz, M. K., Kessler, H. B., Engstrom, P. F. & Rosan, J. R. (1989). Why women resist screening mammography: patient-related barriers. *Radiology*, **172**, 243–246.

Roberts, M. M., Alexander, F. E., Anderson, T. J., Chetty, U., Donnan, P. T., Forrest, P., Hepburn, W., Huggins, A., Kirkpatrick, A. E. & Lamb, J. et al. (1990). Edinburgh trial of screening for breast cancer: Mortality at seven years. *Lancet*, **335**, 241–246.

Robertson, A., Reid, G. S., Stoker, C. A., Bissett, C., Waugh, N., Fenton, I., Rowan, J. & Halkerston, R. (1989). Evaluation of a call programme for cervical cytology screening in women aged 50–60. *British Medical Journal*, **299**, 163–166.

Rundall, T. G. & Bruvold, W. H. (1988). A meta-analysis of school-based smoking and alcohol use prevention programs. *Health Education Quarterly*, **15**, 317–334.

Russell, M. A. H., Merriman, R., Stapleton, J. & Taylor, W. (1983). Effect of nicotine chewing gum as an adjunct to general practitioner's advice against smoking. *British Medical Journal*, **287**, 1782–1785.

Russell, M. A., Stapleton, J. A., Jackson, P. H., Hajek, P. & Belcher, M. (1987). District programme to reduce smoking: Effect of clinic supported brief intervention by general practitioners. *British Medical Journal*, 295, 1240–1244.

Schwartz, M., Savage, W., George, J. & Emohare, L. (1989). Women's knowledge and experience of cervical screening. A failure of health education and medical organization. *Community Medicine*, 11(4), 279–289.

Schofield, M. S., Tripodi, D. A., Girgis, A. & Sanson-Fisher, R. W. (in press). Solar protection issues for schools: Policy, practice and recommendations.

Shapiro, S., Venet, W., Strax, P. & Venet, L. (1988). Current results of the breast cancer screening randomised trial: The Health Insurance Plan (HIP) of Greater New York. In N. E. Day & A. B. Miller (Eds). *Screening for breast cancer* (pp. 3–15).

Shapiro, S., Venet, W., Strax, P., Venet, L. & Roeser, R. (1982). Ten to fourteen-year effect of screening on breast cancer mortality. *Journal of the National Cancer Institute*, 69, 349–353.

Shelley, J. & Irwig, L. Unpublished data. School of Public Health, University of Sydney, Australia.

Shipley, R., Orleans, C., Wilbur, C., Piserchia, P. & McFadden, D. (1988). Effect of the Johnson & Johnson Live For Life program on employee smoking. *Preventive Medicine*, 17, 25–34.

Slama, K., Redman, S., Cockburn, J. & Sanson-Fisher, R. (1989). Community views about the role of general practitioners in disease prevention. *Family Practice*, 6, 203–209.

Slama, K., Redman, S., Perkins, S., Reid, A. L. & Sanson-Fisher, R. W. (1990). The effectiveness of two smoking cessation programmes for use in general practice: A randomised clinical trial. *British Medical Journal*, 300, 1707–1709.

Smith, A., Elkind, A. & Eardley, A. (1989). Making cervical screening work. *British Medical Journal*, 298, 1662–1664.

Standing, P. & Mercer, S. (1984). Quinquennial cervical smears: Every woman's right and every general practitioner's responsibility. *British Medical Journal*, 289, 883–886.

Stern, R. S., Weinstein, M. C. & Kiviranta, H. (1986). Melanoma and other tumours of the skin among indoor and outdoor workers in Sweden 1961–1969. *British Journal of Cancer*, 20, 91–92.

Tabar, L., Fagerberg, G., Duffy, S. & Day, N. E. (1989). The Swedish two county trial of mammography screening for breast cancer: Recent results and calculation of benefit. *Journal of Community Health*, 43, 107–114.

Taplin, S. H., Thompson, R. S., Schnitzer, F., Anderman, C. & Immanuel, V. (1990). Revisions in the risk-based breast cancer screening program at Group Health Cooperative. *Cancer*, 66, 812–818.

Temoshok, L., DiClemente, R. J., Sweet, D. M., Blois, M. S. & Sagebiel, R. W. (1984a). Factors related to patient delay in seeking medical attention for cutaneous malignant melanoma. *Cancer*, 54, 3048–3053.

Temoshok, L., DiClemente, R. J., Sweet, D. M., Blois, M. S. & Sagebiel, R. W. (1984b). Prognostic and psychosocial factors related to delay behaviour in patients with cutaneous malignant melanoma. *Advances in Cancer Control: Epidemiology & Research*, 156, 169–179.

Tomatis, L. (1990). *Cancer: Causes, occurrence and control*. Lyon: International Agency for Research on Cancer.

US Preventive Services Task Force. (1989). *Guide to Clinical Preventive Services*. Baltimore: Williams and Wilkins.

Verbeek, A. L. M., Hendriks, J. H. C. L., Holland, R., Mravunac, M., Sturmans, F. & Day, N. E. (1984). Reduction of breast cancer mortality through mass screening with modern mammography. First results of the Nijmegen Project, 1975–1981.

Lancet, **1**, 1222–1224.

Verbeek, A. L. M., Straatman, H. & Hendriks, J. H. C. L. (1988). Sensitivity of mammography in Nijmegen women under age 50: Some trials with the Eddy model. In N. E. Doy & A. B. Miller (Eds), *Screening for breast cancer*. (pp. 29–32). Toronto: Hans Huber Publishers.

Vernon, S. W., Laville, E. A. & Jackson, G. (1990). Participation in breast screening programs: A review. *Social Science and Medicine*, **30**, 1107–1118.

Vogel, V. G. (1991). High risk populations as targets for breast cancer prevention trials. *Preventive Medicine*, **20**, 86–100.

Vogel, V. G., Graves, D. S., Vernon, S. W., Lord, J. A., Winn, R. J. & Peters, G. W. (1990). *Cancer*, **66**, 1613–1620.

Waard, F. de., Collette, H. J. A., Rombach, J., Baanders-van-Halewijn, E. A. & Honing, C. (1984). The DOM project for the early detection of breast cancer, Utrecht, The Netherlands. *Journal of Chronic Disability*, **37**, 1–44.

Wakefield, M. & Bonett, A. (1990). Preventing skin cancer in Australia. *The Medical Journal of Australia*, **152**, 60–61.

Walter, S. D., Clarke, E. A., Hatcher, J. & Stitt, L. W. (1988). A comparison of physician and patient reports of Pap smear histories. *Journal of Clinical Epidemiology*, **41**(4), 401–410.

Ward, J., Boyle, K., Redman, S. & Sanson-Fisher, R. W. (1990). Increasing women's compliance with opportunistic cervical cancer screening: A randomised trial. Unpublished data. Faculty of Medicine, University of Newcastle, Australia.

Williams, E. & Vessey, M. (1989). Randomised trial of two strategies offering women mobile screening for breast cancer. *British Medical Journal*, **299**, 158–159.

Wilson, D. M., Taylor, D. W., Gilbert, J. R., Best, J. A., Lindsay, E. A., Willms, D. G. & Singer, J. (1988). A randomized trial of a family physician intervention for smoking cessation. *Journal of the American Medical Association*, **260**, 1570–1574.

Wilson, D., Wood, G., Johnston, N. & Sicurella, J. (1982). Randomised clinical trial of supportive follow-up for cigarette smokers in a family practice. *Canadian Medical Association Journal*, **126**, 127–129.

Winett, R. A., King, A. C. & Altman, D. G. (1989). *Health Psychology and Public Health: An Integrative Approach*. New York: Pergamon Press.

World Health Organization (1986). *Ottawa Charter for Health Promotion*. Ottawa: Canadian Public Health Association.

Part III

ILLNESS BEHAVIOUR AND HEALTH CARE

6 Health-related Screening: Psychological Predictors of Uptake and Impact

THERESA M. MARTEAU
Health Psychology Unit, Royal Free Hospital School of Medicine, London, UK

INTRODUCTION

There is a growing literature concerning the behavioural aspects of screening, particularly in North America where screening programmes are an established part of health care. Most of the studies have been descriptive, focussing either upon uptake, to describe who undergoes screening and who does not, or upon impact, describing the behavioural consequences, both intended and unintended, or undergoing a screening test. Where theoretical models have been used to guide the studies, they have tended to be cognitive–behavioural models. Their use has been most evident in studies concerning the uptake, the first area in which the health belief model was applied (Rosenstock, 1974). The predominant models used have been the Health Belief Model and Social Learning Theory. There has however been relatively little development or application of these models that goes beyond considering the individual.

People's behaviour may be conceptualised at different levels: individual, small group, at the level of the organisation or community (Rappaport, 1977). To date many of the models, theories or frameworks guiding research have tended to be individually oriented as part of the prevailing paradigm within psychology of the "contextless individual" (Sarason, 1981). Karoly (1985) has argued that given no genuinely integrative systems model is yet available,... "health psychology is best served by those who are ecumenical in orientation." (Karoly, 1985, p. 15). In working towards such a model it is perhaps helpful to consider the variables such a model may incorporate. Winett (1985) suggests the importance of the economic and legal as well as political influences upon health and health-related behaviours.

In the following review, the organisational factors that influence people's behaviour in the context of screening will be considered, alongside the cognitions, emotions and behaviours of both health professionals and those eligible for screening. The organisational factors include economic, legal, cultural and political influences.

International Review of Health Psychology. Volume 2. Edited by S. Maes, H. Leventhal and M. Johnston
© 1993 John Wiley & Sons Ltd

A pre-requisite to determining which model(s) may be the most suitable for explaining and predicting behaviour in relation to screening, is an accurate description of the behaviour and its meaning to the actor. Screening is a heterogeneous activity, whose meaning is likely to vary both between people and for any individual across time and tests. Health screening covers many conditions, and is offered to different groups in the population at different stages of their life cycles. It is sometimes aimed at the detection of potentially fatal diseases such as breast cancer, and at other times at potentially correctable problems, such as myopia. A screening test may be used to detect disease in the individual, their risk of developing a disease (such as hypertension screening), or the chances that any children they have may inherit a disease (Safer, 1986).

Health screening takes place in many settings including health clinics, places of work, schools, and more recently in the high street. Thus people will arrive for a screening test by a variety of routes. Some will have received a letter of invitation, others will have been invited opportunistically while attending a health professional for another reason. Others may be self-referred. While much screening in Britian is available under the National Health Service, some people will undergo screening in the private sector.

The nature of a screening test itself varies from the taking of a history to the use of complex technology such as ultrasound scanning. Some forms of screening, such as taking blood pressure, are more acceptable than others, such as faecal occult screening for cancer of the bowel.

These different features of screening programmes will influence uptake as well as the impact of taking part.

The main intended purpose of health-related screening is to detect disease or an increased risk of disease before symptoms present in order to reduce the morbidity and mortality associated with the disease. A further aim includes reassuring those for whom no problem is detected. The extent to which any screening programme achieves these aims depends upon whether the screening test is effective at detecting cases, and early detection and treatment can improve outcome. While necessary, they are not sufficient criteria for success. Success depends critically upon how people behave, i.e. whether they attend, and if they do, how they respond to the screening. The aim of this paper is to review the studies that have examined psychological aspects of screening, and to develop a theoretical context for explaining people's responses to screening.

UPTAKE OF SCREENING

The number of people who undergo any particular screening test ranges from a small minority to a vast majority. Uptake rates vary between conditions for which screening is offered. But as much if not more variation is to be found within the same condition, between different centres and different countries. For example, rates of cervical screening varied between two hospitals in the same State in North America. Neither patient nor provider beliefs accounted for these differences (Wheat, Kunitz & Fisher, 1990). The uptake of HIV screening in pregnant women is lower in North America and Britain where a minority of women undergo testing (Meadows et al., 1990; Minkoff et al., 1988) in contrast with Sweden and France, where uptake rates of over 99% have been reported (Larsson et al., 1990; Moatti et al., 1990). The major factors influencing uptake can be broadly categorised as individual and organisational. Individual factors include patients' and doctors' cognitions. Organisational factors, which will influence and be influenced by doctors' and patients' behaviour, include local or national screening policies, the setting in which screening is offered, and how participation in a screening programme is sought.

Individual factors

Patient factors

Many studies attempt to explain uptake of screening with a view to increasing uptake. Studies vary in both their theoretical perspectives and study designs. Studies which tend to provide more useful data are those that are prospective, in which all those eligible for screening are included, measures are taken before the issue of invitations for screening, and the choice of standardised measures is guided by psychological model(s) of behaviour. Examples of studies that meet these criteria are those of King (1982) and Norman and Fitter (1989).

Many studies have attempted to explain uptake of screening by comparing the characteristics of attenders with non-attenders. For example, McLean et al. (1984) found that those who attended for breast screening differed from those who did not in being of higher socioeconomic status, were more sympathetic to screening and were less likely to have been made anxious by the invitation. Owens et al. (1987) in another retrospective study of attenders for breast screening also found that attenders had higher socioeconomic status and were older than a comparison group. Lack of information from non-attenders limit the conclusions that can be drawn from studies such as this. Fear of undergoing a screening test was reported as a reason for not undergoing HIV screening during pregnancy by a fifth of those not undergoing the test (Larsson et al., 1990). Not only are the most fearful least likely to attend, but also those who are least healthy (Waller et al., 1990).

Some studies of uptake have been used as an empirical test of a particular model (e.g. Becker et al., 1975; King, 1982; Kristiansen, 1985; Seydel, Taal & Wiegman, 1990), while others have used one or more models to guide selection of variables (e.g. Marteau et al., 1992). Uptake or attendance for screening is conceptualised differently in different models. At least three different conceptualisations of attending or undergoing a health-related screening test are discernable: as engaging in a preventive health behaviour; as a behaviour aimed at avoiding or reducing a health threat; and as a decision to minimise likelihood of regret from not attending. All these perspectives are based on an expectancy-value model of motivation which asserts that individuals are motivated to maximize gains and minimize losses. Behavioural choice and persistence are a function of the expected success of the behaviour in attaining a goal and the value attached to that goal. These different views of uptake of screening may be used to explain uptake across different screening tests and programmes, as well as explaining uptake for different people undergoing the same screening test.

Screening as a health behaviour.   Some investigators have considered attending for screening as undertaking a preventive health behaviour, and attempted to predict it alongside a range of other health-related behaviours. There is however much concern regarding the usefulness of a general concept of health behaviour. Much evidence suggests that behaviours that promote health or reduce risk of ill health are not undimensional, and hence need to be predicted individually (for review, see Anderson, 1988).

Kasl & Cobb (1966) defined health behaviour as "any activity undertaken by a person believing himself to be healthy for the purpose of preventing disease or detecting it at an asymptomatic stage" (Kasl & Cobb, 1966, p. 246). Although Kasl and Cobb defined health behaviour by the intentions of the person, Anderson (1988) argues that most researchers have interpreted this in terms of medically approved practices designed to prevent disease. Failure to consider the individual's perception of a health behaviour is one reason why attempts to predict health behaviours using health-related predictors are frequently weak. For example, Kristiansen (1985) found that the value people attached to health was a weaker predictor of indirect risk behaviours, such as not attending for general health screening and not brushing teeth on a regular basis, than of direct ones, such as smoking or excessive alcohol intake. These results suggest that value attached to health will not predict behaviours that are not perceived as health-related.

Uptake of screening to avoid or reduce a health threat.   The predominant approach to predicting uptake of screening is one that considers attendance for health screening as a behaviour to reduce or avoid threat. This is evident in the health belief model, Weinstein's precaution adoption model (Weinstein, 1988), protection motivation theory and social learning theory. The health belief model has been found to predict attendance for a range of screening programmes, including general health screening (Norman & Fitter, 1989), hypertension screening (King, 1982), screening for carriers of Tay-Sachs disease (McQueen, 1975), prenatal screening for haemoglobinopathies (Rowley et al., 1991), and colorectal cancer (Jansen, 1984; Hoogewerf et al., 1990). The strongest predictors from the health belief model are perceived barriers to attendance and perceived susceptibility to the screened condition (for review, see Janz & Becker, 1984). Yet the predictive power of the model is relatively weak.

These models however are unable to account for the fact that appraising a health threat as threatening may prevent attendance at screening. Seydel, Taal & Weigman (1990) found that intention to attend mass cancer screening was negatively associated with perceived susceptibility, that is, those who saw themselves as more vulnerable to cancer were least likely to attend for screening. As discussed above, non-participants in screening may often be more afraid than participants. One explanation for these results concerns the way people conceptualise vulnerability within the context of an action recommended to reduce the threat. It may be for example, that people undergoing a recommended action rate their vulnerability as lower than those not attending because they will be undergoing an action likely to reduce the threat. Ronis (1992) suggests the need to distinguish between how susceptible to a disease a person thinks he or she would be if that person were and were not able to take a preventive action.

An alternative explanation is one derived from Leventhal's (1970) parallel response model, which predicts that if fear of a health threat is too great, people will avoid screening. This model postulates that reactions to health information entail efforts to reduce unpleasant effects (i.e. fear control) as well as action planning (i.e. danger control). Although these processes may be mutually facilitative, as when fear of illness motivates giving up smoking, fear control may inhibit danger control. This may occur when an individual is invited to be screened for an illness to which he or she feels vulnerable (Leventhal, Meyer & Nerenz, 1983). In this case, efforts to control the fear may be incompatible with undertaking the recommended action. Grady, Kegeles & Lund (1982) found that participants in a breast self-examination programme reported being less frightened by this early-detection practice than those who refused to participate.

Screening as a behaviour to minimize anticipated regret. Several authors have suggested that people have an almost insatiable appetite for medical interventions, including screening (van Lith, Tymstra & Visser, 1989; Woo et al., 1985; Tymstra, 1989). Tymstra (1989) argues from decision theory that avoiding feelings of regret is an important motivational factor in the choices people make. Thus, not to attend screening allows the possibility of not detecting disease, a situation likely to cause much regret. Attendance minimises the chances of experiencing this regret. Thus far this remains a possible explanation of screening attendance; its ability to predict attendance has not been tested.

Several factors limit the conclusions from studies of the uptake of screening. More information is available on attenders than non-attenders (Jansen, 1984). Aside from differing in attendance, non-attenders may be more heterogeneous than attenders (Hunt, Alexander & Roberts, 1988). Aside from the methodological limitations of many studies in this area, failure to predict more than a quarter of the variance in uptake is most likely a result of the theoretical perspective used. The majority of studies define the dependent variable as attendance for screening, and assume that predictors will be cognitions related to screening. While attendance may be a unitary behaviour, it reflects different considerations. For example for some it may reflect consideration of the health threat. For others it may follow a decision to undergo any test offered by a health professional (Marteau et al., 1992). Thus, if uptake of screening is examined not as a dichotomous variable, but as a group of behaviours, predictive models can be identified accordingly. Failure to consider factors other than those relating to the screenee is another reason for the weak predictive power of most studies. Consideration of health professionals and how screening is organised is likely to explain more of the variance in uptake of screening.

Health-professional factors

There is increasing recognition of the need to consider the health-related beliefs and behaviour of health professionals alongside those of patients in order to explain larger amounts of variance in patients' behaviour and health outcomes (for review, see Marteau & Johnston, 1990). The majority of studies conducted in this area are correlational. Care should therefore be taken not to infer causality from any reported associations.

Health-professionals' beliefs and attitudes towards screening may affect uptake of screening by influencing whether and how a screening programme is set up. That general practitioners' attitudes may influence screening is illustrated in a study of the organisation of cervical screening in general practice (Havelock et al., 1988). A belief in the effectiveness of cervical screening and a positive view of the time spent on screening were both associated with an organised approach to cervical screening within a practice. In a study of uptake of prenatal testing, the lower physicians' beliefs in the accuracy of prenatal testing, the lower their referral rates (Lippman-Hand & Cohen, 1980). Willingness to recommend mammographic screening outweighed the radiation risks (Cockburn et al., 1989).

Several studies however have failed to find attitudes towards screening predicting behaviour in doctors (Ziffer, Song & Mandleblatt, 1987; Commonwealth AIDS Research Grant Committee Working Party, 1990). While beliefs, including knowledge, are one set of factors influencing screening-related behaviour of physicians, situational factors are also important. Availability of equipment, perceived time, and remembering to initiate screening, as well as overcoming a reluctance to initiate screening may all be relevant.

Evidence suggesting that how health professionals present a screening test will influence whether those eligible undergo it was obtained in a study of the uptake of HIV testing in antenatal clinics. The overall uptake rate was around 17%, but the uptake rates obtained by different midwives varied from 3% to 82% (Meadows et al., 1990). Variation in presentation of the test is likely to have been one factor accounting for this wide variation in uptake. Both the amount of information presented and the manner in which it was presented may account for this observed variation. As predicted by Ley's cognitive hypothesis (Ley, 1982), information is a necessary prerequisite to performing many health-related activities. Using data derived from tape-recorded consultations, uptake of prenatal screening was correlated with the amount of information provided about the test, those undergoing the test having received significantly more information about the test during their consultations (Marteau et al., 1992). How information is presented has also been found to influence choice (McNeil et al., 1982). For example, in an analogue study, people were more likely to choose to undergo a prenatal test (amniocentesis) if the likelihood of the condition being screened for was framed negatively (e.g. 20% chance of abnormality) than if the likelihood was framed positively (e.g. 80% chance that there is no abnormality); (Marteau, 1989).

Sources of variation in physicians' beliefs and behaviour in relation to screening have not been the subject of much research. Personal experience of a disease influences estimates of its prevalence in health professionals, as well as non-health professionals (Jemmott, Croyle & Ditto, 1988). For example, physicians who had had herpes simplex estimated the population prevalence of the disorder to be 52% in contrast to an estimate of 15% provided by doctors who had not experienced the problem. Woo et al. (1985) found that physicians with a family history of cancer were significantly more likely to recommend two cancer screening procedures: sigmoidoscopy and mammography.

Another factor that may influence beliefs and in turn practice is knowledge. Health professionals' knowledge of various screening programmes have been found to be less than optimal. For example in a study of midwives involved in routine screening of pregnant women for risk of spina bifida, 45% were found to lack the basic knowledge necessary to inform women about this test (Sanden, 1985). Comparison of physicians' attitudes towards cholesterol and heart disease in 1983 with those obtained in 1986 indicated that physicians were more convinced in 1986 of the benefits of lowering high blood cholesterol levels and were treating patients accordingly (Schucker et al., 1987). The authors attributed these changes largely to a change in knowledge following the release of results from a large North American trial of the effects of reducing blood cholesterol levels.

The importance of focussing upon physicians and other health professionals in explaining and reducing the short-fall between recommended levels of screening and actual screening is emphasised by Woo and colleagues (1985):

> Thus, the principal problem rests not with the patient, not with major discrepancies in recommendations, but rather with the frequent failure of physicians in our study and others to live up to either the published recommendations or their own expectations. (p. 1484)

Organisational influences

Method of invitation

A major factor influencing uptake of a screening test is the method by which the test is offered. High rates of uptake are recorded when the test is presented as routine, requiring patients to opt out of a programme rather than to opt in (e.g. Smith et al., 1990), if the invitation is issued in person (e.g. Mann et al., 1988), and if the test is offered to those already receiving care, and hence not needing to make a separate journey to undergo the test (e.g. Watson et al., 1991). It is however important to distinguish between attendance rates and screening rates. For example, one general practice reporting an attendance rate of 94% from opportunistic invitations only managed to screen 25% of the target population after a period of two and a half years (Sacks & Marsdon, 1989).

The content of the invitation is also likely to influence responses. Prospect theory (Tversky & Kahneman, 1981) suggests that perceived losses of an option motivate action in risky situations more than perceived gains. Support for this hypothesis was obtained in a study of breast self-examination (BSE): women who received a message about the potential losses or disadvantages of not performing BSE had higher rates of BSE than those who received a message about the gains or advantages of performing BSE (Meyerowitz & Chaiken, 1987). However, no such effects were observed in a study of attendance following an abnormal smear result (Lauver & Rubin, 1990).

Others report that stressing gains rather than losses is more likely to motivate people to act to reduce health threats. For example, perceiving benefits from attending for a general health screen was the largest predictor of intention to attend, accounting for around 50% of the variance in intention to attend (Norman & Fitter, 1989). Gintner and colleagues (Gintner et al., 1987) compared the effects on attendance for hypertension screening of different messages given to those with and without a parental history of hypertension. Those with a parental history of hypertension were more than twice as likely to attend for screening following a message emphasising the benefits of attending, in contrast to a message stressing the threat of hypertension. These contrasting messages had no effect upon attendance of those without a family history of hypertension. These findings are in accord with those of Leventhal and Watts (1966) who found that low-risk subjects (i.e. nonsmokers) were equally likely to attend for a chest x-ray regardless of the fear level of the appeal, whereas high risk individuals (i.e. smokers) were less likely to in the fear condition. These findings are compatible with Leventhal's (1970) parallel response model, described above.

While this model predicts the importance of tailoring health messages to the individual, this is unlikely to be a cost-effective approach in population-based screening programmes. If only one message can be issued in an invitation for screening, the evidence would suggest that more people will respond if the message stresses the advantages of attendance, as opposed to the disadvantages of not attending.

Setting of screening

Screening may take place in many settings. Aside from the more common settings of health centres and hospitals, screening may also be available in pharmacies, at the work site, at school, and in the form of mobile screening services (Koran, Sox & Marton, 1984; Thornton & Chamberlain, 1989; Zeesman et al., 1984; Garcia & Moodie, 1989). Offering screening to people in the high street, at work and at school has the advantage of making attendance more convenient with a resulting higher screening coverage. Some possible disadvantages include a danger that those eligible may feel coerced to undergo screening. There is also a concern that screening offered outside of a health-care context is less likely to include any pre- or post-test counselling. Hence people are less likely to be well informed about the purpose of the test and the meaning of any possible results. A further problem that needs to be resolved is how to communicate the results to the person screened and his or her general practitioner (Rubin et al., 1990).

Legislation

Regulations that govern the running of screening programmes are likely to have a large influence upon uptake of screening. Uptake of screening is likely to be higher in mandatory as opposed to voluntary screening programmes. No such programmes exist in the UK. In Cyprus premarital testing to detect whether either partner carries a gene for thalasaemia is mandatory (Royal College of Physicians, 1989). While this approach has in part contributed to the success of the control of thalassaemia in the Mediterranean, the use of mandatory testing for sexually transmitted diseases, namely syphilis and AIDS, in the US has not been successful (Silverman,1990). Several states require screening of HIV status prior to the granting of a marriage licence. During the first six months of legislatively mandated premarital HIV testing in Illinois, eight seropositive individuals were identified out of over 70 000 applicants. The number of marriage licenses issued decreased by 22.5%, while the number isued to Illinois residents in surrounding States increased significantly (Dykers, 1990; Turnock & Kelly, 1989).

In the UK, the General Practitioner's New Contract (1990) makes payment of general practitioners partly dependent upon reaching pre-set targets for cervical screening (80% of the female population aged between 21 and 65), and general health screening (80% of the population). Prior to this legislation uptake of cervical screening in the UK ranged from 17% (Nathoo, 1988) to over 80% (National Audit Office, 1992). While it is too soon to evaluate the impact of this change, preliminary information shows that providing financial incentives for doctors to screen increases uptake (Duncan Nicholls, *The Independent*, February 1991).

Increasing uptake of screening

Attempts to increase the uptake of screening have ranged from the use of mass communications, to contacting individuals. The aim behind many interventions, particularly mass communications, is to heighten awareness of the particular threat, and increase perceived susceptibility towards it. But while interventions may alter these attitudes they do not necessarily lead to a change in behaviour. In a study attempting, unsuccessfully, to increase home radon testing amongst those living in a high risk area, Weinstein, Sandman & Roberts (1991) highlight two key barriers to encouraging people to undertake preventive health behaviours, including attending for screening: an enduring sense of invulnerability despite information to the contrary; and a poor understanding of the factors that determine undertaking preventive actions.

In a review of studies addressing behavioural methods of increasing uptake of cancer-related screening, Kegeles (1983) concluded that while individual contacts, such as letters and telephone calls, have been the most successful of all methods in obtaining single and repeat visits, they are too labour intensive for population-based screening programmes. He stresses the need for methods to establish long-term habits of health behaviour, which would include attending for regular screening.

Perhaps more effective and efficient ways of increasing uptake are those that attempt to alter the behaviour of health professionals presenting the screening, or the organisation of a screening programme. For example, uptake of screening for cystic fibrosis carrier status increased seven-fold, from 14% to 70% when those issuing the invitation returned after providing initial information, to ask if an individual wished to be tested (Bekker et al., 1992). Providing free screening at worksites can also result in high uptakes of screening. While such approaches may achieve high uptake, there may be some unexpected adverse consequences of doing so. MacDonald and colleagues (MacDonald et al., 1984) suggest that the negative consequences of learning of raised blood pressure from a routine screening test are more likely to occur in studies achieving higher uptake rates.

The individuals attending for screening following a low profile campaign will differ from those who attend following a high profile one (Rogers, 1983). Participation in the latter instance may be due to persuasive communication, rather than an appreciation of the threat and a desire to reduce it, as may antecede attendance with a lower profile campaign. Those unwittingly entering a screening programme may as a consequence have more difficulty dealing with being recalled.

By contrast, Havas has argued that the adverse effects of being labelled hypertensive would be less likely to occur if large numbers of people were so labelled, as is expected to occur with cholesterol screening (Havas, 1988). To explain the impact of screening it is therefore important to know amongst other things, how recruitment was instigated, and the uptake rate.

While we have some knowledge of the factors associated with uptake, these are not necessarily the basis for interventions to alter behaviour. In attempts to alter uptake, it may be illuminating to study a range of consequences following an alteration of precursors. For example, what are the effects of increasing a sense of vulnerability in people in order to increase the likelihood that they will attend for screening?

IMPACT OF SCREENING

The widespread availability of screening has implications for participants as well as non-participants in a programme. This section will consider first the impact of screening upon those participating in a screening programme. The implications for non-participants as well as the general population will then be considered.

Impact of undergoing screening

Receipt of an invitation to attend for screening

The behavioural consequences of different invitations have most usually been studied to determine the most effective way of encouraging uptake of different screening tests, as discussed in the previous section. The cognitive and emotional consequences have been less frequently studied. Receipt of an invitation to be screened for a disease or risk of a disease will raise some concern about the health threat. For example, in a retrospective study of responses to breast screening, while the majority (93%) of those attending were pleased that they had received an invitation, 55% reported feeling worried (Fallowfield, Rodway & Baum, 1990). But for some, albeit a minority of recipients, this concern may be extreme. In a follow-up study of non-attenders for cervical screening, Nathoo (1988) found that 12 of the 17 women he was able to trace expressed terror at having received the invitation. They did not understand the reason for it, but all assumed that they had cancer of the cervix and that their doctor knew this. The nature and extent of this response is difficult to study given that non-attenders for screening are also unlikely to respond to questionnaires. A study design that will overcome some of these difficulties is one that involves comparisons between an invited and a matched uninvited group.

Negative results

Meaning of a negative result.   The meaning of a negative result will vary for different screening tests, according primarily to the sensitivity of the test (i.e. the extent to which it will detect all cases), and whether it is detecting a fixed or changing risk. For screening tests assessing an unchangeable risk, such as one determining the presence of a gene where all mutations are known or an inherited disease evident at birth such as phenylketonuria, a negative result means that the individual is free from risk of ever developing the disease or passing it on to any offspring. In genetic tests where not all mutations are known, as is the case for cystic fibrosis, a negative result means that there is a residual risk that the individual is a carrier. In tests that screen for diseases for which an individual is vulnerable across a period of time, a negative result means no evidence of disease or risk of disease was found at the time of the test. A life-time free of disease or risk of disease is not implied by a negative result. This applies to screening for several different types of cancer, including breast, cervical and bowel.

In tests that screen for risk of disease, it is a misnomer to describe any result as negative. Such screening tests assess relative risk of a disease. The most common of these is screening for risk of coronary heart disease. Amongst the risk factors assessed are blood pressure, blood cholesterol, smoking, diet, exercise and family history of heart disease. Individuals undergoing such screening are commonly categorised as being at low, average or higher than average risk. Other screening tests that detect risk of disease include the prenatal biochemical tests to detect fetal abnormalities (Drife & Donnai, 1991). Such tests may be used to revise the risk determined on the basis of family history and maternal age that a woman's fetus has spina bifida or Down's syndrome.

While the implications of a negative result will vary in theory, according to whether the test screens for disease or risk of disease, in practice this is less evident. One reason for this is that staff tend to convey test results in a categorical manner, i.e. as being either positive or negative (Marteau et al., 1993). This is reinforced by the presence of precise points at which treatment plans alter. For example, with cholesterol levels of higher than 6.5, dietary advice is frequently given; with levels above 7.8 mmol/l, drug treatment may be offered. In screening for Down's syndrome, a woman would be offered amniocentesis if the results of a screening test indicated a risk higher than 1 in 250. Such practices encourage screeners and screenees alike to consider results below any cut-off points as negative.

Receiving a negative result. Most of those undergoing population-based screening will receive a negative test result. An exception to this is screening for risk factors for coronary heart disease in Western societies, where the majority of individuals have some risk factors. The most commonly investigated outcomes of participating in a health-related screening programme are anxiety or its converse, reassurance. Receipt of a negative result on screening has been found to be associated with raised levels of anxiety (Stoate, 1989), no change in anxiety (Dean et al., 1984; Berne-Fromell, Kjessler & Josefson, 1983; Burton, Dillard & Clark, 1985), reassurance (Orton et al., 1991), as well as inappropriately high levels of reassurance (Tymstra & Bieleman, 1987; Kinlay & Heller, 1990).

These studies vary in the measures used, study designs, as well as the types of screening tests investigated. A better understanding of the factors determining responses to a negative result of screening is likely to follow from carefully controlled comparative studies which consider the effects of screening within the contexts of the processes of screening as well as participants' perceptions of screening.

False negative results. Some of those who undergo screening, despite a negative result, will develop the disease or have an affected child. The number of people who receive such false negative results will vary according to the sensitivity of a screening test. There have been no studies documenting the psychological effects of false negative results. Effects may be evident in initial reactions to a diagnosis, as well as the longer-term adjustment to the condition.

Positive results

Receipt of a positive result on certain screening tests, later confirmed by diagnostic investigations, is frequently associated with a mixture of shock, anger, and anxiety. There are several personal accounts of such experiences from screening for cervical cancer and fetal abnormalities (Quilliam, 1988; Britten, 1988; Brown, 1989; Statham, 1987). The extent and duration of adverse responses to a positive result vary. It would seem that if there is a time-limited resolution to an abnormal result, then adverse responses will similarly be time-limited. The majority of cervical abnormalities detected during routine screening can be treated relatively easily. Although receipt of a positive result and undergoing further investigations is associated with much anxiety (Marteau et al., 1990; Posner & Vessey, 1988), longer-term studies suggest that for the majority of women there are no lasting adverse psychological effects (Reelick, De Haes & Schuurman, 1984). Women's responses to the detection of fetal abnormalities and subsequent termination of pregnancy show a similar process of attrition over time (Black, 1989; Iles, 1989).

Little is known about whether people respond differently to a diagnosis if it is detected during routine screening than if it is detected from clinical signs or symptoms. In one study where this question was considered, no differences in psychological states were found between 30 women with breast cancer whose cancer had been detected during routine screening, and 30 women whose cancer had been diagnosed following self-referral for breast symptoms (Farmer, Payne & Royle, 1992).

Sometimes reactions to a positive result on a screening test are more extreme or pervasive than expected on the basis of the prognosis attached to the condition. For example, in the year following detection of hypertension during screening, those found to have elevated blood pressure were absent twice as frequently as they had been in the preceeding 12 months (Haynes et al., 1978). A further example of how a positive result on screening may have effects that spread beyond expected effects comes from genetic screening. People identified as carriers of a recessive gene for Tay-Sachs disease, which confers no risk to their own health, viewed their future with less optimism than those who were not found to carry the gene (Marteau, van Duijn & Ellis, 1992). This may reflect the tendency of people to seek symptoms or explain symptoms within the context of a label: ". . . given symptoms, an individual will seek a diagnostic label, and given a label, he or she will seek symptoms" (Leventhal et al., 1980). Thus, any symptoms experienced by carriers may be more likely to be noticed and attributed to their carrier status. An alternative explanation for the finding is that receipt of one piece of bad news about one's health (that is, learning that one is a carrier) reduces the general tendency for people to be optimistic when considering the chances of becoming ill or experiencing any misfortune.

False positive results. Depending upon the specificity of a screening test, many of those recalled after one positive result will subsequently receive a result indicating no problem. For those receiving such false positive results, reports vary in the extent and duration of concern documented. In some studies it would appear that once the seeds of doubt have been sown they are difficult to remove. Bloom and Monterossa (1981) studied people who had initially been told that they were hypertensive but who after three more tests were judged normal. Such patients reported more symptoms of depression and a lower state of general health than a matched group initially found to be normotensive. In a study of women receiving false positive results on routine screening for fetal abnormalities, raised anxiety and concern about the baby were evident after further testing had shown that no abnormalities were detected (Marteau et al., 1988), and for some women even after the baby was born (Marteau et al., 1992). The parents of newborn children who were falsely diagnosed on routine screening as having congenital hypothyroidism reported greater strain on their marriages and difficulties in their relationships with their children (Tymstra, 1986). Although they knew that the results of subsequent testing were negative, they continued to be plagued by questions and uncertainties about their children's health. Women recalled after an initial breast screening mammography subsequently increased the frequency with which they practiced breast self-examination (Bull & Campbell, 1990). The frequency of breast self-examination remained unchanged in women who underwent screening but were not recalled. This suggests that being recalled for further tests heightens awareness of, or anxiety about a threat.

Other studies however have failed to find any evidence of sustained concern after an initial positive result has been shown to be false. Such differences may reflect study methods, sustained effects being more apparent in prospective than retrospective studies. Two studies that failed to detect differences were retrospective (Mant et al., 1990; Orton et al., 1991). Lack of a sustained effect of a positive result may also reflect the manner in which screening is conducted. Effects of being labelled hypertensive were minimal when accompanied by regular supportive follow up as part of a controlled trial (Mann, 1984).

Interventions following positive results on screening. One purpose of screening for risk factors for disease is, having identified those at risk, to intervene to reduce that risk. There have been several reviews of the psychological effects of screening for risk factors of coronary heart disease (Lefebvre, Hursey & Carleton, 1988; MacDonald et al., 1984; Tymstra, 1990; Havas, 1988). Many of the earlier studies focussed on the emotional and behavioural consequences of screening for hypertension. Haynes et al. (1978) reported a two-fold increase in absenteeism the year after identification of previously unknown hypertension. Bloom and Monterossa (1981) found more symptoms of depression amongst those labelled hypertensive than those not so labelled.

Not all of those detected through screening as being at increased risk of disease receive an intervention to reduce their risks. The percentages of those with raised blood cholesterol detected at screening contacting a doctor for advice varies from 33% (Wynder, Field & Haley, 1986) to 82% (Kinlay & Heller, 1990). Rastam et al. (1988) followed up 107 of the 35% of those with raised blood cholesterol who had not seen a doctor. Twenty-five per cent reported having made life-style changes on their own, 21% expected to go at a later date, and 21% regarded the results as unimportant.

Of those who do attend a health professional following a problem detected on screening, not all will be offered advice or an intervention. For example, between 25% and 71% of those with raised cholesterol levels were either told not to worry or given no specific advice (Wynder, Field & Haley, 1986; Rastam et al., 1988; Kinlay & Heller, 1990).

Of those receiving interventions to reduce risk of coronary heart disease, there are at least three possible outcomes: the risk is reduced, the risk is unaltered, or the risk is increased. Each of these outcomes may follow from the patient either following or not following any advice given. We do not know how people respond particularly to a failure to reduce a level of risk detected through screening. Possible reactions to risk reduction following change in behaviour include reassurance, and intention to sustain the behaviour change. Alternatively, reassurance may reduce perceived need to sustain behaviour change. Of those who change their behaviour and whose risk is unaltered or even increased, several reactions are possible. These include minimisation of the threat, self-blame, anger and learned helplessness (Abramson, Seligman & Teasdale, 1978). While there has been no study of the responses to the outcomes of interventions following screening, studies of patients' responses to treatments that have failed illustrate some of these different responses (Seligman, 1975; Wortman & Brehm, 1975; Wagener & Taylor, 1986). It is important to know the cognitive, emotional and behavior consequences for at least two reasons. First, because they are likely to influence responses to any future health-related advice; and second, it is important to know what these are in evaluating the effects of population-based risk factor screening programmes.

Implicit in the notion of risk-factor screening is the fact that a number of those "at risk" will not develop the condition. As pointed out by Kristiansen, Eggen & Thelle (1991), measurement of blood cholesterol levels in a population will result in over half the population being labelled "at risk" unnecessarily. These authors argue that the quality of life for these individuals will be reduced. Studies are needed that address this question.

Factors influencing the impact of screening

Aside from the test result received, several other factors are likely to mediate and moderate the effects of participating in a screening programme. These will include how testing and results are communicated, social support, beliefs about the condition detected, perceptions of risk, perceptions of self, and the reactions of others.

The way that results of screening are presented will influence the impact of screening. Following detection of raised blood pressure, subjects given a reassuring message about the implications of this finding were significantly less anxious than those given a traditional message about hypertension, the silent killer (Rudd et al., 1986). Both general social support and specific support from health professionals will affect responses to screening (Robinson, Hibbard & Laurence, 1984; Mann, 1984).

In a series of elegant laboratory-based studies (for review, see Croyle & Jemmott, 1991), Croyle, Jemmott and colleagues have demonstrated how reactions to screening positive on a risk factor for disease is influenced by prevalence information: a hypothetical deficiency was perceived as more serious when subjects believed that only one in five students had tested positive, than when subjects believed that four in five students had tested positive. Given that the majority of women underestimate the likelihood of being recalled following routine cervical screening, this may be one factor accounting for the very high levels of anxiety in women recalled in this screening programme (Marteau & Thwaites, 1992).

A further factor influencing how people respond to screening is their perception of threat or risk. Most people underestimate their vulnerability to adverse events, including illness (Weinstein, 1984). Participation in a screening programme albeit receiving a negative result, may alert some people for the first time that they may be vulnerable to a particular condition. This may be one explanation for an adverse response to a negative result on screening, as found by Stoate (1989). Perceptions of risk are influenced not only by probabilistic information but also by certainty. The salience of certainty over probability is illustrated in a study of predictive testing for Huntington's disease, when a woman became distressed when her pre-testing probability of having the gene changed from a 50% probability to a certain 11% probability (Huggins et al., 1992). Several analogue studies demonstrate how the framing of probability information also influences reactions to that information (McNeill et al., 1982; Marteau, 1989; Shiloh & Sagi, 1989). Interactions between information presented and threat perceived warrant more studies in this area.

People's identity or image of themselves is determined both by how they view themselves and how they are viewed by others. Given that these views are influenced by how healthy an individual is or appears to be, results of screening will influence an individual's identity. Evidence to support this is found in several studies of screening, demonstrating first, that a positive result on screening affects an individual's perception of their health, and second, studies documenting the differential emotional effects of screening results.

Compared with a normotensive sample, people incorrectly identified as being hypertensive perceived their present health as significantly poorer although there was no evidence that their health was poorer (Bloom & Monterossa, 1981). Some unpredicted effects of genetic screening may be explained by recourse to their effects upon individual's identities. In several studies of predictive testing for Huntington's disease, adverse effects have been found for those receiving a negative test result as well as for those receiving a positive one. In the Canadian collaborative study of predictive testing for Huntington's disease, 10% of those who received a negative result experienced some difficulty in the first year adjusting to this result (Huggins et al., 1992). A study in the Netherlands (Tibben et al., 1990) found that of 18 people screened, the nine found to be carriers responded initially with shock, followed by a rapid recovery. Eight of the non-carriers responded with guilt and depression. Six were avoided by members of their family, including four who were actually rejected by their families. There are several possible reasons for these difficulties. First, many had lived their lives "as if they would develop Huntington's": removal of the threat removed an important part of their identity, and justification for past life decisions; second, it served to cut one tie with families where the threat of a disease was an important theme.

In a study of responses to sickle-cell trait testing, when the husband was found to be a carrier this created more upset both for the men and their wives than when the wives were found to be carriers (Childs et al., 1976). One possible explanation is that men's identity is more closely linked to their perceived health or ability to reproduce. Another is that men are more likely to be the family bread-winner, and hence any perceived threat to their health may be of greater concern to the family.

The reactions of those other than close family may also affect responses to screening, particularly amongst those who obtain a positive result. Both health professionals and others hold negative attitudes towards people with a wide variety of illnesses, handicaps and disabilities (Tringo, 1970; Margolies et al., 1983). Much of the work on stigma and disease has been conducted in the area of genetic screening. Some of this research was prompted by concern in the US over employment discrimination amongst carriers for sickle-cell disease (Wilfond & Fost, 1990). Carriers and non-carriers of sickle-cell trait were asked to describe what it felt like to be a carrier, using a series of semantic differential scales. Non-carriers perceived carriers as more bad, less happy, less healthy and less active than non-carriers (Woolridge & Murray, 1989). Fear of such a negative reaction may explain why carriers of sickle-cell trait were far less likely than non-carriers to tell their friends that they had been screened (Stamatoyannopoulous, 1974).

As most studies of screening programmes have not used experimental design, it is difficult to infer causality from some of the associations reported. This is an area requiring attention in future studies. The studies of Croyle, Jemmott and colleagues provide one model for research in this area. Using experimental laboratory-based studies they develop hypotheses to be tested in field research. Research questions need to evolve from those which focus purely upon outcome, to ones that encompass the process as well. Rather than considering what the effect of screening is, research questions should consider the effects of screening under a pre-defined set of experimentally manipulated conditions.

Impact of the presence of screening programmes

Alongside the specific effects for those participating in screening programmes, the widespread availability of screening may have a sphere of influence that extends beyond those participating in screening programmes.

Screening may alter our views of who and what is healthy. That screening programmes may alter people's attitudes towards the screened condition is suggested in a study of attitudes towards justifiable termination of babies with a range of abnormalities (Faden et al., 1987). The threshold for conditions seen as justifying termination was lower after the introduction of a screening programme than before. The availability of prenatal screening may similarly, by enhancing perceived control over outcomes, lead to blame over negative outcomes. Given the option of prenatal screening and abortion of affected fetuses, some parents may feel that to produce a child with a potentially diagnosable handicap is to be blame-worthy for the child's birth. In North America, disabled children including some with Down's syndrome have been awarded for wrongful life (for review, see Marteau, 1991).

Widespread screening may also affect attributions for illness, and by extension, attitudes and behaviour towards those who are affected. If people are being encouraged to believe more strongly that they can control their health, an extension of this is the view that illness is caused by a failure to act appropriately (Sontag, 1983). Evidence to support this hypothesis comes from a study of doctors' and nurses' attitudes to caring for different types of patient (Marteau & Riordan, 1992). For example, staff held more negative attitudes towards patients with cervical cancer who had not attended for screening, compared with patients who had attended for such screening. It appeared that these effects were mediated by perceived controllability of the illness, as predicted by an attributional model of helping behaviour.

It is difficult to determine the causal nature of any associations between the presence of screening programmes and health-related attitudes. The existence of such programmes, for example, may reflect certain attitudes, reinforce them as well as shape them. Nonetheless, studies addressing the wider psychological effects of screening could further our understanding of this area.

CONCLUDING COMMENTS

This chapter has focussed upon two behavioural aspects of screening: uptake and impact. Other aspects of screening for which psychological perspectives are relevant include explaining why some screening tests are introduced while others are not. Alongside a historical perspective on screening (Reiser, 1978), notions of acceptable and unacceptable risk are applicable (Fischoff et al., 1981), ethnocentrism and racial prejudice (France-Dawson, 1986), financial incentives for the drug industry (Vines, 1989), as well as politically motivated desires to emphasise the role of individual behaviour in causes of ill health rather than economic factors.

Another aspect of screening that lends itself to psychological enquiry concerns the reliability of tests that are determined by human judgment (Ennis, 1990). Training following the identification of cognitive biases has for example been used to improve the accuracy of radiographers in reading screening mammograms (Gale & Walker, 1990).

There is some debate over the role of health psychology, in particular whether its prime aim is to explain or to change behaviour. Most of the work to date in the area of screening has been to describe uptake or impact of screening, although some have attempted to increase uptake or alter the impact. Caution is needed for psychologists attempting to change behaviour given the rocky epidemiological and clinical foundations upon which some screening tests are based. The criteria for screening proposed by Wilson and Junger (1968) are frequently ignored. Skrabanek and McCormick (1989) argue that screening reflects a preoccupation with health, perpetuating a fallacy of cheating death. It is too easy for health psychologists to accept the prevailing ideology that prevention is better than cure. Health psychologists can perhaps best contribute to the area of screening by helping to evaluate proposed and existing programmes, thereby contributing to the debates concerning the benefits and harm in which screening can result. In addition, health-related screening presents an area of health-related activity within which many different psychological concepts and models may be developed and tested.

The next wave of research in this area requires a refinement of the major research questions. Hitherto studies have addressed such unqualified questions as: "What is the uptake of screening for a particular condition?" and "What is the impact of undergoing screening for a particular condition?" Both our theoretical and empirical understanding of this area will be enhanced by considering outcomes within the context of processes and individual differences. Examples of research questions reflecting this stance are: What is the uptake or impact for people varying on different psychological dimensions, of screening for particular conditions, when offered in different ways? Such an elaboration of research questions will facilitate the immense contribution that psychology can make to the theory and practice of health-related screening.

REFERENCES

Abramson, L. Y., Seligman, M. E. P. & Teasdale, J. D. (1978). Learned helplessness in humans: Critique and reformulation. *Journal of Abnormal Psychology*, 87, 49–74.

Anderson, R. (1988). The development of the concept of health behaviour and its application in recent research. *Health Behavour Research and Health Promotion*, 22–23.

Becker, M. H., Kaback, M. M., Rosenstock, I. M. & Ruth, M. V. (1975). Some influences on public participation in a genetic screening program. *Journal Community Health*, 1, 3–14.

Bekker, H., Modell, M., Denniss, G., Mathew, C., Silver, A., Bobrow, M. & Marteau, T. M. (1992). Evaluation of alternative screening strategies for detecting carriers of cystic fibrosis in a primary care setting. Paper to be presented at the British Medical Genetics Conference, September 1992.

Berne-Fromell, K., Kjessler, B. & Josefson, G. (1983). Anxiety concerning fetal malformations in women who accept or refuse alpha fetoprotein screening in pregnancy. *Journal of Psychosomatic Obstetrics and Gynaecology*, 2, 94–95.

Black, R. B. (1989). A 1 and 16 month follow-up of prenatal diagnosis patients who lost pregnancies. *Prenatal Diagnosis*, 9, 795–804.

Bloom, J. R. & Monterossa, S. (1981). Hypertension labelling and sense of well-being. *American Journal of Public Health*, 71, 1228–1232.

Booth, C. S., Safer, M. A. & Leventhal, H. (1986). Use of physician services following participation in a cardiac screening programme. *Public Health Reports*, 101, 315–319.

Britten, N. (1988). A personal view. *British Medical Journal*, 292, 1191.

Brown, J. (1989). The choice: A piece of my mind. *Journal of the American Medical Association*, 262, 2735.

Bull, A. R. & Campbell, M. J. (1990). Assessment of the psychological impact of a breast screening programme. *British Medical Journal of Radiology*, 64, 510–515.

Burton, B. K., Dillard, R. G. & Clark, E. N. (1985). Maternal Serum alpha fetoprotein screening: The effect of participation on anxiety and attitude toward pregnancy in women with normal results. *Americal Journal of Obstetrics and Gynaecology*, 152, 540–543.

Childs, B., Gordis, L., Kabach, M. M. & Kazazian, H. H. (1976). Tay-Sachs screening: Social and psychological impact. *American Journal of Human Genetics*, 28, 550–558.

Cockburn, J., Irwig, L., Turnbull, D., Simpson, J. M., Mock, P. & Tattersall, M. (1989). Encouraging attendance at screening mammography: Knowledge, attitudes and intentions of general practitioners. *The Medical Journal of Australia*, 151, 391–396.

Commonwealth AIDS Research Grant Committee Working Party (1990). Attitudes, knowledge and behaviour of general practitioners in relation to HIV infection and

AIDS. *The Medical Journal of Australia*, 153, 5–12.

Croyle, R. T. & Jemmott, J. B. (1991). Psychological reactions to risk factor testing. In: J. A. Skelton and R. T. Croyle (Eds), *Mental Representation in Health and Illness* (pp. 85–107). New York: Springer-Verlag.

Dean, C., Roberts, M. M., French, K. & Robinson, S. (1984). Psychiatric morbidity after screening for breast cancer. *Journal of Epidemiology and Community Health.*, 40, 71–75.

Drife, J. O. & Donnai, D. (Eds) (1991). *Antenatal Diagnosis of Fetal Abnormalities*. London: Springer-Verlag.

Dykers, J. R. (1990). Mandatory premarital HIV testing: The Illinois experience. *Journal of the American Medical Association*, 263, 1917.

Ennis, M. (1990). Over confidence in the interpretation of traces used to diagnose fetal wellbeing. Paper presented at the BPS Conference, 17 December 1990.

Faden, R. R., Chwalow, A. J., Quaid, K., Chase, G. A., Lopes, C., Leonard, C. O. & Holtzman, N. A. (1987). Prenatal screening and pregnant women's attitudes toward the abortion of defective fetuses. *American Journal of Public Health*, 77, 3, 288–290.

Fallowfield, L. J., Rodway, A. & Baum, M. (1990). What are the psychological factors influencing attendance, non-attendance and re-attendance at a breast screening centre? *Journal of the Royal Society of Medicine*, 83, 547–551.

Farmer, A. J., Payne, S. & Royle, G. T. (1992). A comparative study of psychological morbidity in women with screen detected and symptomatic breast cancer. *The British Psychological Society Abstracts*, p. 10.

Fischhoff, B., Lichenstein, S., Slovic, P., Derby, S. L. & Kenney, R. L. (1981). *Acceptable Risk*. Cambridge: Cambridge University Press.

France-Dawson, M. (1986). Sickle cell disease: Implications for nursing care. *Journal of Advanced Nursing*, 11, 729–737.

Gale, A. G. & Walker, G. E. (1991). Cognitive factors in breast cancer screening. In: M. Johnston, M. Herbert & T. Marteau (Eds), *European Health Psychology*. Leicester: British Psychological Society and Bogardo Press.

Garcia, R. E. & Moodie, D. S. (1989). Routine cholesterol surveillance in childhood. *Paediatrics*, 84, 751–755.

Gintner, G. G., Rectanus, E. F., Achord, K. & Parker, B. (1987). Prenatal history of hypertension and screening attendance: Effects of wellness appeal versus threat appeal. *Health Psychology*, 6, 431–444.

Grady, K. E., Kegeles, S. S. & Lund, A. K. (1982). Experimental studies to increase BSE—preliminary findings. In C. Mettlin & G. P. Murphy (Eds), *Issues in Cancer Screening and Communications*. New York: Liss A.R. Inc.

Havas, S. (1988). The challenge of lowering blood cholesterol levels. *Archives of Internal Medicine*, 148, 1910–1913.

Havelock, C., Edwards, R., Cuzlick, J. & Chamberlain, J. (1988). The organisation of cervical screening in general practice. *Journal of the Royal College of General Practitioners*, 38, 207–211.

Haynes, B. R., Sackett, D. L., Taylor, W. D., Gibson, E. S. & Johnson, A. L. (1978). Increased absenteeism from work after detecting and labeling of hypertensive patients. *The New England Journal of Medicine*, 299(14), 741–744.

Hoogewerf, P. E., Hislop, T. G., Morrison, B. J., Burns, S. D. & Sizto, R. (1990). Health belief and compliance with screening for fecal occult blood. *Social Science and Medicine*, 30, 721–726.

Huggins, M., Bloch, M., Wiggins, S. et al. (1992). Predictive testing for Huntington Disease in Canada. Adverse effects and unexplained results on those receiving a decreased risk. *American Journal of Medical Genetics*, 42, 508–515.

Hunt, S. M., Alexander, F. & Roberts, M. M. (1988). Attenders and non-attenders at a breast screening clinic: A comparative study. *Public Health*, 102, 3–10.

Iles, S. (1989). The loss of early pregnancy. In: M. Oates (Ed), Psychological Aspects of Obstetrics and Gynaecology. *Clinical Obstetrics and Gynaecology*, 3, 769–790.

Jansen, J. H. (1984). Participation in the first and second round of a mass-screening for colorectal cancer. *Social Science and Medicine*, 18, 633–636.

Janz, N. K. & Becker, M. H. (1984). The health belief model: A decade later. *Health Education Quarterly*, 11, 1–47.

Jemmott, J. B., III, Croyle, R. T. & Ditto, P. H. (1988). Commonsense epidemiology: Self-based judgements from laypersons and physicians. *Health Psychology*, 7, 55–73.

Karoly, P. (1985). The logic and character of assessment in health psychology: Perspectives and possibilities. In P. Karoly (Ed), *Measurement Strategies in Health Psychology*, pp. 3–45. New York: Wiley.

Kasl, S. V. & Cobb, S. (1966). Health behaviour, illness behaviour and sick role behaviour. *Archives of Environmental Health*, 12, 246–266.

Kegeles, S. S. (1983). Behavioural methods for effective cancer screening and prevention. *Behavioural Medicine Update*, 5, 36–44.

King, J. B. (1982). The impact of patient's perceptions of high blood pressure on attendance at screening: An extension of the health belief model. *Social Science and Medicine*, 16, 1079–1091.

Kinlay, S. & Heller, R. F. (1990). Effectiveness and hazards of case finding for a high cholesterol concentration. *British Medical Journal*, 300, 1545–1547.

Koran, L. M., Sox, H. C. & Marton, K. I. (1984). Mobile medical screening. *Hospital Community Psychiatry*, 35, 1151–1153.

Kristiansen, C. M. (1985). Value correlates of preventive health behaviour. *Journal of Personality and Social Psychology*, 49, 748–758.

Kristiansen, I. S., Eggen, A. E. & Thelle, D. S. (1991). Cost effectiveness of incremental programmes for lowering serum cholesterol concentration: Is individual intervention worth while? *British Medical Journal*, 302, 1119–1122.

Larsson, G., Spangberg, L., Lindgren, S. & Bohlin, A. B. (1990). Screening for HIV in pregnant women: A study of maternal opinion. *Aids Care*, 2, 223–228.

Lauver, D. & Rubin, M. (1990). Message framing, dispositional optimism, and follow-up for abnormal papanicolaou tests. *Research in Nursing and Health*, 13, 199–207.

Lefebvre, R. C., Hursey, K. G. & Carleton, R. A. (1988). Labelling of participants in high blood pressure screening programmes: implications for blood cholesterol screenings. *Archives of Internal Medicine*, 148, 1993–1997.

Leventhal, H. (1970). Findings and theory in the study of fear communications. In L. Berkowitz (Ed), *Advances in Experimental Social Psychology* (pp. 119–186). New York: Academic Press.

Leventhal, H., Meyer, D. & Nerenz, D. (1980). The commonsense representation of illness danger. In: S. Rachman (Ed), *Medical Psychology*, 2, pp. 7–30. New York: Pergamon Press.

Leventhal, H. & Watts, J. (1966). Sources of resistance to fear-arousing communications on smoking and lung cancer. *Journal of Personality*, 34, 155–175.

Ley, P. (1982). Satisfaction, compliance, and communication. *British Journal of Clinical Psychology*, 21, 241–254.

Lippman-Hand, A. & Cohen, D. I. (1980). Influence of obstetrician's attitudes on their use of prenatal diagnosis for the detection of Down's Syndrome. *Canadian Medical Association Journal*, 122, 1381–1386.

MacDonald, L. A., Sackett, D. L., Haynes, R. B. & Taylor, D. W. (1984). Labelling in hypertension: A review of the behavioural and psychological consequences. *Journal of Chronic Diseases*, 37, 933–942.

MacLean, U., Sinfield, D., Klein, S. & Harnden, B. (1984). Women who decline breast screening. *Journal of Epidemiology and Community Health*, 24, 278–283.

McNeil, B. J., Pauker, S. G., Sox, H. C. & Tversky, A. (1982). On elicitation of preferences for alternative therapies. *New England Journal of Medicine*, 306, 1259–1262.

McQueen, D. V. (1975). Social aspects of genetic screening for Tay-Sachs disease: The pilot community screening program in Baltimore and Washington. *Social Biology*, 22, 125–133.

Mann, A. H. (1984). Hypertension: psychological aspects and diagnostic impact in a clinical trial. *Psychological Medicine*, 5 (suppl. 5), 3–35.

Mann, J. I., Lewis, B., Shepherd, J., Winder, A. F., Fenster, S., Rose, L. & Morgan, B. (1988). Blood lipid concentrations and other cardiovascular risk factors: Distribution, prevalence and detection in Britain. *British Medical Journal*, 296, 1702–1706.

Mant, D., Fitzpatrick, R., Hogg, A., Fuller, A., Farmer, A., Verne, J. & Northover, J. (1990). Experiences of patients with false positive results from colorectal cancer screening. *British Journal of General Practice*, 40, 423–425.

Margolies, R., Wachtel, A. B., Sutherland, K. R. & Blum, R. H. (1983). Medical students' attitudes towards cancer: Concepts of professional distance. *Journal of Psychosocial Oncology*, 1, 35–49.

Marteau, T. M. (1989). Framing of information: Its influence upon decisions of doctors and patients. *British Journal of Social Psychology*, 28, 89–94.

Marteau, T. M. (1991). Psychological implications of prenatal diagnosis. In J. O. Drife & D. Donnai (Eds) *Antenatal Diagnosis of Fetal Abnormalities*. London: Springer-Varlag. (pp. 243–254).

Marteau, T. M., Cook, R., Kidd, J., Michie, S., Johnson, M., Slack, J. & Shaw, R. W. (1992). The psychological effects of false positive results in prenatal screening for fetal abnormality. A prospective study. *Prenatal Diagnosis*, 12, 205–214.

Marteau, T. M. & Johnston, M. (1990). Health professionals: A source of variance in patient outcomes. *Health Psychology*, 5, 47–58.

Marteau, T. M., Johnston, M., Kidd, J., Michie, S., Cook, R., Slack, J. & Shaw, R. W. (1992). Psychological models in predicting uptake of prenatal screening. *Psychology and Health*, 6, 13–22.

Marteau, T. M., Kidd, J., Cook, R., Johnston, M., Michie, S., Shaw, R. W. & Slack, J. (1988). Screening for Down's syndrome. *British Medical Journal*, 297, 1469.

Marteau, T. M., Plenicar, M. & Kidd, J. (1993). Obstetricians presenting amniocentesis to pregnant women: practice observed. *Journal of Reproductive and Infant Psychology*, 11, 3–10.

Marteau, T. M. & Riordan, D. C. (1992). Staff attitudes to patients: The influence of causal attributions for illness. *British Journal of Clinical Psychology*, 31, 107–110.

Marteau, T. M., Slack, J., Kidd, J. & Shaw, W. (1992). Presenting a routine screening test in antenatal care: Practice observed. *Public Health*, 106, 131–141.

Marteau, T. M. & Thwaites, S. (1992). Presenting cervical screening in primary and secondary care: Practice observed. Paper presented at the 1992 AUTGP Annual Scientific Meeting, July, 1992.

Marteau, T. M., van Duijn, M. & Ellis, I. (1992). Effects of genetic screening on perceptions of health: A pilot study. *Journal of Medical Genetics*, 24, 24–26.

Marteau, T. M., Walker, P., Giles, J. & Smail, M. (1990). Anxieties in women undergoing colposcopy. *British Journal of Obstetrics and Gynaecology*, 97, 859–861.

Meadows, J., Jenkinson, S., Catalan, J. & Gazzard, B. (1990). Voluntary HIV testing in the antenatal clinic: Differing uptake rates for individual counselling midwives. *AIDS Care*, 2, 229–233.

Meyerowitz, B. E. & Chaiken, S. (1987). The effect of message framing on breast self-examination: Attitudes, intentions and behaviour. *Journal of Personality and Social Psychology*, **52** (3), 500–510.

Minkoff, H. L., Holman, S., Beller, E., Delkie, I., Fishbone, A. & Landesman, S. (1988). SUNY Health Science Centre routinely offered prenatal HIV testing. *New England Journal of Medicine*, **319**, 1018.

Moatti, J-P., Le Gales, C., Seror, V., Papiernik, E. & Henrion, R. (1990). Social acceptability of HIV screening among pregnant women. *Aids Care*, **2** (3), 213–222.

Nathoo, V. (1988). Investigation of non-responders at a cervical screening clinic in Manchester. *British Medical Journal*, **296**, 1041–1042.

National Audit Office (1992). Cervical and Breast Screening in England. London: HMSO.

Norman, P. & Fitter, M. (1989). Intention to attend a health screening appointment: Some implications for general practice. *Counselling Psychology Quarterly*, **2**, 261–272.

Orton, M., Fitzpatrick, R., Fuller, A., Mant, D., Mlynek, C. & Thorogood, M. (1991). Factors affecting women's response to an invitation to attend for a second breast cancer screening examination. *British Journal of General Practice*, **41**, 320–323.

Owens, R. G., Daly, J., Heron, K. & Leinster, S. J. (1987). Psychological and social characteristics of attenders for breast screening. *Psychology and Health*, **1**, 303–313.

Posner, T. & Vessey, M. (1988). *Prevention of Cervical Cancer: The patient's view*. London: King Edward's Hospital Fund for London.

Quilliam, S. (1988). *Positive Smear*. Penguin Books.

Rappaport, J. (1977). *Community Psychology: Values, Research, Action*. New York: Rinehart and Winston.

Rastam, L., Luepker, Russell V. & Pirie, P. L. (1988). Effect of screening and referral on follow-up and treatment of high blood cholesterol levels. *American Journal of Preventive Medicine*, **4**, 244–249.

Reelick, N. F., DeHaes, W. F. M. & Schuurman, J. H. (1984). Psychological side-effects of the mass screening on cervical cancer. *Social Science and Medicine*, **18**, 1089–1093.

Reiser, S. J. (1978). The emergence of the concept of screening for disease. *Milbank Memorial Fund Quarterly*, **56**, 403–425.

Robinson, J., Hibbard, B. M. & Laurence, K. M. (1984). Anxiety during a crisis: Emotional effects of screening for neutral tube defects. *Journal of Psychosomatic Research*, **28**, 163–169.

Rogers, E. M. (1983). *Diffusion of Innovations* (3rd edn). New York: The Free Press.

Ronis, D. L. (1992). Conditional health threats: Health beliefs, decisions and behaviour among adults. *Health Psychology*, **11**, 127–134.

Rosenstock, I. M. (1974). Historical origins of the health belief model. *Health Education Monographs*, **2**, 328–335.

Royal College of Physicians of London (1989). Prenatal Diagnosis and Genetic Screening. Community and Service Implications. September.

Rowley, P. T., Loader, S., Sutera, C. J., Walden, M. & Kozyra, A. (1991). Prenatal Screening for Hemoglobinopathies. III. Applicability of the Health Belief Model. *American Journal of Human Genetics*, **48**, 452–459.

Rubin, E., Frank, M. S., Stanley, R. J., Bernreuter, W. K. & Han, S. Y. (1990). Patient-initiated mobile mammography: Analysis of the patients and the problems. *Southern Medical Journal*, **83**, 178–184.

Rudd, P., Price, M. G., Graham, L. E., Beilstein, B. A., Tarbell, S. J. H., Bacchetti, P. & Fortmann, S. P. (1986). Consequences of worksite hypertension screening. *American Jounal of Medicine*, **80**, 853–60.

Sacks, G. & Marsden, R. (1989). Evaluation of a practice-based programme of health checks: Financial costs and success at risk reduction. *Journal of the Royal College of*

General Practitioners, **39**, 369–372.

Safer, M. (1986). A comparison of screening for disease detection and screening for risk factors. *Health Education Research*, **1**, 131–138.

Sanden, M. L. (1985). Midwives' knowledge of the alpha fetoprotein test. *Journal of Psychosomatic Obstetrics and Gynaecology*, **4**, 23–30.

Sarason, S. B. (1981). *Psychology Misdirected*. New York: Free Press.

Schucker, B., Wittes, J. T., Cutler, J. A., Bailey, K., MacKintosh, D. R., Gordon, D. J. et al. (1987). Change in physician perspective on cholesterol and heart disease. *Journal of the American Medical Association*, **258**, 3521–3531.

Seligman, M. E. P. (1975). Helplessness: *On Depression, Development and Death*. San Francisco: Freeman.

Seydel, E., Taal, E. & Wiegman, O. (1990). Risk-appraisal, outcome and self-efficacy expectancies: Cognitive factors in preventive behaviour related to cancer. *Psychology and Health*, **4**, 99–109.

Shiloh, S. & Sagi, M. (1989). Effect of framing on the perception of genetic recurrence risks. *American Journal of Medical Genetics*, **33**, 130–135.

Silverman, C. (1990). Mandatory premarital HIV testing: The Illinois Experience. *Journal of the American Medical Association*, **263**, 1917.

Skrabanek, P. & McCormick, J. (1989). Follies and Fallacies in Medicine. Glasgow: Tarragan Press.

Smith, R. A., Williams, D. K., Sibert, J. R. & Harper, P. S. (1990). Attitudes of mothers to neonatal screening for Duchenne muscular dystrophy. *British Medical Journal*, **300**, 1112.

Sontag, S. (1983). *Illness as Metaphor*. Harmondsworth: Penguin.

Stamatoyannopoulous, G. (1974). Problems of screening and counselling in the hemoglobinopathies. In A. H. Motulsky, & . J. G. Ebling (Eds). Birth defects: Proceedings of the Fourth International Conference. Vienna, Austria: *Excerpta Medica*, (pp. 268–276).

Statham, H. (1987). Cold Comfort. *The Guardian*, March 24.

Stoate, H. (1989). Can health screening damage your health? *Journal of the Royal College of General Practitioners*, **39**, 193–195.

Thornton, J. & Chamberlain, J. (1989). Cervical screening in the workplace. *Community Medicine*, **11**, 290–298.

Tibben, A., Vliss, M. V. v.d., Niermeijer, M. F. et al. (1990). Testing for Huntington's disease with support for all parties. *Lancet*, **335**, 553.

Tringo, J. L. (1970). The hierarchy of preference toward disability groups. *The Journal of Special Education*, **4**, 295–306.

Turner, G., Robinson, H., Laing, S. & Purvis-Smith, S. (1986). Preventive screening for the fragile X syndrome. *New England Journal of Medicine*, **315**, 607–609.

Turnock, B. J. & Kelly, C. J. (1989). Mandatory premarital testing for human immuno deficiency virus: the Illinois experience. *Journal of the American Medical Association*, **261**, 3415–3418.

Tversky, A. & Kahneman, D. (1981). The framing of decisions and the psychology of choice, *Science*, **211**, 453–458.

Tymstra, T. (1986). False positive results in screening tests: experiences of parents of children screened for congenital hypothyroidism. *Family Practice*, **3**, 883–887.

Tymstra, T. (1989). The imperative character of medical technology and the meaning of "anticipated decision regret". *International Journal of Technology Assessment in Health Care*, **5**, 207–213.

Tymstra, T. (1990). Psychological and social implications of serum cholesterol screening. *International Journal of Risk and Safety in Medicine*, **1**, 29–44.

Tymstra, T. & Bieleman, B. (1987). The psychosocial impact of mass screening for cardiovascular risk factors. *Family Practice*, 4, 287–290.

van-Lith, J. M., Tymstra, T. J. & Visser, G. H. (1989). Attitudes of pregnant women concerning testing for HIV. *Ned-Tijdschr-Geneeskd*, 133, 1237–123?.

Vines, G. (1989). Diet, Drugs and Heart Disease (1989). *New Scientist*, 121, 44–49.

Wagener, J. J. & Taylor, S. E. (1986). What else could I have done? Patients' responses to failed treatment decisions. *Health Psychology*, 5, 481–496.

Waller, D., Agass, M., Mant, D., Coulter, A., Fuller, A. & Jones, L. (1990). Health checks in general practice: another example of inverse care? *British Medical Journal*, 300, 1115–1118.

Watson, E. K., Mayall, E., Chapple, J., Dalziel, M., Harrington, K., Williams, C. & Williamson, R. (1991). Screening for carriers of cystic fibrosis through primary health care services. *British Medical Journal*, 303, 504–507.

Weinstein, N. D. (1984). Why it won't happen to me: Perceptions of risk factors and susceptibility. *Health Psychology*, 3, 431–457.

Weinstein, N. D. (1988). The Precaution Adoption Process. *Health Psychology*, 7, 355–386.

Weinstein, N. D., Sandman, P. M. & Roberts, N. E. (1991). Perceived susceptibility and self-protective behaviour: A field experiment to encourage home radon testing. *Health Psychology*, 10, 25–33.

Wheat, M. E., Kunitz, G. & Fisher, J. (1990). Cancer screening in women: A study of house staff behaviour. *American Journal of Preventive Medicine*, 6, 130–137.

Wilfond, B. S. & Frost, N. (1990). The cystic fibrosis gene: medical and social implications for heterozygote detection. *Journal of the American Medical Association*, 263, 2777–2783.

Wilson, J. M. G. & Junger, G. (1968). Principles and practice of screening for disease. *Public Health Papers*, no. 34, WHO, Geneva.

Winett, R. A. (1985). Ecobehavioural assessment in health life-styles: Concepts and methods. In P. Karoly (Ed), *Measurement Strategies in Health Psychology*. New York: Wiley, (pp. 147–181).

Woo, B., Woo, B., Cook, F., Weisberg, M. & Goldman, L. (1985). Screening procedures in the asymptomatic adult: Comparison of physicians' recommendations, patients' desires, published guidelines, and actual practice. *Journal of the American Medical Association*, 254, 1480–1484.

Woolridge, E. Q. & Murray, R. F. (1989). The health orientation scale: A measure of feeling about sickle cell trait. *Social Biology*, 35, 123–136.

Wortman, C. V. & Brehm, J. W. (1975). Responses to uncontrollable outcomes: An integration of reactance theory and the learned helplessness model. In L. Berkowitz (Ed), *Advances in Experimental Social Psychology*, 8.

Wynder, E. L., Field, O. D. & Haley, N. J. (1986). Population screening for cholesterol determination: A pilot study. *Journal of the American Medical Association*, 256 (20), 2839–2841.

Zeesman, S., Clow, C. L., Cartier, L. & Scriver, C. R. (1984). A private view of heterozygosity: Eight-year follow-up on carriers of Tay-Sachs gene detected by high school screening. *American Journal of Medical Genetics*, 18, 769–778.

Ziffer, A., Song, P. & Mandleblatt, J. (1987). Preventive health practices in a teaching hospital: House staff attitudes and performance on gynaecological screening. *American Journal of Preventive Medicine*, 3, 142–146.

7 Psychological Aspects of Diabetes in Adults

STEWART M. DUNN

Medical Psychology Unit, Department of Psychiatry, Endocrinology and Cancer Medicine, Royal Prince Alfred Hospital and Department of Medicine, University of Sydney, NSW 2006

The field of psychological factors in diabetes is vast and there have been some excellent reviews of the earlier literature (e.g. Fisher et al., 1982). Rather than repeat material which has been presented elsewhere, this review of psychological aspects of diabetes in adults is restricted largely to literature published during the years 1985 to 1990. It is important to clarify at the outset that the earlier classification of diabetes as "juvenile-onset" or "maturity-onset" is now outmoded. While all juvenile-onset patients are dependent on injected insulin to control their disease, patients diagnosed in adulthood may be treated with diet and insulin, diet and oral hypoglycemic agents (tablets), or diet alone. The current classification of diabetes is discussed briefly below, but for a fuller exposition the reader is referred to Harris et al. (1985), Anonymous (1985) and Bradley (1988b).

The literature on psychological aspects of diabetes in adults has expanded rapidly since the early 1970s when major efforts were beginning to be directed at the development and evaluation of diabetes patient education programs. Program evaluation identified two important deficits: first, a lack of information about the psychological variables which intervene between educational activities and metabolic outcomes and, second, a lack of objective instruments for their scientific assessment. The pioneering instruments focussed on the relatively simpler task of measuring diabetes knowledge. As the inadequacies of knowledge for predicting behavioural or metabolic outcomes became apparent, more attention was directed to the measurement of other psychological aspects and to the design of more widely defined interventions.

The ordering of the contents for this review reflects this historical development, beginning with patient education and the gradual expansion of the range of "educational" interventions, and commenting on the earlier and most recent developments in psychometric instrumentation. The literature on

International Review of Health Psychology. Volume 2. Edited by S. Maes, H. Leventhal and M. Johnston
© 1993 John Wiley & Sons Ltd

coping and emotional adjustment is seen as a natural consequence of the failure of formal patient education to impact as expected on the control of diabetes. The research which emerged through the 1980s constitutes potentially the most influential psychological input to date: studies of cognitive deficits associated with diabetes and the impact of stress and its management, and, most recently, the recognition of the special psychosocial needs of the increasing number of adults who can expect to live for many years with the complications of the disease. Finally, we review briefly the large range of interventions which target behavior as the means to more effective self-management and long-term control of diabetes.

THE EPIDEMIOLOGY OF DIABETES

Diabetes mellitus is a disease characterized by high blood sugar levels. The typical symptoms of diabetes are unusual thirst, excessive urination, weight loss and fatigue, but in middle-aged and older people the disease may have no early warning symptoms and the diagnosis is often made in the course of a routine check-up.

The two common forms of diabetes in developed countries are insulin dependent diabetes (IDDM) and non-insulin dependent diabetes (NIDDM); which were previously know respectively as juvenile diabetes and maturity-onset diabetes. IDDM affects predominantly young people with an abrupt and potentially life-threatening onset of symptoms and requires long-term treatment with insulin injections. NIDDM is a more common condition, affecting mostly middle-aged and elderly people and accounts for 80–85% of all diabetic persons. It has a gradual onset and is often treated by diet or tablets, although insulin injections may be necessary to control symptoms in some cases, particularly after many years. People with this form of diabetes are just as prone to develop the same complications as those with IDDM and, being older, may have a greatly increased risk of heart and blood vessel disease.

The exact cause of the disease is unknown. In IDDM an inherited susceptibility is believed to interact with an external "trigger" such as a viral infection. In NIDDM, heredity has a major influence together with "lifestyle factors" including obesity, lack of physical activity and stress (Zimmet, 1982).

The frequency of diabetes is increasing in both developed and undeveloped countries around the world and it is now a common cause of blindness, kidney failure and accelerated atherosclerotic disease. During this century, non-communicable diseases, including NIDDM, have replaced infectious diseases as the major causes of morbidity and mortality (Zimmet, Finch & Dowse, 1990). A Western Australian study showed that almost 50% of all survey subjects with diabetes had clinical evidence of large vessel disease including coronary heart disease, stroke and peripheral vascular disease (Welborn et al., 1984). About 30% of all diabetic patients surveyed had diabetic changes in the eye and, in 13% of cases, these were vision-threatening (Constable et al., 1984).

In the USA, stroke is four times more common in diabetes and lower limb amputation is 10 to 20 times more common, with the majority of these being due to peripheral vascular disease and/or chronic infections in NIDDM (US DHHS, 1985).

DEVELOPING CONCEPTS IN PATIENT EDUCATION

Much of the impetus for research into the psychological aspects of diabetes in adults during the 1980s was a direct consequence of the increased attention directed to quality assurance and program evaluation in diabetes patient education. The initial practice of diabetes patient education was simply an extension of the information transfer approach found in most schools, in which lack of knowledge and skills were presumed to account for the major portion of poor self-care behavior (Anderson, 1986). The early emphasis on information transfer was probably attributable in part to the fact that knowledge is relatively easier to measure and evaluate. Anderson argued that effective diabetes education programs must facilitate changes in the "personal meaning of diabetes".

Inconsistent results from controlled trials of patient education (e.g. Mazzuca et al., 1986; Raz, Soskolne & Stein, 1988), and the failure to demonstrate that increased knowledge leads to improved diabetic control, were partially explained by the untested assumption that intervening behavioral changes do, in fact, take place. It is likely that there is a minimum threshold for diabetes knowledge, beyond which other factors like attitude and motivation are likely to be of much greater importance (Lockington et al., 1988). Clearly education programs may affect many aspects of psychosocial functioning which have the potential ultimately to alter metabolic parameters, but the mechanisms by which such pathways operate are never spelt out and, until recently, a very limited theoretical basis was applied to research in the area. The model of knowledge change is inadequate and inconsistent with observed human behavior and there is a need to develop educational models, as well as treatment regimens, which fit better with human behavior. The lack of theoretical models in the area of patient education contrasts sharply with the theory-driven approach of research to behavioral change in diabetes (described later in this chapter).

Wing et al. (1986) conceptualized the diabetic regimen in terms of a behavioral self-regulation model based on a negative feedback control system. The four components of this system are: (a) blood glucose monitoring behavior; (b) corrective responses (such as insulin administration or sugar ingestion); (c) modification of diet, exercise and stress; and (d) self-reinforcement of self-regulatory behavior. The authors reviewed intervention studies separately for IDDM and NIDDM within the framework provided by this model, and provided positive recommendations for future research in this important area.

Psychosocial function is now recognized as an important outcome for educational intervention. Rubin, Peyrot & Saudek (1989) measured self-care behaviors and emotional well-being for 165 participants in a week-long program. Increased self-esteem and self-efficacy, and reduced anxiety and depression were reported immediately after the program and these improvements were maintained in 124 patients re-assessed after six months. Self-care behaviors and metabolic control were also improved from pre-program levels. Yet, studies such as this are prone to important selection biases and are frequently taken as support for the prescription of patient education as a panacea for all types of problems. Despite these positive results, we have no definitive evidence that families or individuals selected on the basis of identified psychosocial dysfunction, will benefit from educational intervention.

Interventions involving groups offer the dual benefits of more cost-effective use of available resources, and enhancement of attitude change through group interaction (Dunn, 1985; Dunn et al., 1982). Tattersall et al. (1985) reviewed the need for psychosocial support in the treatment of diabetes and proposed group psychotherapy as a neglected alternative. Nevertheless, the majority of psychological interventions have been clinical studies with patients treated individually.

The difficulties of promoting primary and secondary risk reduction behaviors in areas like smoking cessation are just as critical in the adult with diabetes (Ardon et al., 1988). Smoking is a major preventable risk factor contributing to the development of diabetes complications and is associated with impaired metabolic control. A Swedish study of 192 patients with IDDM of at least two years duration found 31% were smokers and the prevalence of smoking increased with increasing HbA1c (Lundman, Asplund & Norberg, 1990). In a case-referent study of 25 matched patients, the odds ratio gave a six-fold likelihood of smoking associated with poor metabolic control. Fowler et al. (1989) concluded that recruitment to their anti-smoking program was best two months after diagnosis. However, the combination of low enrolment, a high drop-out rate and minimal smoking cessation, verified by plasma cotinine levels, led them to conclude that the strategy was not cost-effective in the context of a specialized diabetes centre.

It is essential that changes in diabetes health care delivery systems are evaluated for their impact on psychological function. To take one example, the advent of outpatient education and stabilization programs in the mid-1980s was greeted with considerable enthusiasm because of the perceived benefits in cost-savings and individual heatlh outcomes (Hamman et al., 1985; Hoskins et al., 1985; Ling et al., 1985; Adamson & Gulion, 1986). Little attention was directed initially at psychosocial responses among patients treated in outpatient settings. Gorman, Ludemann & Reichle (1988) corrected this in their study of patient satisfaction with inpatient versus outpatient education. There were no differences on perceived understanding of diabetes management, life satisfaction and the influence of recommendations on future health; but satisfaction was higher among inpatients who felt that more interest and concern were shown towards them and that they were treated more like individuals.

PSYCHOMETRIC INITIATIVES

Perhaps the most critical benefit flowing from the involvement of health psychologists in the planning, delivery and evaluation of interventions in diabetes, was the rapid development of a catalogue of diabetes-specific psychometric tests. Relative to the pioneering work of Etzwiler (1962) and others, the range of measurement tools for diabetes knowledge in the 1990s is highly sophisticated. In addition to several well-standardized instruments designed for comprehensive knowledge assessment (Windsor et al., 1981; Hess & Davis, 1983; Garrard et al., 1987), parallel forms of multiple-choice questionnaires are now available for the serial assessment of knowledge in adult populations (Dunn et al., 1984). Most of the papers cited above report data on content, concurrent, and discriminant validity, reliability, internal consistency, readability and sensitivity to instructional gains. Assal & Aufseesser-Stein (1986) have reviewed several of the published questionnaires of diabetes knowledge.

Attitude assessment instruments have focussed on the cognitive component in terms of diabetes-specific health beliefs and perceived control of diabetes (Bradley et al., 1984; Harris & Linn, 1985; Hurley, 1990; Lewis et al., 1990) and on emotional adjustment to diabetes (Dunn et al., 1986). Emotional adjustment, measured on this latter scale in 128 patients, was correlated with diabetes type, complications status and sex, but not with metabolic control or diabetes duration; consistent relationships were found between adjustment scores and other personality and performance measures in a separate sample of 34 IDDM patients (Szabo-Kallai, Gyimesi & Ivanyi, 1990).

Bradley and Lewis (1990) published diabetes-specific scales designed specifically for tablet-treated NIDDM patients to measure well-being and treatment satisfaction. The three well-being subscales and satisfaction scale had internal reliability (Cronbach alpha) coefficients of 0.70–0.88. Construct validity was demonstrated by consistent relationships between scale scores and degree of overweight and metabolic control.

Quality of life is another important component for comprehensive evaluation of alternative interventions in diabetes care. Quality of life assessment has a rigorous research base in hypertension and clinical oncology but it has only very recently achieved prominence in diabetes. In an 18-month follow-up study, Kaplan et al. (1987) reported improved quality of life on a general measure of well-being in 70 NIDDM volunteers randomized to diet and exercise interventions. The combination group showed steady improvement in quality of life while controls showed modest declines.

The Diabets Control and Complications Trial (DCCT) Research Group published a diabetes quality of life scale for patients with IDDM and reported initial validity and reliability data (DCCT Research Group, 1988). This group is conducting a long-term prospective randomized trial of conventional versus intensive insulin treatment in order to test the hypothesis that near-normal maintenance of blood glucose reduces the incidence of retinopathy and other diabetic complications. The impact of this intensity of treatment on quality of life is seen as a critical issue for its future feasibility.

The emergence of these scales raises the interesting possibility of comparing quality of life in NIDDM and IDDM patients. The first such study (Mayou, Bryant & Turner, 1990) found minimal differences in psychological morbidity with overall little disruption to most areas of life, although 27% of NIDDM patients reported considerable loss of enjoyment and reduction in social life. The pattern of social consequences differed for the two groups with NIDDM patients reporting difficulties with leisure and IDDM patients describing greater impact on work related activities. High fasting plasma glucose was associated with fatigue and leisure difficulties in the NIDDM sample. The authors reported that a nearly one-fifth of their sample of NIDDM women showed considerable distress on the profile of mood states; moreover, psychological state was correlated with social difficulties in this sub-group.

Technological innovation has played a major role in educational intervention and assessment. Interactive, computer-based instruments for the teaching and monitoring of diabetes knowledge (e.g. Meadows et al., 1988) have been followed by computerized behavioural assessment (Schlundt, 1988) and a variety of software programs for calculating insulin dosage or dietary requirements, storage and analysis of diabetes management data, and instruction and simulation in a variety of tasks for patients and professionals (Smith et al., 1988; Sivitz et al., 1989).

EMOTIONAL ADJUSTMENT

Psychological functioning in diabetic patients has been a focus for research for at least the past 50 years. Comparisons between diabetic samples and controls have never satisfactorily resolved the question of whether observed differences are a function of chronic illness in general or specific to diabetes.

Coping strategies in a sample of 151 older patients with chronic illness (principally arthritis and diabetes) were found to vary as a function of age in a study by Felton & Revenson (1987). Older adults were less likely to use emotional expression or information seeking strategies than were middle-aged adults and this relationship persisted after controlling for the effects of physical disability and other illness characteristics. When the disease was perceived as extremely serious, older patients were more likely to minimize the threat of the illness.

Emotional expression, specifically the expression of anger, was studied in hypertensive, diabetic, and non-patient normotensive groups (Deshields, Jenkins & Tait, 1989). Both chronic illness groups reported more anger experience and anger expression than non-patient controls, and diabetic patients revealed a greater level of current anger than hypertensives.

Depression has been proposed as a characteristic of diabetes in adults since at least the nineteenth century. The true incidence and prevalence of depression in diabetes remain unknown. A UK study reported a prevalence rate of 8.5% for both IDDM and NIDDM adult patients with a further 14–19% borderline depression (Robinson, Fuller & Edmeades, 1988). These prevalence rates were similar in a non-diabetic control group. Depression was unrelated to diabetes variables but patients with symptoms were more likely to have current complications.

It has been reported that the symptoms which diabetic patients typically report may be unreliable indicators of poor metabolic control when features suggestive of depression are present. Scores of 114 adult patients on the Beck Depression Inventory were moderately correlated with 9 of 11 diabetes symptoms, including thirst, polyuria and weight loss, but only polyuria was associated with HbAlc (Lustman, Clouse & Carney, 1988). A five-year follow-up of major depression in 37 adults with NIDDM suggested that the course of depression in diabetes is malevolent and possibly more so than the course of depression in the medically well (Lustman, Griffith & Clouse, 1988).

Wing et al. (1990) compared depressive symptomatology in 32 obese NIDDM patients and their obese non-diabetic spouses attending a behavioral weight loss program. Diabetic subjects were reported to have significantly higher scores on 15 of the 20 Beck Depression Inventory (BDI) items. A continuing problem with this line of research, however, has been the confounding of depression symptomatology, in instruments like the Beck Depression Inventory, with symptoms of poor diabetic control (Dunn & Turtle, 1981). Any instrument which relies heavily on somatic symptoms will be inherently biased in favour of over-diagnosing depression in most samples of diabetic patients.

A Danish group (Jensen, 1986) explored the sexual relationships in 51 couples where one partner has IDDM and reported that the couple's acceptance of diabetes was a better predictor of sexual dysfunction than was the presence of peripheral neuropathy in the diabetic partner; sexual dysfunction in women was also predicted by indices of psychological adjustment to diabetes.

The sex- and age-adjusted prevalence of affective and anxiety disorders and drug/alcohol abuse was reported to be higher in a sample of individuals with chronic medical disorders compared to a non-chronic disease sample (Wells, Golding & Burnam, 1989). People with diabetes were reported to have an increased adjusted prevalence of lifetime affective and anxiety disorders, but not substance abuse.

The prevalence of eating disorders in diabetes is controversial. Because the majority of reported cases involve young women with IDDM the topic is strictly beyond the scope of this review. However, there are important implictions from this research for the adult with diabetes whose "normal" dietary intake is being restricted. A mail survey of approximately 385 young women with IDDM found that only 1% of patients met the criteria for lifetime prevalence of anorexia nervosa, 16% for bulimia and 5% for induced glycosuria (Birk & Spencer, 1989). The rates for anorexia and bulimia were at the upper end of the normal range within the general population. The authors concluded that deliberate attempts to deplete the body of glucose as a means of losing weight represent a significant and dangerous problem in young women with diabetes. A smaller survey reported a bulimia prevalence rate of 12% and these authors also noted a positive relationship between bulimic symptoms and reports of hospitalizations, ketoacidosis and pathological scores on the Eating Disorders Inventory (Stancin, Link & Reuter, 1989). Another survey concluded that rapid weight gain following initiation of insulin therapy, and the dietary preoccupation associated with diabetes treatment, may contribute to the development of abnormal eating attitudes in young diabetic women (Steel et al., 1989).

A prospective study of eating attitudes in a cohort of newly-diagnosed IDDM patients noted changes over 12 months of insulin therapy in items on the Eating Attitudes Test and the Eating Disorders Inventory which were consistent with the changes in diet and weight control required for good diabetes management; but the authors also noted changes in body image which could predispose to the development of eating disorders (Steel et al., 1990).

Given the strong evidence of lifestyle disruption associated with diabetes, it is possible that psychosocial factors may be associated with survival, independent of disease control. Davis et al. (1988) completed a study of five-year mortality in a sample of 343 NIDDM patients: the psychosocial impact of diabetes, measured on the Diabetes Educational Profile, was included in a list of five predictor variables (which were, in order of significance, patient age, psychosocial impact, renal function, diet complexity, and history of smoking) which were more closely related to mortality than HbAlc and other more traditional biomedical measures.

COGNITIVE FUNCTION

The large volume of research into cognitive deficits in children with diabetes has reached a degree of consensus on some issues: five years is generally regarded as the critical age at onset below which damage is most likely to occur. The question of cognitive impairment associated with prolonged hyper-glycaemia or hypoglycemia in diabetic adults remains unresolved. The literature was recently reviewed by Perlmuter et al.(1990). Holmes, Koepke & Thompson (1986), using a simple reaction time versus complex choice reaction time paradigm in 24 male subjects, showed that complex cognitive processing is significantly impaired (i.e. longer response latencies) in hypoglycemia, whilst simple motor and perceptual skills were not affected by blood glucose alterations. The performance impairments were independent of diabetes duration and control and without documented neuropathy.

Perlmuter et al. (1987) examined immediate and secondary memory performance in 159 NIDDM patients and 35 non-diabetic controls in two age groups (55–64 and 65–74 years). Digit symbol performance was poorer for older subjects and for diabetic subjects, while serial learning was poorer only for the NIDDM group. Verbal fluency was the same for all groups. The observation that older subjects and NIDDM subjects produced more repetitions in the fluency task was interpreted as evidence for a possible failure to monitor behavior adequately which, in turn, could contribute to cognitive decline. These authors have also shown that triglyceride levels may contribute to decreased short-term memory performance in NIDDM, independent of blood glucose control (Perlmuter et al., 1988).

Reaven et al. (1990) examined 29 healthy, elderly NIDDM subjects and 30 controls. Diabetic subjects performed more poorly on measures of verbal learning, abstract reasoning and complex psychomotor function. Within the diabetic group, poorer control was associated with lower performance on these tasks. However there were no between-group or within-group differences on tasks involving pure motor speed or simple verbal abilities. The authors concluded that even healthy elderly NIDDM patients display significant deficits in processing complex verbal or non-verbal material. Parker et al. (1989) also addressed this issue.

However, longitudinal studies of aging have reported contrary results. Robertson-Tchabo et al. (1986) found no differences on two cognitive performance tests (a measure of non-verbal memory and the Wechsler Adult Intelligence Scale) between men with NIDDM and age-matched controls, and no support for an accelerated cognitive aging effect of diabetes. Several of the longitudinal comparisons in this study extended over 6 and 12 years. The authors compared their study with cross-sectional studies which have reported contrary findings, and suggested that only specific aspects of cognitive functioning are adversely affected by diabetes. They also discussed the possibility that lower SES may be a risk factor in the effect of diabetes on cognitive performance, perhaps by delaying diagnosis and treatment.

STRESS AND STRESS MANAGEMENT IN DIABETES

Stress research in diabetes has addressed two principal hypotheses: (a) stress is a potential causative agent in the onset of the disease, and (b) acute and chronic stress have an adverse effect on metabolic control. Research on chronic stress has concentrated mostly on the impact of life events, while acute stress research has generated a large, clinically-oriented literature regarding the impact of stress management techniques on blood glucose. For a comprehensive review of stress research in diabetes the reader is referred to chapters by Bradley (1988b) and Czyzewski (1988).

Diabetes poses a variety of stresses beginning with the diagnosis of a chronic, life-threatening illness and including the daily tasks of self-management. Many patients who monitor their blood glucose regularly believe that stress does influence their diabetic control (Cox et al., 1984); however the reported direction of influence is not consistent.

One of the earliest observations on the stress response in diabetes was published by Hinkle and Wolf (1952). However, the evidence from empirical studies is conflicting (Carter et al., 1985; Naliboff, Cohen & Sowers, 1985; Kemmer et al., 1986). These studies, using mental arithmetic and public speaking as stressors, showed that blood glucose change was idiosyncratic across subjects but reliable within subjects. Kemmer et al. (1986) concluded that sudden, transient stress is unlikely to disturb metabolic control in patients with IDDM. Yet the skin temperature response to the stress of mental arithmetic was recently proposed as a test for autonomic neuropathy in type 1 diabetes (Locatelli et al., 1989).

Studies which have attempted to reduce stress levels, using relaxation techniques and stress management programs, have met with varied success. Relaxation therapy, principally progressive muscle relaxation (PMR), has consistently been shown to reduce mean blood glucose in NIDDM patients; but the results of such therapy in IDDM are inconsistent.

Surwit and Feinglos (1983) showed improved glucose tolerance, following relaxation training in NIDDM, which could not be accounted for by changes in plasma insulin or catecholamine levels. These authors suggested that central nervous system manipulations have an impact on metabolic control in type II diabetes. Laboratory studies support this hypothesis, as benzodiazepines, given prior to a stress event, have been shown to modify hyperglycemic effects in the ob/ob mouse, an animal model of NIDDM (Surwit et al., 1986). However, these authors were unable to show any effect on glucose tolerance or other indices of diabetic control, using the same technique with 10 poorly controlled IDDM patients (Feinglos, Hastedt & Surwit, 1987). They commented that the response of blood glucose to stress is more difficult to evaluate in IDDM than NIDDM, as the effects of insulin, diet, exercise and non-psychological stressors, such as illness, give rise to a highly variable baseline. Conversely, it may be argued that variability in endogenous insulin levels in NIDDM may contribute to baseline variability in that group beyond that evidenced in IDDM. Another study using PMR obtained a decrease in mean blood glucose in NIDDM patients, but no decrease in mean blood glucose or insulin dose in IDDM (Landis et al., 1985). However, the IDDM sample did record a clinically significant decrease in the range of blood glucose.

Lustman et al. (1983) disputed the belief that stress causes poor diabetic control. They found hyperglycemia itself resulted in a stress-like state, with elevated cortisol, glucagon, heart rate, frontalis electromyograms and skin conductance levels; this implied that hyperglycemia-induced sympathetic nervous system arousal made patients more susceptible to environmental stress, thus setting up a positive feedback cycle. The important role of sympathetic nervous system functioning is supported by Surwit and Feinglos

(1984), who showed exaggerated suppression of insulin secretion and profound hyperglycemia in response to adrenalin in animal models of NIDDM.

There is much evidence to suggest that psychological stress adversely affects diabetic control, particularly in the case of NIDDM, and various mechanisms have been proposed, but none convincingly proven, in human diabetic subjects. Interest in this area has led to many attempts at improving diabetic control by lowering stress levels, but as yet no large, well controlled studies have been carried out. The reasons for this failure lie in the difficulties of quantifying psychological stress, of controlling for the many confounding variables, such as insulin dose, diet and exercise, and of developing adequate control procedures.

THE PATIENT WITH DIABETIC COMPLICATIONS

Complications are an unpleasant fact of diabetes although patients generally do want information about this aspect. In view of the traumatic impact of diabetic complications affecting almost all organ systems of the body, it is surprising to find very little research in this area. A survey of 845 patients throughout Italy (Porta et al., 1988) found most interest in complications (84%), diet (74%), control (63%), intercurrent illnesses (61%) and inheritance (59%). Yet the regular injunction to strive for normal blood glucose levels as a means to minimize or avoid the debilitating complications of diabetes is not based on sound scientific data (hence the need for prospective studies like the Diabetes Control and Complications Trial). As recently as 1988, an international expert concluded thus:

> Some patients under apparently good control or with only impaired glucose tolerance develop severe complications rapidly, while others after decades of poor control are left without complications ... There is no indication that *normalization* of blood glucose is necessary for the prevention of the late diabetic complications (Deckert, 1988).

In 1985 the Joslin Group (Jacobson, Rand & Hauser, 1985) reported data suggesting that the onset of proliferative retinopathy (severe, ultimately vision-threatening damage to the retina) represents a life crisis which renders metabolic control more sensitive to additional life stress, and that the association between metabolic control and life stress is not found among patients whose diabetes is more stable. Sjoberg et al. (1988) noted an association between residual insulin secretion and lower HbAlc with lower "perceived" risk of kidney disease.

Bernbaum, Albert & Duckro (1988) compared patients with stable visual impairment and patients with fluctuating and transitional impairment and found the stable group performed better relative to the transitional group on the MMPI and the Zung Depression Scale. Scores of both groups were significantly improved following a 12-week rehabilitation program offering physical exercise training, diabetes self-management skills for the visually impaired, and group support. The authors suggested that such interventions may be of most clinical benefit early in the course of vision loss associated with diabetic retinopathy (Bernbaum et al., 1989).

BEHAVIOURAL MONITORING OF DIABETES CONTROL

Interest in the potential for training subjects to discriminate different levels of blood glucose is intense. Gross, Magalnick & Delcher (1985) showed that a small sample of patients could improve the accuracy of their blood glucose estimation substantially, although no effects were shown on metabolic control. Cox et al. (1989) trained young IDDM patients to improve their estimation of blood glucose levels with a resultant 31% reduction in dangerous estimation errors; however trained subjects' estimations were still significantly less accurate than machine-monitoring.

In view of these promising results, a study by Jacobson et al. (1990) suggests an important qualification. These authors compared patients in chronically poor control with those in good control. There were no differences in diabetes knowledge, self-esteem or psychiatric symptomatology, but patients in chronic poor control reported feeling physically best at higher blood glucose levels and had a higher threshold for hyperglycemic symptoms. The authors suggest that these results may indicate post hoc rationalization or unreliable beliefs, but they may also be accurate perceptions of physical symptom experiences.

Another area for behavioral intervention which continues to attract research interest is SMBG, or self-monitoring of blood glucose (Wysocki, 1989). Wing et al. (1985) demonstrated, with their objective, marked-item measure of SMBG compliance, that subjects' self-reports significantly overestimated actual compliance rates. Mazze et al., in research with blood glucose monitoring equipment modified by the addition of a memory chip (unknown to the patient), confirmed the unreliability of patient-generated data (1984), and showed that this performance could be improved by appropriately-designed intervention (1986).

Technological advances like the memory-modified blood glucose meter have the potential to improve considerably the quality and accessibility of SMBG data, even in informed older patients (Gilden et al., 1990). A randomized study using memory meters with microcomputer interface found no between-group differences in HbA1c, SMBG testing behavior or dosage self-adjustment; however, experimental group subjects (who used the meter/microcomputer system) reported better understanding of their treatment, and an increased perception of the importance of monitoring and of the quality of interaction with their physician (Marrero et al., 1989). Morrish et al. (1989) found no significant differences in blood glucose, HbA1c or fructosamine between IDDM patients randomized to computer-aided analysis of SMBG or to conventional diary recording.

Hoskins et al. (1988) argued that SMBG records are such an important source of clinical data for management decision-making that different educational models must be developed and evaluated for their impact on SMBG compliance. Thirty-four patients, unaware of the memory capacity of the glucose meters, were randomized to one of three experimental groups: mutual decision-making, didactic teaching, and authoritarian instruction. The results were contrary to the hypothesis of higher compliance in the mutual decision-making group. Higher compliance was predicted by higher perceived intelligence (rated subjectively by the nurse educator) and the patient's private health insurance status; experimental group assignment was not significant. However, the potential for mutual decision-making approaches to improve SMBG compliance should not be dismissed on the basis of this study. Patients were exposed to only one trial of mutual decision-making at the first visit and subsequent contacts were identical for all three groups.

Unfortunately, technologies like SMBG, which offer profound advantages in the monitoring of disease control, often have psychological consequences. Learned helplessness refers to the psychological state of motivational loss, emotional disturbance, and cognitive impairment, which is induced in any person exposed repeatedly to an uncontrollable and unpleasant situation (Seligman, 1975). Diabetes poses many such situations, and SMBG is a common example which has been linked to the onset and maintenance of learned helplessness (Dunn, 1987) and to the development of a specific "neurosis" (Beer, Lawson & Watkins, 1989).

BEHAVIOR CHANGE IN DIABETES

Compliance has been defined as the extent to which a person's behavior coincides with medical advice. There is no doubt that patient-generated data on compliance are notoriously unreliable, but such data are often a predictable response to the context and the individual participants (Dunn, 1989) and it has been demonstrated that patients will admit to non-compliance under conditions of anonymity (Davis, Strong & Bloom, 1988). A meta-analysis of diabetes compliance (Nagasawa et al., 1990) concluded, from the 26 studies surveyed, that emotional stability, motivation, perceived benefit and supportive structures were consistently correlated positively with compliance, while perceived barriers and negative social environments were correlated negatively.

Specific models have been proposed to describe behaviour changes in diabetes in terms which are extensively grounded within the health psychology literature. The Health Belief Model continues to generate data suggesting that diabetes-specific beliefs and cognitions are a potent influence on compliance, and (possibly) directly on metabolic control (Bradley et al., 1984; Harris & Linn, 1985). Rosenstock (1985) reviewed studies on patient compliance and proposed a comprehensive framework based on the Health Belief Model expanded to include the learning theory concept of perceived self-efficacy.

Long-term maintenance of changed behavior, in this framework, is addressed in terms of the relapse prevention model derived from social learning theory.

The Marlatt and Gordon model of relapse was tested in 89 diabetic adults who were interviewed regarding their most recent dietary violations (Kirkley & Fisher, 1988). Most non-adherence situations fitted with the predictions of the model, occurring in a limited range of high-risk situations. However, approximately one-third of the lapses did not fit into the coding schema and these were errors of omission rather than errors of commission. The authors concluded that most episodes of dietary non-adherence in diabetes should be interpreted as intermittent lapses that typically do not develop further.

The Fishbein-Ajzen theory of human behavior asserts that a person's intention is the primary determinant of action, and that attitudes and social norms are precursors of intention. The predictive value of the theory was assessed in relation to self-care behaviors in a sample of 558 insulin-treated diabetic patients (de Weerdt et al., 1990). Attitudes were found to be the most important predictors of behavior, with adequate knowledgte and a low orientation on the powerful others health locus of control scale predicting a positive attitude.

Wilson and Glasgow, and their colleagues, have published several articles on aspects of compliance in diabetes with particular reference to diabetes-specific social learning variables (Wilson et al., 1986; Glasgow, McCaul & Schafer, 1986; Glasgow & Toobert, 1988; Glasgow, Toobert et al., 1989). They assessed four different self-care behaviors in 184 NIDDM patients: medication taking, glucose testing, diet, and exercise. Multiple measures were collected of psychosocial variables including knowledge, stress, depression, anxiety, diabetes-specific health beliefs, and social support, and metabolic control was measured by HbA1c. They concluded that approximately 25% of the variance in self-care behaviors can be explained by psychosocial and demographic variables, but psychosocial variables were not significant predictors of diabetic control. A value of 25% variance translates to a substantial clinical effect size (Wolf & Cornell, 1986). The diabetes-specific measures were the most consistent and strongest predictors of self-care behavior across all areas studied.

Another study (Kirkley & Fisher, 1988) classified patient nonadherence to diet and concluded that most episodes represent intermittent lapses (errors of omission) which do not typically develop into full relapse. IDDM patients were more likely to lapse in situations characterized by negative emotions than were NIDDM patients. Finally, Uhlmann et al. (1988) studied the relationship between the extent to which adult IDDM patients' needs are met in the consultation and their compliance, glycemic control and several other health care outcomes. Patients whose needs were fulfilled were more satisfied, rated themselves as in better health and had fewer hypos, and were more reliable at self-injection, although the improved control in fulfilled patients did not reach statistical significance.

The interpretation of non-compliance has altered during the 1980s and the emphasis of responsibility is shifting away from the patient alone to other members of the health care team and the quality of the patient–professional interaction. The understandable frustration that non-compliance arouses in clinicians was classified by Heszen-Klemens (1987), who showed that two-thirds of doctors react with frustration and ego-defensive responses and only one-third react with task-oriented responses. Some authors attribute their failure to improve diabetic control with new technologies to patient non-compliance rather than to a flaw in the therapeutic approach (e.g. Belmonte et al., 1988). The expectation that human behavior should measure up to technology, and not vice versa, is endemic: a better model for compliance in adults with diabetes adopts human behavior as the independent variable and technology as the dependent variable.

Communication problems in the consultation are confirmed by the finding that physicians are not good at estimating non-compliance or other difficulties with self-management in their patients. For example, Fowler et al. (1987) assessed the management skills of 125 patients, 50 of whom had been referred by physicians or other staff specifically because of subjectively-assessed coping difficulties or compliance problems. The remaining 75 patients were selected from the clinic waiting list by random number generation and studied at the same time. The performance of referred patients was no different from that of the randomly selected group in insulin dosage and technique, urinalysis technique, understanding of sick day management principles, and recognition and treatment of hypoglycemia. Other research (Pendleton, House & Parker, 1987) identified clear discrepancies between the ways patients view difficulties complying with behavioral aspects of diabetes treatment and the views of their physicians.

The relationship between the diabetic patient and other members of the health care team is at the core of diabetes care. D'Eramo-Melkus and Demas (1989) suggest that poor compliance may be partially a result of problems in doctor–patient communication. A 53% discrepancy rate was found between patients and their doctors in the area of overall treatment goals with similar rates for the specific goals of weight loss and blood glucose levels.

A small body of research in the area of diabetes patient–professional communication is developing and the next decade will bring a substantial increase in our understanding of the factors which contribute to the effectiveness of this component of diabetes care. Greenfield et al. (1988) randomized 59 patients to either non-intervention controls or a 20-minute pre-consultation session designed to increase patient involvement in medical decision-making. Mean post-intervention HbA1c levels were significantly lower in the experimental group and they were shown to be twice as effective as controls in eliciting information from the physician. Experimental patients also reported fewer function limitations.

Gillespie and Bradley (1988) investigated the level of congruence in causal attributions and perceived control of diabetes between doctors and patients. Adult patients with poorly controlled insulin-treated diabetes were assigned to one of three types of clinic consultations: (a) routine consultation; (b) explicit negotiation and agreement between doctor and patient of the nature of the problem; and (c) the latter plus agreement on the causes of the problems. The experimental manipulations were successful in improving problem and attribution congruence across the groups. However, there were no clinical implications of this improved congruence: metabolic control improved in all three groups after six weeks but there were no between-group differences. Satisfaction with the consultation was unchanged. The authors concluded their results support an increasing body of evidence indicating that biomedical and health outcomes, including diabetic control, are multiply determined.

Finally, the crucial mind–body relationship in diabetes justifies a brief comment by way of conclusion. There are many potential dimensions for the impact of psychosocial factors on diabetes control, extending from the individual level of neuropsychological, cognitive, affective and behavioral events through to interactions within the family, work and social environments. In many of these areas prescriptive models are being proposed which will lead to more co-ordinated and directed research. Recent developments have already gone some way to redressing the problems of a lack of validated psychometric instruments, the difficulties involved in measuring specific function as distinct from generalized trait, and the need for solid theoretical foundations to support and integrate research (Bradley, 1988; Dunn & Turtle, 1988). The question of how much variance in diabetic control is due to psychosocial factors is confounded with the related question of how much of this variance is amenable to personal control. In psychosocial impact studies from 1985–1988, using standardized instruments, the 95% confidence interval for the mean effect size on diabetes control varied between 13% and 37% (Dunn, 1989). Despite the fact that the evidence for the impact of some psychological factors on diabetes control is increasingly consistent, there remains significant individual variation which it is critical to address (Bradley, 1988b).

EPILOGUE

The frequency of diabetes is increasing in both developed and undeveloped countries around the world. It is a common cause of blindness, kidney failure and accelerated atherosclerotic disease. NIDDM is the most common form of diabetes, accounting for 80–85% of all diabetic persons, and people with this form of diabetes may have a greatly increased risk of heart and blood vessel disease. Diabetes has generated a large volume of high-quality research in pure and applied psychology, mostly directed at the more exotic IDDM form, and it is now critical that similar attention be directed to the multiple issues affecting this large and expanding NIDDM majority of the diabetic population. The last two decades of health psychology applied to diabetes have seen a rapid transition from the earlier focus on more proscribed areas like educational evaluation, knowledge assessment, and psychological adjustment in juveniles, towards the complexities of primary and secondary prevention, and intervention studies with adult populations. Almost all disciplines within psychology are relevant to the diagnosis and treatment of diabetes and, ultimately, to its prevention.

ACKNOWLEDGMENT

The author is grateful for the support of the National Health and Medical Research Council of Australia during the preparation of this chapter.

REFERENCES

Adamson, T. E. & Gulion, D. S. (1986). Assessment of diabetes continuing medical education. *Diabetes Care*, **9** (1), 11.

Anderson, R. M. (1986). The personal meaning of having diabetes: Implications for patient behavior and education or kicking the bucket theory. *Diabetic Medicine.*, **3**, 85.

Anonymous (1985). Diabetes Mellitus. Report of WHO Study Group. Geneva, WHO, TRS 727.

Ardon, M., McFarlane, I. A., Robinson, C. et al. (1988). Anti-smoking advice for young diabetic smokers: Is it a waste of breath? *Diabetic Medicine*, **5** (7), 667–670.

Assal, J-Ph & Aufseesser-Stein, M. (1986). Patient education in diabetes therapy. In: *Diabetes Annual/3*. K.G.M.M. Alberti & L. P. Krall (Eds). Elsevier, Amsterdam & New York- Oxford: 156.

Beer, S. F., Lawson, C. & Watkins, P. J. (1989). Neurosis induced by home monitoring of blood glucose concentrations. *British Medical Journal*, **298**, 362.

Belmonte, M. M., Schiffrin, A., Dufresne, J. et al. (1988). Impact of SMBG on control of diabetes as measured by HbA1c. 3-year survey of a juvenile IDDM clinic. *Diabetes Care*, **11** (6), 484–488.

Bernbaum, M., Albert, S. G., Brusca, S. R. et al. (1989). A model clinical program for patients with diabetes and vision impairment. *Diabetes Educator*, **15** (4), 325–330.

Bernbaum, M., Albert, S. G. & Duckro, P. N. (1988). Psychosocial profiles in patients with visual impairment due to diabetic retinopathy. *Diabetes Care*, **11** (7), 551–557.

Birk, R. & Spencer, M. L. (1989). The prevalence of anorexia nervosa, bulimia, and induced glycosuria in IDDM females. *Diabetes Educator*, **15** (4), 336–341.

Bradley, C. (1988a). Psychological factors and metabolic control: time for collaboration [letter]. *Diabetic Medicine*, **5** (7), 710–711.

Bradley, C. (1988b). Stress and diabetes. In: S. Fisher & J. Reason (Eds), *Handbook of Life Stress, Cognition and Health*. London: John Wiley.

Bradley, C., Brewin, C., Gamsu, D. S., & Moses, J. L. (1984). Development of scales to measure perceived control of diabetes mellitus and diabetes-related health beliefs. *Diabetic Medicine*, **1** (3), 213–218.

Bradley, C. & Lewis, K. S. (1990). Measures of psychological well-being and treatment satisfaction developed from the responses of people with tablet-treated diabetes. *Diabetic Medicine*, **7** (5), 445–451.

Carter, W. R., Gonder-Frederick, L. A., Cox, D. J., Clarke, W. L. & Scott, D. (1985).

Effect of stress on blood glucose in IDDM. *Diabetes Care*, 8 (4), 411–412.

Constable, I. J., Knuiman, M., Welborn, T. A., Cooper, R. L., Stanton, K., McCann, V. & Gross, G. C. (1984). Assessing the risk of diabetic retinopathy. *American Journal of Ophthalmology*, 97, 53–61.

Cox, D. J., Gonder-Frederick, L. A., Lee, J. H., Julian, D. M., Carter, W. R. & Clarke, W. L. (1989). Effects and correlates of blood glucose awareness training among patients with IDDM. *Diabetes Care*, 12 (5), 313–318.

Cox, D. J., Taylor, A. G., Nowacek, G. et al. (1984). The relationship between psychological stress and insulin-dependent diabetic blood glucose control: preliminary investigations. *Health Psychology*, 3 (1), 63–75.

Czyzewski, D. (1988). Stress management in diabetes mellitus. In: M. Russell (Ed). *Stress management for chronic disease*. Oxford: Pergamon, 270–289.

D'Eramo-Melkus, G. A. & Demas, P. (1989). Patient perceptions of diabetes treatment goals. *Diabetes Educator*, 15 (5), 440–443.

Davis, W. K., Hess, G. E., Hiss, R. G. (1988). Psychosocial correlates of survival in diabetes. *Diabetes Care*, 11 (7), 538–545.

Davis, T. M. E., Strong, J. A. & Bloom, S. R. (1988). Compliance in diabetes mellitus: A self-assessment study. *Practical Diabetes*, 5 (4), 170–172.

DCCT Research Group (1988). Reliability and validity of a diabetes quality-of-life measure for the diabetes control and complications trial (DCCT). *Diabetes Care*, 11 (9), 725–732.

Deckert, T. (1988). In K. G. M. M. Alberti & L. P. Krall (Eds). *Diabetes Annual/4*: Elsevier, Excerpta Medica, 496–518.

Deshields, T. L., Jenkins, J. O. & Tait, R. C. (1989). The experience of anger in chronic illness: A preliminary investigation. *International Journal of Psychiatry in Medicine*, 19 (3), 299–309.

de Weerdt, I., Visser, A. P., Kok, G. & van der Veen, E. A. (1990). Determinants of active self-care behavior of insulin treated patients with diabetes: Implications for diabetes education. *Social Science and Medicine*, 30 (5), 605–615.

Dunn, S. M. (1986). Reactions to educational techniques: Coping strategies for diabetes and learning. *Diabetic Medicine*, 3, 419–429.

Dunn, S. M. (1987). Psychological issues in diabetes management: I. Blood glucose monitoring and learned helplessness. *Practical Diabetes*, 4 (3), 109–111.

Dunn, S. M. (1989). Overview—psychosocial impact on diabetes control. 13th Congress, International Diabetes Federation, Sydney. In: R. Larkins, P. Zimmet & D. Chisholm (Eds). *Diabetes*, 1988. Elsevier, 1019–1020.

Dunn, S. M., Bryson, J. M., Hoskins, P. L. et al. (1984). Development of the diabetes knowledge scales (DKN): Forms DKNA, DKNB and DKNC. *Diabetes Care*, 7, 36–41.

Dunn, S. M., Hoskins, P. L., Alford, J. B. & Turtle, J. R. (1982). Cost-benefit analysis of audiovisual techniques in diabetes education. Proceedings, International Diabetes Federation. *Excerpta Medica*, Amsterdam- Oxford, 577, 17.

Dunn, S. M., Smartt, H. H., Beeney, L. J. & Turtle, J. R. (1986). Measurement of emotional adjustment in diabetic patients: Validity and reliability of the ATT39. *Diabetes Care*, 9, 480–489.

Dunn, S. M. & Turtle, J. R. (1981). The myth of the diabetic personality. *Diabetes Care*, 4 (6), 640–646.

Dunn, S. M. & Turtle, J. R. (1988). Education. In: K. G. M. M. Alberti & L. P. Krall (Eds), *Diabetes Annual/4*. Elsevier, Excerpta Medica: 144–161.

Etzwiler, D. D. (1962). What the juvenile diabetic knows about his disease. *Pediatrics*, 29, 135.

Feinglos, M. N., Hastedt, P. & Surwit, S. (1987). Effects of relaxation therapy on patients with Type I diabetes mellitus. *Diabetes Care*, **10** (1), 72–74.

Felton, B. J. & Revenson, T. A. (1987). Age differences in coping with chronic illness. *Psychology and Aging*, **2** (2), 164–170.

Fisher, E. B., Delamater, A. M., Bertelson, A. D. & Kirkley, B. G. (1982). Psychological factors in diabetics and its treatment. *Journal of Consulting and Clinical Psychology*, **50** (6), 993–1003.

Fowler, P. M., Hoskins, P. L., Dunn, S. M. et al. (1987). Factors determining the self-management skills of diabetic patients. *Practical Diabetes*, **4** (2), 63–65.

Fowler, P. M., Hoskins, P. L., McGill, M. et al. (1989). Anti-smoking program for diabetic patients: The agony and the ecstasy. *Diabetic Medicine*, **6** (8), 698–702.

Garrard, J., Joynes, J. O., Mullen, L. et al. (1987). Psychometric study of patient knowledge test. *Diabetes Care*, **10**, 500.

Gilden, J. L., Casia, C., Hendryx, M. & Singh, S. P. (1990). Effects of self-monitoring of blood glucose on quality of life in elderly diabetic patients. *Journal of the American Geriatric Society*, **38** (5), 511–515.

Gillespie, C. R. & Bradley, C. (1988). Causal attributions of doctor and patients in a diabetes clinic. *British Journal of Clinical Psychology*, **27** (1), 67–76.

Glasgow, R. E., McCaul, K. D. & Schafer, L. C. (1986). Barriers to regimen adherence in persons with insulin-dependent diabetes. *Journal of Behavioural Medicine*, **9**, 65.

Glasgow, R. E. & Toobert, D. J. (1988). Social environment and regimen adherence among type II diabetic patients. *Diabetes Care*, **11** (5), 377–386.

Glasgow, R. E., Toobert, D. J., Riddle, M. et al. (1989). Diabetes-specific social learning variables and self-care behaviors among persons with type II diabetes. *Health Psychology*, **8** (3), 285–303.

Gorman, A. R., Ludemann, M. A. & Reichle, S. C. (1988). Comparing satisfaction levels of inpatients and outpatients with a diabetes teaching program. *Patient Education and Counseling*, **12** (2), 121–129.

Greenfield, S., Kaplan, S. H., Ware, J. E. et al. (1988). Patients' participation in medical care: Effects on blood sugar control and quality of life in diabetes. *Journal of General Internal Medicine*, **3** (5), 458–463.

Gross, A. M., Magalnick, L. J. & Delcher H. K. (1985). Blood glucose discrimination training and metabolic control in insulin-dependent diabetics. *Behavior Research & Therapy*, **23** (5), 507.

Hamman, R. F., Cook, M., Keefer, S. et al. (1985). Medical care patterns at the onset of insulin-dependent diabetes mellitus: Association with severity and subsequent complications. *Diabetes Care*, **8** (supplement 1), 94.

Harris, M. I. et al. (1985). International criteria for the diagnosis of diabetes and impaired glucose tolerance. *Diabetes Care*, **8**, 562–567.

Harris, R. & Linn, M. W. (1985). Health beliefs, compliance, and control of diabetes mellitus. *Southern Medical Journal*, **8**, 562–567.

Hess, G. E. & Davis, W. K. (1983). The validation of a diabetes patient knowledge test. *Diabetes Care*, **6**, 591.

Heszen-Klemens, I. (1987). Patients' non-compliance and how doctors manage this. *Social Science and Medicine*, **24** (5), 409–416.

Hinkle, L. E. Jr. & Wolf, S. (1952). Importance of life stress in course and management of diabetes mellitus. *Journal of the American Medical Association*, **148**, 513–520.

Holmes, C. S., Koepke, K. M. & Thompson, R. G. (1986). Simple versus complex performance impairments at three blood glucose levels. *Psychoneuroendocrinology*, **11**, 353.

Hoskins, P., Alford, J., Fowler, P. et al. (1985). Outpatient stabilization program—an innovative approach in the management of diabetes. *Diabetes Research*, **2** (2), 85.

Hoskins, P. L., Alford, J. B., Handelsman, D. J. et al. (1988). Comparison of different models of diabetes care on compliance with self-monitoring of blood glucose by memory glucometer. *Diabetes Care,* **11** (9), 719–724.

Hurley, A. C. (1990). The health belief model: Evaluation of a diabetes scale. *Diabetes Educator,* **16** (1), 44–48.

Jacobson, A. M., Adler, A. G., Wolfsdorf, J. I., Anderson, B. & Derby, L. (1990). Psychological characteristics of adults with IDDM. Comparison of patients in poor and good glycemic control. *Diabetes Care,* **13** (4), 375–381.

Jacobson, A. M., Rand, L. I. & Hauser, S. T. (1985). Psychologic stress and glycaemic control: A comparison of patients with and without proliferative diabetic retinopathy. *Psychosomatic Medicine,* **47** (4), 372–381.

Jensen, S. B. (1986). The natural history of sexual dysfunction in diabetic women. A 6-year follow-up study. *Acta Medica Scandinavica,* **219** (1), 73.

Kaplan, R. M., Hartwell, S. L., Wilson, D. K. & Wallace, J. P. (1987). Effects of diet and exercise interventions on control and quality of life in non-insulin-dependent diabetes mellitus. *Journal of General Internal Medeicine,* **2**, 220–227.

Kemmer, F. W., Bisping, R., Steingruber, H. J. et al. (1986). Psychological stress and metabolic control in patients with Type I diabetes mellitus. *New England Journal of Medicine,* **314** (17), 1078–1084.

Kirkley, B. G. & Fisher, E. B. (1988). Relapse as a model of nonadherence to dietary treatment of diabetes. *Health Psychology,* **7** (3), 221–230.

Landis, B., Jovanovic, L., Landis, E. et al. (1985). Effect of stress reduction on dialy glucose range in previously stabilized insulin-dependent diabetic patients. *Diabetes Care,* **8** (6), 624–626.

Lewis, K. S., Jennings, A. M., Ward, J. D. & Bradley, C. (1990). Health belief scales developed specifically for people with tablet-treated type 2 diabetes. *Diabetic Medicine,* **7** (2), 148–155.

Ling, P., Lovesay, J. M., Mayon-White, V. A. et al. (1985). The diabetic clinic dinosaur is dying: Will diabetic day units evolve? *Diabetic Medicine,* **2** (3), 163.

Locatelli, A., Franzetti, I., Lepore, G., Maglio, M. L., Gaudio, E., Caviezel, F. & Pozza, G. (1989). Mental arithmetic stress as a test for evaluation of diabetic sympathetic autonomic neuropathy. *Diabetic Medicine,* **6** (6), 490–495.

Lockington, T. J., Farrant, S., Meadows, K. A. et al. (1988). Knowledge profile and control in diabetic patients. *Diabetic Medicine,* **5** (4), 381–386.

Lundman, B. M., Asplund, K. & Norberg, A. (1990). Smoking and metabolic control in patients with insulin-dependent mellitus. *Journal of Internal Medicine,* **227** (2), 101–106.

Lustman, P. J., Clouse, R. E. & Carney, R. M. (1988). Depression and the reporting of diabetes symptoms. *International Journal of Psychiatry in Medicine.* **18** (4), 295–303.

Lustman, P. J., Griffith, L. S. & Clouse, R. E. (1988). Depression in adults with diabetes. Results of 5-yr follow-up study. *Diabetes Care,* **11** (8), 605–612.

Lustman, P. J., Skor, D. A., Carney, R. M., Santiago, J. V. & Cryer, P. E. (1983). Stress and diabetic control [letter]. *Lancet,* **1** (8324), 588.

Marrero, D. G., Kronz, K. K., Golden, M. P., Wright, J. C., Orr, D. P. & Fineberg, N. S. (1989). Clinical evaluation of computer-assisted self-monitoring of blood glucose system. *Diabetes Care,* **12** (5), 345–350.

Mayou, R., Bryant, B. N. & Turner, R. (1990). Quality of life in non-insulin-dependent diabetes and a comparison with insulin-dependent diabetes. *Journal of Psychosomatic Research,* **34** (1), 1–11.

Mazze, R. S., Pasmantier, R., Murphy, J. A. & Shamoon, H. (1986). Self-monitoring of capillary blood glucose: Changing the performance of individuals with diabetes. *Diabetes Care,* **8** (3), 207.

Mazze, R. S., Shamoon, H., Pasmantier, R. et al. (1984). Reliability of blood glucose monitoring by patients with diabetes mellitus. *American Journal of Medicine*, 77, 211.

Mazzuca, S. A., Moorman, N. H., Wheeler, M. L. et al. (1986). The Diabetes Education Study: A controlled trial of the effects of diabetes patient education. *Diabetes Care*, 9 (1), 1–10.

Meadows, K. A., Fromson, B., Gillespie, C. et al. (1988). Development, validation and application of computer-linked knowledge questionnaires in diabetes education. *Diabetic Medicine*, 5 (1), 61–67.

Morrish, N. J., Cohen, D. L., Hicks, B. & Keen, H. (1989). A controlled study of the effect of computer-aided analysis of home blood monitoring on blood glucose control. *Diabetic Medicine*, 6 (7), 591–594.

Nagasawa, M., Smith, M. C., Barnes, J. H. & Fincham, J. E. (1990). Meta-analysis of correlates of diabetes patients' compliance with prescribed medications. *Diabetes Education*, 16 (3), 192–200.

Naliboff, B. D., Cohen, M. J. & Sowers, J. D. (1985). Physiological and metabolic responses to brief stress in non-insulin dependent diabetic and control subjects. *Journal of Psychosomatic Research*, 29 (4), 367–374.

Parker, L., Kim, C. L., Hess, E., Rabelo, J. & Charter, R. (1989). Does moderate hyperglycemia adversely affect mentation? [letter]. *Diabetes Care*, 12 (10), 750–751.

Pendleton, L., House, W. C. & Parker L. E. (1987). Physicians' and patients' views of problems of compliance with diabetes regimens. *Public Health Reports*, 102, 21.

Perlmuter, L. C., Nathan, D. M., Goldfinger, S. H., Russo, P. A., Yates, J. & Larkin, M. (1988). Triglyceride levels affect cognitive function in noninsulin-dependent diabetics. *Journal of Diabetic Complications*, 2 (4), 210–213.

Perlmuter, L. C., Tun, P., Sizer, N., McGlinchey, R. E. & Nathan, D. M. (1987). Age (and diabetes-related changes in verbal fluency. *Experimental Aging Research*, 13 (1), 9–14.

Perlmuter, L. C. et al. (1990). Cognitive function in non-insulin-dependent diabetes. In C. S. Holmes (Ed), *Neuropsychological and Behavioral Aspects of Diabetes*. London: Springer Verlag.

Porta, M., Rudelli, G., Colarizi, R. et al. (1988). A survey of patients acceptability of diabetes education programs in Italy. *Diabete Metabolisms*, 14 (3), 247–252.

Raz, I., Soskolne, V. & Stein, P. (1988). Influence of small-group education sessions on glucose homeostasis in NIDDM. *Diabetes Care*, 11 (1), 67–71.

Reaven, G. M., Thompson, L. W., Nahum, D. & Haskins, E. (1990). Relationship between hyperglycemia and cognitive function in older NIDDM patients. *Diabetes Care*, 13 (1), 16–21.

Robertson-Tchabo, E. A., Arenberg, D., Tobin, J. D. & Plotz, J. B. (1986). A longitudinal study of cognitive performance in noninsulin dependent (Type II) diabetic men. *Experimental Gerontology*, 21, 459.

Robinson, N., Fuller, J. H. & Edmeades, S. P. (1988). Depression and diabetes. *Diabetic Medicine*, 5 (3), 268–274.

Rosenstock, I. M. (1985). Understanding and enhancing patient compliance with diabetic regimens. *Diabetes Care*, 8 (6), 610.

Rubin, R. R., Peyrot, M. & Saudek, C. D. (1989). Effect of diabetes education on self-care, metabolic control, and emotional well-being. *Diabetes Care*, 12 (10), 673–679.

Schlundt, D. G. (1988). Computerized behavioral assessment of dietary compliance in IDDM patients. *Diabetes Educator*, 14 (6), 567–570.

Seligman, M. E. (1975). *Helplessness*. San Francisco: W. H. Freeman.

Sivitz, W. I. et al. (1989). Computer-assisted instruction in intense insulin therapy using a mathematical model for clinical simulation with a clinical algorithm and flow sheet.

Diabetes Educator, **15** (1), 77–79.

Sjoberg, S., Carlson, A., Rosenqvist, U. & Ostman, J. (1988). Health attitudes, self-monitoring of blood glucose, metabolic control and residual insulin secretion in type I diabetic patients. *Diabetic Medicine*, **5** (5), 449–453.

Smith, J. M. et al. (1988). Survey of computer programs for diabetes management and education. *Diabetes Educator*, **14** (5), 412–415.

Stancin, T., Link, D. L. & Reuter, J. M. (1989). Binge eating and purging in young women with IDDM. *Diabetes Care*, **12** (9), 601–603.

Steel, J. M., Lloyd, G. G., Young, R. L. & MacIntyre, C. C. (1990). Changes in eating attitudes during the first year of treatment for diabetes. *Journal of Psychosomatic Research*, **34** (3), 313–318.

Steel, J. M., Young, R. J., Lloyd, G. G. & Macintyre, C. C. (1989). Abnormal eating attitudes in young insulin-dependent diabetics. *British Journal of Psychiatry*, **155**, 515–521.

Surwit, R. S. & Feinglos, M. N. (1983). The effects of relaxation on glucose tolerance in non-insulin-dependent diabetes mellitus. *Diabetes Care*, **6**, 176–179.

Surwit, R. S. & Feinglos, M. N. (1984). Stress and diabetes. *Behavioral Medicine Update*, **6** (1), 8–11.

Surwit, R. S., McCubbin, J. A., Kuhn, C. M. et al. (1986). Alprazolam decreases stress hyperglycaemia in Ob/Ob mice. *Psychosomatic Medicine*, **48** (3–4), 278–282.

Szabo-Kallai, K., Gyimesi, A. & Ivanyi, J. (1990). Role of emotional factors in diabetes. *Acta Diabetologia Latina* **27** (1), 23–29.

Tattersall, R. B., McCulloch, D. K. & Aveline, M. (1985). Group therapy in the treatment of diabetes. *Diabetes Care*, **8** (2), 180.

Uhlmann, R. F., Inui, T. S., Pecoraro, R. E. & Carter, W. B. (1988). Relationship of patient request fulfillment to compliance, glycemic control, and other health care outcomes in insulin-dependent diabetes. *Journal of General. Internal Medicine*, **3** (5), 458–463.

US Department of Health & Human Services (1985). Diabetes in America: Diabetes Data Compiled 1984. NIH Publication No. 85–1468.

Welborn, T. A., Knuiman, M., McCann, V., Stanton, K. & Constable, I. J. (1984). Clinical macrovascular disease in Caucasoid diabetic subjects: Logistic regression analysis of risk variables. *Diabetologia*, **27**, 568–573.

Wells, K. B., Golding, J. M. & Burnam, M. A. (1989). Affective, substance use, and anxiety disorders in persons with arthritis, diabetes, heart disease, high blood pressure, or chronic lung conditions. *General Hospital Psychiatry*, **11** (5), 320–327.

Wilson, W., Ary, D. V., Biglan, A., Glasgow, R. E., Toobert, D. J. & Campbell, D. R. (1986). Psychosocial predictors of self-care behaviors (compliance) and glycemic control in non-insulin-dependent diabetes mellitus. *Diabetes Care*, **9**, 614.

Windsor, R. A., Roseman, J., Gartseff, G. & Kirk, K. A. (1981). Qualitative issues in developing educational diagnostic instruments and assessment procedures for diabetic patients. *Diabetes Care*, **4**, 468.

Wing, R. R., Epstein, L. H., Blair, E. & Nowalk, M. P. (1985). Psychologic stress and blood glucose levels in nondiabetic subjects. *Psychosomatic Medicine*, **47** (6), 558–564.

Wing, R. R., Epstein, L. H., Nowalk, M. P. et al. (1985). Compliance to self-monitoring of blood glucose: a marked-item technique compared with self-report. *Diabetes Care*, **8** (5), 456.

Wing, R. R., Epstein, L. H., Nowalk, M. P. & Lamparski, D. M. (1986). Behavioral self-regulation in the treatment of patients with diabetes mellitus. *Psychological Bulletin*, **99** (1), 78.

Wing, R. R., Marcus, M. D., Blair, E. H., Epstein, L. H. & Burton, L. R. (1990).

Depressive symptomatology in obese adults with type II diabetes. *Diabetes Care*, **13** (2), 170–172.

Wolf, F. M. & Cornell, R. G. (1986). Interpreting behavioral, biomedical, and psychological relationships in chronic disease from 2 × 2 tables using correlation. *Journal of Chronic Diseases*, **39**, 605.

Wysocki, T. (1989). Impact of blood glucose monitoring on diabetic control: obstacles and interventions. *Journal of Behavioral Medicine*, **12** (2), 183–205.

Zimmet, P. (1982). Type 2 (non-insulin dependent) diabetes—an epidemiological overview. *Diabetologia*, **22**, 399–411.

Zimmet, P., Finch, C. & Dowse, G. (1990). The epidemiology of diabetes mellitus. In K. G. M. M. Alberti & L. P. Krall (Eds), *Diabetes Annual/5*, 1–21. Elsevier, Excerpta Medica.

8 Effects of Asthma Patient Education upon Psychological and Behavioural Outcomes

ADRIAN BAUMAN
School of Community Medicine, University of New South Wales, PO Box 1, Kensington 2033, Australia

INTRODUCTION

Childhood and adult asthma are important chronic health problems, which are associated with increasing rates of morbidity and mortality (Sears, 1986; Buist, 1989). In Australia, for example, 20% of children and 10% of adults have asthma at any one time, which are prevalence rates more than twice as high as those reported in the USA and Europe (NHMRC, 1988). Asthma is the leading cause of hospital admission in Australian children (AIH, 1988), and is a leading cause of time off school, restricted activity and disturbed sleep (Ford, Dawson & Cowie, 1988; Schneider, Melton & Reisch, 1980; Lewis et al., 1984). By its chronic and variable course, and by its effect on the families of those with asthma, it is also associated with considerable psycho-social distress and disruption (Sibbald, 1989).

Management by both patient and physician is considered crucial in the prevention of asthma mortality and morbidity. Studies have assessed patient and physician delays in recognising asthma severity as an important factor in asthma deaths (BTS 1982) and others have identified considerable under-recognised and under-treated asthma in the community (Anderson, 1983; Avery, 1980; Mitchell et al., 1990). Less is known about the short and long-term psychological consequences of having asthma, and methods for their prevention and amelioration.

The first section of this review traces the history of asthma education programmes, and the role played in asthma care by health psychologists and behavioural researchers. The development of "asthma self-management programmes" (ASMPs) has occurred over the past decade, replacing traditional health education approaches which only provided information to patients, rather than teaching skills or changing attitudes and coping styles. Recently, medical, psychological and educational perspectives have converged, leading to a multi-disciplinary approach to this health problem.

The second half of this chapter attempts to answer the question whether

International Review of Health Psychology. Volume 2. Edited by S. Maes, H. Leventhal and M. Johnston
© 1993 John Wiley & Sons Ltd

these asthma self-management programmes have been effective. A meta-analysis pooled data from 24 studies, and assessed the outcomes of primary relevance to health psychologists, namely, psychological and behavioural outcomes. The future roles of health psychologists in asthma education can be more easily seen in this context.

BACKGROUND: THE PRINCIPLES AND DEVELOPMENT OF ASTHMA EDUCATION PROGRAMMES

Early attempts at asthma education occurred as a small part of the primary school curriculum in "health education" (Willson, 1958; Smith, 1976). More recently, the principles of adult learning have been used in educational programmes for asthmatic patients (Knowles, 1978). Psychological interventions for asthma have comprised three phases, two of which focused on psychological therapies for asthma. The three stages were the eras of psychosomatic research and treatment for asthma, the period where asthma was seen as a learned response, and the contemporary "cognitive-coping" approach. It is the latter developments which have contributed to asthma education programmes, and are most relevant to the present review.

A considerable amount of explanatory research has been carried out into psychological factors associated with asthma. Recent researchers have addressed patient denial and perceived stigma of asthma (Sibbald et al., 1988; Sibbald, 1989), personality factors in asthma management (Dirks et al., 1982; Jones et al., 1976; Kinsman et al., 1977), the need for assertiveness training (Bauman & Browne, 1987), and cognitive coping with asthma (Maes & Schlösser, 1988; Maes and Schlösser, 1988a). There have also been studies which have observed a relationship between psychosocial distress and the risk of asthma death (Yellowlees et al., 198; Strunk et al., 1985).

During the 1980s, asthma self-management (ASM) training developed, based largely upon self-regulation and self-control theory (Kanfer, 1988; Ormiston, 1979; Bruhn, 1983; Thoresen, 1983). Some of these approaches were derived from social learning theory (Creer, 1991; Bruhn, 1983), and others have suggested family and social systems approaches to (childhood) asthma (Bruhn, 1983; Hindi-Alexander, 1985).

The principles of asthma self-management programmes (ASMPs) include training adults and children with asthma about their disease (knowledge), teaching them specific behavioural skills to monitor and manage their asthma, and developing self-confidence about managing their asthma (Bauman & Browne, 1987).

There are numerous applications of psychological theory used in the development of ASMPs. These include behavioural skills development through the use of goal setting, behavioural contracting and self-observation (Bruhn, 1983). Other cognitive-behavioural (social learning theory based) approaches focus on increasing an individual's level of self-efficacy, which is defined as a

Figure 8.1 Asthma self-management skills and competencies (derived from Bauman and Browne, 1987; Wilson-Pessano, 1985).

person's level of confidence or conviction that he/she can perform specific behaviours in a specific context (Clark, 1987; Clark & Zimmerman, 1990). Efficacy enhancing strategies are highly relevant for asthma self-management programmes. These include performing the target behaviour (enactive learning), observing credible role models performing the behaviour (vicarious learning), encouragement (exhortation), and learning coping skills to deal with the performance of the behaviour in anxiety provoking and/or social situations (Hindi-Alexander, Throm & Middleton, 1987). One example of this was the study by Maiman & Green (1979) which demonstrated that modelling of behaviours by (credible) asthmatic nurse educators, was an effective intervention strategy.

Asthma self-management education focuses upon the skills of inhaler use, peak flow monitoring and the assessment of asthma severity, the avoidance of precipitating factors and prevention of attacks, and the early initiation of help-seeking behaviours in severe asthma. Early health education programmes for asthma, such as the audio-visual interventions described by Moldofsky et al. (1979) and Darr et al. (1981), focused on information transfer alone. More recent ASMPs are distinguished from these early interventions by the presence of specific self-management competencies and skills, which are summarised in Figure 8.1. It is these latter programmes which are the focus of the present review, as informational strategies alone are unlikely to have any effect upon psychological or behavioural outcomes (Lorig & Laurin, 1985).

Figure 8.1 divides asthma competencies into three potential groups, namely preventive medication use, acute episode management, and psychological dimensions, such as coping. All three are inter-related, and also depend, in part, on the relationship between patient and health care provider. The objective has been to develop collaborative and interactive relationships between patient and health providers.

The development and use of asthma action plans and portable peak flow meters (PFMs) to measure asthma severity have become important behavioural self-management goals for many asthmatics. These strategies have been recognised as important components of an overall approach to asthma management in Australia, Britain and the USA (Woolcock et al., 1989; BTS, 1990; NAEP, 1991). The importance of self-assessment and monitoring of asthma severity, linked to a specific behavioural plan (action plan or crisis plan) enables patients to take a more active role in the control of their chronic illness.

Prevention of asthma symptoms is also an important component of behavioural self-management. Knowledge of, and avoidance of provoking agents which trigger asthma attacks is important for both adults and children with asthma. Avoidable triggers in some asthmatics include specific foods and food colourings, some pollens and moulds, and cigarette smoke. Anticipation of attacks may be prevented with appropriate use of preventive medications, and monitored using PFMs.

The management of acute asthma attacks is also linked to peak flow meter self-monitoring and to the action plans individually tailored to each patient's needs. In addition, some ASMPs address the problems of denial, embarrassment, anxiety, and assertiveness as they relate to or hinder self-management.

It is essential for every asthmatic to learn to use their inhaler medications correctly. Although new devices have been developed to facilitate the administration of aerosol medications, there remains much scope for patient skills training in this area. The issue of adherence to medications is a vexed question in asthma management, as flexible dosage regimens are required during acute attacks. Preventive medication use, particularly before physical activity, is another *ad hoc* situation for the asthmatic patient. Regular preventive medication use suffers from the same problems as all medication regimen in chronic disease. It is likely that poor adherence is widespread, although population measures of asthma medication adherence are not known. Clinical studies have documented poor adherence (Glanz, 1984; Marion, Creer & Burns, 1983), particularly in mid-day doses of inhaled medications, when social barriers to medication use may be maximal (Smith et al., 1986).

The virtues of these asthma self-management principles have been described before (Clarke, 1989; Creer, 1991). The crucial question is whether, in practice, asthma education interventions produce the behavioural and psychological effects, which theoretically, they should. One method to answer this question is to conduct a pooled analysis of data from published asthma interventions, using the technique of meta-analysis [see also chapter 1, this volume. Eds]. This analysis constitutes the second half of this chapter.

A META-ANALYSIS OF ASTHMA EDUCATION PROGRAMMES: PSYCHOLOGICAL AND BEHAVIOURAL EFFECTS

Meta-analyses in health education

Meta-analysis is the process of pooling the results of several studies to assess their average effectiveness in influencing those exposed to particular interventions (Wolf, 1986). The first phase of any meta-analysis is to assemble relevant studies. The present meta-analysis identified asthma self-management programme evaluations, published since 1980, and assessed their overall effectiveness in influencing psychological and self-management outcomes. By pooling data, meta-analysis increases the power of a review to detect programme effects.

Previous meta-analyses of arthritis and diabetes patient education programmes have suggested overall improvements in those who attended programmes, particularly in knowledge outcomes, but also in self-management skills (Brown, 1990; Mullen, 1987). Mazzuca (1982) reviewed over 300 patient education programmes for chronic disease and demonstrated that a greater effect (on any outcome) if the education programme was behaviourally based, rather than simply didactic. Similar results for cognitive behaviour therapies were reported by Miller & Berman (1983).

Four recent reviews of asthma programmes have reached different conclusions about programme effectiveness, with less favourable qualitative reviews by Klingelhofer & Gershwin (1987) and Howland (1988), and more favourable reviews by Clark (1989) and Creer et al. (1990). None of these papers assessed outcome effects in a quantitative manner, and none highlighted the overall change in psychological outcomes. These tasks are the subject of the present study.

Method of meta-analysis

Published asthma education programmes were sought up to December 1990 using appropriate electronic databases, including MEDLINE and SOCIAL SCIENCE ABSTRACTS and PSYCH-LIT. All possible programmes were considered, but were only included if the study employed a randomised or quasi-experimental design, and used a behaviourally-based intervention for adults or children with defined asthma. Small group interventions, and those that used behaviourally-oriented one-to-one counselling were included in the present review, but didactic programmes based solely on information transfer were not.

Some meta-analysts (Glass, 1981) have suggested the use of overall pooled assessments of programme success; another approach, taken in this preliminary analysis, is to compare similar categories of measurement between studies. In this synthesis, the ASMP outcomes were divided into three conceptually congruent groups, namely asthma self-management behaviours, asthma adherence behaviours, and psychological measures (cognitive and attitudinal measures). Self-management behaviours have been measured using specific indices or scores (Whitman et al., 1985; Evans et al., 1987). Adherence or compliance behaviours were usually assessed by medication use or inhaler technique (Creer, 1991; Heringa et al., 1987; Smith et al., 1986), but have also been assessed by appointment-keeping behaviours (Jones, Jones & Katz, 1987). Psychological outcomes comprised measures of attitudes and beliefs

(Sibbald, 1989; Richards et al., 1989; Creer, Kotses & Reynolds, 1989; Creer et al., 1989), asthma coping scales (Maes & Schlösser, 1988), general measures of sense of control (Parcel, Nader & Tiernan, 1980; Rubin et al., 1986; Taggart et al., 1987), and specific asthma self-efficacy measures (Tobin et al., 1987; Evans et al., 1987, Snyder et al., 1987). These three groups of outcomes were considered in the present analysis, and there were too few studies to further refine the outcome categories.

An effect size (ES) is defined as the standardised mean difference between intervention and control groups; it is a unitless measure which may be compared between groups (Glass, 1981; Light & Pillemer, 1984). It may be derived from intervention and control group means, or from t- or F-statistics or proportions reported in study results (Mullen & Ramirez, 1987). The ES represents the improvement, in standard deviation units, of the intervention group over the control group. Effect sizes of more than 0.2–0.3 are considered educationally important (Wolf, 1986).

Three specific difficulties were encountered in the present study. The estimation of effect size from single group before–after design (no control group) studies was estimated using the method described by Light, where post-test means were compared with pre-test means (1984, 56). Approximate ES values were estimated less accurately in studies which reported, for example, F-statistics derived from (multiple) repeat-measures analyses of variance (Hindi-Alexander & Cropp, 1984). Other data produced ES values with a lower limit only (Mayo, Richman & William-Harris, 1990, and a conservative estimate of ES = 2.0 was made). Finally, some studies (e.g. Maes and Schlösser, 1988), reported 15 psychological outcomes; only the first nine were used, as these were asthma-specific cognitive and attitudinal measures, and an average ES value over these nine outcome measures was estimated.

Crude mean ES values are reported. Each ES value was then weighted in relation to its sample size, and weighted ES values calculated (using the method of Hedges & Olkin, 1985), and outlier (non-heterogeneous) estimates considered for exclusion.

Results of the meta-analysis

Data from 24 asthma education programmes are shown in Table 8.1. The effect sizes are shown for each category of outcome reported. Self-management was measured in nine studies, compliance in 13 studies, and psychological outcomes in ten studies. Studies are divided into randomised controlled trials, and quasi-experimental designs, with patients-as-their-own-controls being included in the latter category.

The significance of the crude mean effect sizes are not interpretable, as their standard error may not be calculated. All the weighted mean effect sizes were significantly greater than zero, as evidenced by the 95% confidence intervals (CI) for each outcome (Table 8.2). Weighted ES values were also reported only

Table 8.1. Results of meta-analysis of ASMPs: the pooled effect sizes obtained for psychological measures, self-management behaviour and compliance

Author* (year)	Measures of self-management	Compliance measures	Psychological measures
Randomised controlled studies			
Self, 1983		1.37	
Lewis, 1984		0.52	
Rakos, 1985	0.33		
Lebaron, 1985		0.07	
Whitman, 1985	0.81		0.23 (c)
Smith, 1986		0.54	
Rubin, 1986	0.72		0.21 (a)
Mitchell, 1986	0.12	0.30	
Evans, 1987	0.28		0.30 (b)
Jones, 1987		1.65	
Heringa, 1987		3.8	
Mayo, 1990	2.0 (d)	1.50	
Ringsberg, 1990		1.77	
Quasi-experimental designs			
Parcel, 1980			0.63 (a)
Hindi-Alexander, 1984		0.35	1.07 (a)
Robinson, 1985			0.83 (a)
Hilton, 1986	−0.39		
Taggart, 1987			1.62 (a)
Indinnimeo, 1987	1.80	0.15	
Hindi-Alexander, 1987a		0.44	
Maes, 1988			0.68 (c)
Bauman, 1989	2.12		0.55 (b)
Windsor, 1990		1.29 (e)	
Taggart, 1991			0.81 (a)

(a) (Child) health locus of control
(b) measures of self-efficacy
(c) other attitudinal or psychological measures
(d) conservative estimate of ES from Mayo et al. (1990) paper, as proportion performing behaviour at follow-up was 100%
(e) ES derived for total adherence score

* first-named authors are cited only

Table 8.2. Weighted mean effect sizes (ES) for asthma self-management behaviours, compliance and psychological outcomes.

Effect size (ES)	Self-management	Compliance	Psychological measures
Crude mean ES	0.86	1.06	0.69
Weighted mean ES	0.49	0.71	0.62
(95% confidence interval)	(0.39–0.59)	(0.64–0.78)	(0.54–0.70)
Weighted mean ES (randomised trials only)	0.46	0.71	0.44

for randomised controlled studies, but were only reduced significantly for psychological outcomes (from 0.62 to 0.44). However, the latter estimate, ES = 0.44, was only based on three studies.

The weighted ES for psychological outcomes was 0.62, which suggests that the average intervention subject had a psychological outcome measure score better than 72% of controls. The 95% CI imply that the universe of underlying effect sizes for psychological outcomes is likely to lie between about 0.54 and 0.70.

In order to assess the possibility of undetected or unpublished studies with negative findings (publication bias), the "fail-safe N" approach was used. For example, this procedure estimates how many negative studies needed to exist in order to overturn the observation of ES = 0.62 for psychological outcomes (Wolf, 1986). For the ES for psychological outcomes to be reduced to 0.1, more than 46 negative studies would have been required (and it was unlikely that this many were not found or published, using standard literature search procedures). Similarly, 35 negative self-management outcomes and 73 negative compliance studies would have been required to overturn the observed ES values for these outcomes.

Discussion of meta-analysis of asthma education

Most of the asthma self-management programmes which measured them showed an effect upon self-management behaviours and psychological effects. The pooled effects were likely to be both clinically as well as statistically significant. The larger ES for compliance was noteworthy, but included several small clinical studies conducted by pharmacists. These results indicate that positive psychological and behavioural outcomes are achievable following exposure to asthma self-management education programmes. It confirms the need for behavioural expertise in the development and conduct of programmes aimed at educating people with asthma.

However, clear deficiencies exist in the field. Of 38 ASMPs identified, only 24 used here reported data of psychological or self-management measures (Table 8.1). Others collected extensive psychological data or self-management data, but did not report them (for example, McNabb et al., 1985, and Snyder et al., 1987). In addition to the need for further refinements to psychological outcome measures, there is the real need to report psychological outcome data—both to enhance our understanding of the psychological and behavioural effects of ASMPs, and to enhance the standing of these outcomes in the minds of asthma physicians. The plea for randomised controlled studies persists, although their conduct in the area of asthma education is notoriously difficult (see Lewis & Lewis, 1987). Finally, further analyses are needed to determine whether these psychological changes are maintained, and to assess whether they are related to other indices of morbidity, such as hospital attendance and time off work or school. However, at present, few of these studies assess these outcomes (Howland et al., 1988), and a precise meta-analytic estimate could not be derived.

4. FUTURE DIRECTIONS

The domain of asthma research conducted by psychologistis has been extensive over the past four decades. Initial research focused upon aetiological research and learning theory approaches to asthma treatment (King, 1980). Over the past decade, the theoretical focus has switched towards asthma self-management interventions, which, as shown in the meta-analysis above, have generally produced positive psychological and behavioural effects.

The most recent trends in asthma education are towards a collaborative model, where medicine, psychology and education meet. The medical model has changed by including self-management skills in published guidelines for asthma care (BTS, 1990; NAEP, 1990; NAEP, 1991; Woolcock et al., 1989). The principles of adult learning, namely that adults are capable of self-initiated learning and may learn best from previous experience (Knowles, 1978) have been incorporated into many ASMPs. The integration of these disciplines has led to the notion of "collaborative management" (Conboy, 1989) rather than patient self-management in isolation.

The processes of asthma care are contingent upon both optimal medical assessment and its linkage with patient self-management. This is leading towards an extended model of the determinants of asthma behaviour and morbidity, and towards asthma interventions which aspire to optimise the patient's medical treatment, as well as teaching self-management, cognitive and coping skills. Examples of this combined approach already exist, such as that described by Mayo (1990) in New York. In this study, individualised behavioural skills training was combined with optimal medical care. In this more general framework, psychologists would work within multi-disciplinary teams, rather than individual health professionals each developing their own interpretations of asthma education.

Another important area for future research is the area of psychological and behavioural measurement in asthmatic adults and children. A strength of psychological research is the diversity of measures that may reflect the problems experienced by asthma patients, but this may also be a weakness. There may be useful merit in standardising psychological and behavioural outcome measures, so that replication studies can assess whether asthma education consistently influences self-efficacy or coping style. A further problem is that some asthma-specific measures are developed, and psychometrically validated, and then not reported in intervention studies (Snyder, Winder & Creer, 1987). Finally, the relationship between psychological and physiological morbidity needs further attention, although some researchers (Sibbald, 1989; Clark et al., 1990; Rubin et al., 1989) have conducted some exploratory work in this area.

It would be desirable for psychologists to broaden their involvement in other areas of asthma education. Kaptein et al. (1988) has appropriately suggested that psychologists have a role in health professional training, especially primary care physician education. The task here is to change physicians' behaviour, and to teach them about self-management of asthma in their patients. A major barrier to population peak-flow meter usage is the rate of physician acceptance of this behaviour, and perhaps diffusion theory may have a role in overcoming this problem (Rogers, 1987).

There are new and innovative approaches to asthma education which extend beyond individual or small-group approaches. In the USA, the National Asthma Education programme, and in Australia, the National Asthma Campaign have commenced population-wide approaches to this common health problem (NAEP, 1990; Antic, 1991). These include community-based programmes to increase awareness about asthma, and educate those not usually reached by small group programmes. Community psychologists have an important role to play in the design and evaluation of these public health interventions. These changes are substantial, and will influence the future role of health professionals involved in asthma education and counselling.

REFERENCES

AIH. (1988). Australia's Health. Report by the Australian Institute of Health, Canberra: Aust. Govt Press.

Anderson, H. R., Bailey, P. A., Cooper J. S. et al. (1983). Medical care of asthma and wheezing illness in children: a community survey. *J. Epidemiol. Commun. Health*, 37, 180–186.

Antic, R., Bauman, A., Rubinfeld, A. et al. (1991). Asthma education using the mass media: results from the 1988 pilot national campaign. *Aust. N.Z. J. Med.*, 21, 644 (abstract).

Avery, C. H., March, J. & Brook, R. H. (1980). An assessment of the adequacy of self-care by adult asthmatics. *Journal of Community Health*, 5, 167–180.

Bauman, A. E. & Browne, G. (1987). The role of education in adult asthma management. *Patient management*, 14, 94–103.

Bauman, A., Craig, A. R., Dunsmore, J. et al. (1989). Removing barriers to asthma self management. *Patient Educ. Counsel*, 14, 217–226.

BTS (British Thoracic Society). (1982). Deaths from asthma in two regions of England. *Br. Med. J.*, 285, 1251–1255.

BTS (British Thoracic Society). (1990). Guidelines for the management of asthma in adults: I—chronic persistent asthma. *Br. Med. J.*, 301, 651–653.

Brown, S. A. (1990). Studies of educational interventions and outcomes in diabetes adults: A meta-analysis revisited. *Patient Educ. Counsel*, 16, 189–215.

Bruhn, J. (1983). The Application of Theory in Childhood Asthma Self-help Programs. *J. Allergy Clin. Immunol.*, 72, 561–577.

Buist, A. S. (1989). Asthma mortality: what have we learned? *J. Allerg. Clin. Immunol.*, 84, 275–283.

Clark, N. M. (1987). Social learning theory in current health education practice. In: *Advances in Health Promotion*, Volume 2. Connecticut: JAI Press, 251–277.

Clark, N. M. (1989). Asthma self-management education. *Chest*, 95, 1110–1113.

Clark, N. M. & Zimmerman, B. J. (1990). A social cognitive view of self-regulated learning about health. *Health Education Research*, 5(3), 371–379.

Clark, N. M., Levison, M. J., Evans, D. et al. (1990). Communication within low income families and the management of asthma. *Patient Educ. Counseling*, 15, 191–210.

Conboy, K. (1989). Self-management skills for cooperative care in asthma. *J. Pediatrics*, 115, 863–866.

Creer, T. L., Kotses, H. & Reynolds, V. C. (1989). Living with Asthma: Part 2. Beyond CARIH. *J. Asthma*, 26(1), 31–51.

Creer, T. L., Wigal, J. K., Tobin, D. L. et al. (1989). The Revised Asthma Problem Behaviour Checklist. *J. Asthma*, 26, 17–29.

Creer, T. L., Wigal, J. K., Kotses, H. et al. (1990). A Critique of 19 Self-Management Programs for Childhood Asthma: Part II. Comments Regarding the Scientific Merit of the Programs. *Pediatric Asthma, Allergy and Immunol.*, 4, 41–55.

Creer, T. L. (1991). The application of behavioral procedures to childhood asthma—current and future perspectives. *Patient Educ. Counsel*, 17, 9–22.

Darr, M. S., Self, T., Ryan, M. et al. (1981). Content and retention evaluation of an audiovisual patient-education program on bronchodilators. *Am. J. Hosp. Pharm.*, 38, 672–675.

Dirks, J. F. & Kreischer, H. (1982). The Batery of Asthma Illness Behaviour (BAIB) I: Independence from age of asthma onset. *J. Asthma*, 19, 75–78.

Evans, D., Clark, N. M., Feldman, C. H. et al. (1987). A school health education program for children with asthma aged 8–11 years. *Health Educ. Quart.*, 14, 267–280.

Ford, R. P. K., Dawson, K. P. & Cowie, A. (1988). Asthma: does an accurate diagnosis influence school attendance and performance. *Aust. N.Z. J. Med.*, 18, 134–136.

Glanz, K., Fiel, S. B., Swartz, M. A. & Francis, M. E. (1984). Compliance with an experimental drug regimen for treatment of asthma: its magnitude, importance, and correlates. *J. Chron. Dis.*, 37, 11, 815–824.

Glass, G. V., McGaw, B. & Smith, M. L. (1981). *Meta-analysis in social research*. Beverly Hills, CA: Sage Press.

Hedges, L. V. & Olkin, I. (1985). *Statistical methods for meta-analysis*. New York: Academic Press.

Heringa, P., Lawson, L. & Reda, D. (1987). The effect of a structured education program on knowledge and psychomotor skills of patients using beclomethasone dipropionate aerosol for steroid dependent asthma. *Health Education Quart.*, 14, 309–317.

Hilton, S., Sibbald, B., Anderson, H. R. & Freeling, P. (1986). Controlled Evaluation of the Effects of Patient Education on Asthma Morbidity in General Practice. *Lancet*, Jan. 4, 26–29.

Hindi-Alexander, M. C. (1985). Decision Making in Asthma Self-Management. *Chest*, (suppl), 88, 100S–104S.

Hindi-Alexander, M. & Cropp, G. (1984). Evaluation of a family asthma program. *J. Allergy Clin. Immunol.*, 74, 505–510.

Hindi-Alexander, M. C., Throm, J. & Middleton, E. (1987). Collaborative asthma self-management evaluation designs. *Clin. Rev. Allergy*, 5, 249–258.

Hindi-Alexander, M., Throm, J., Zielezny, M. et al. (1987a). Results of training and education on the course of asthma in adults. *J. Allerg. Clin. Immunol.*, 79, 140 (abstract).

Howland, J., Bauchner, H. & Adair, R. (1988). The impact of pediatric asthma education. *Chest*, 94, 964–969.

Indinnimeo, L., Midulla, F., Hindi-Alexander, M. et al. (1987). Controlled studies of childhood asthma self-management in Italy using the "Open Airways" and "Living with Asthma" programs: A preliminary report. *Health Education Quart.*, **14**, 291–308.

Jones, P. K., Jones, S. L. & Katz, J. (1987). Improving compliance for asthmatic patients visiting the emergency department using a Health Belief Model intervention. *J. Asthma*, **24**, 199–206.

Jones, N. F., Kinsman, R. A., Schum, R. et al. (1976). Personality profiles in asthma. *J. Clin. Psychol.*, **32**, 285–291.

Kanfer, F. & Schefft, B. (1988). *Guiding the process of therapeutic change*. Illinois: Research Press.

Kaptein, A. A., Dekker, F. W., Gill, K. et al. (1988). Health psychology and asthma: current status and future directions. In: S. Maes (Ed.), *Topics in Health Psychology*. London: John Wiley, pp. 157–189.

King, N. J. (1980). The behavioural management of asthma and asthma-related problems in children: A critical review of the literature. *J. Behav. Med.*, **3**, 169–189.

Kinsman, R. A., Dahlem, N. W., Spector, S. et al. (1977). Observations on subjective symptomatology, coping behaviour, and medical decisions in asthma. *Psychosom Med.*, **39**, 102–119.

Klingelhofer, E. L. & Gershwin, M. E. (1988). Asthma self-management programs: premises, not promises. *J. Asthma*, **25**, 89–101.

Knowles, M. (1978). *The Adult Learner—a neglected species*. Houston: Gulf.

LeBaron, S., Zeltzer, L. K., Ratner, P. & Kniker, W. T. (1985). A controlled study of education for improving compliance with cromolyn sodium (Intal): The importance of physician–patient communication. *Ann. Allergy*, **55**, 811–818.

Lewis, C. E. & Lewis, M. A. (1987). Evaluation and implementation of self-management programs for children with asthma. *J. Allergy Clin. Immunol.*, **80**, 498–500.

Lewis, C. E., Rachelefsky, G., Lewis, M. A. et al. (1984). A randomized trial of ACT (Asthma Care Training) for kids. *Pediatrics*, **74**, 478–486.

Light, R. & Pillemer, D. (1984). *Summing up—the science of reviewing research*. Cambridge, MA: Harvard University Press.

Lorig K. & Laurin, J. (1985) Some notions about assumptions underlying health education. *Health Education Quarterly*, **12** (3), 231–243.

McNabb, W. L., Wilson-Pessano, S. R., Hughes, G. W. et al. (1985). Self-management education of Children with Asthma: AIR WISE. *Amer. J. Public Health*, **75**, 1219–1220.

Maes, S. & Schlösser, M. (1988). Changing health behaviour outcomes in asthmatic patients: A pilot intervention study. *Soc. Sci. Med.*, **26**, 359–364.

Maes, S. & Schlösser, M. (1988a). The cognitive management of health behaviour outcomes in asthmatic patients, Chapter 11 in: *Topics in Health Psychology* (Eds S. Maes et al.). London: John Wiley, pp. 171–189.

Maiman, L. A., Green, L. W. et al. (1979). Education for self-treatment by adult asthmatics. *JAMA*, **241**, 1919–1922.

Marion, R. J., Creer, T. L. & Burns, K. (1983). Training Asthmatic Children to Use Their Nebulizer Correctly. *J. Asthma*, **20**, 183–188.

Mayo, P. H., Richman, J. & William-Harris, H. (1990). Results of a Program to Reduce Admissions for Adult. *Ann. Intern. Med.*, **112**, 864–871.

Mazzuca, S. A. (1982). Does Patient Education in Chronic Disease have Therapeutic Value? *J. Chron. Dis.*, **35**, 521–529.

Miller, R. & Berman, J. S. (1983). The efficacy of cognitive behaviour therapies: a quantitative review. *Psychol. Bull.*, **94**, 39–53.

Mitchell, E. A., Anderson, H. R., Feeling, P. & White, P. T. (1990). Why are hospital admission and mortality rates for childhood asthma higher in New Zealand than in the United Kingdom? *Thorax*, **45**, 176–182.

Mitchell, E. A., Ferguson, V. & Norwood, M. (1986). Asthma education by community child health nurses. *Arch. Dis. Child.*, **61**, 1184–1189.

Moldofsky, H. (1979). Videotape educational program for people with asthma. *Canad. Med. Assoc. J.*, **120**, 669–672.

Mullen, P. D. & Laville, E. A. (1987a). Efficacy of psychoeducational interventions on pain, depression and disability in people with arthritis: A meta-analysis. *J. Rheumatol.*, **14** (Suppl. 15), 33–39.

Mullen, P. D. & Ramirez, G. (1987). Information synthesis and meta-analysis. In: *Advances in Health Education and Health promotion* (Ed. A. Ward), vol. 2, 201–239. Connecticut: JAI Press.

NAEP (1990). National Asthma Education Program: Program description and background information. NHLBI Office of Prevention, Education and Control, Washington DC. (Also see: C. Lenfant & S. Hurd, NAEP. *Chest* (1990), **98**, 226–227.)

NAEP (1991). Guidelines for the diagnosis management of asthma—patient education. *Patient Educ. Counsel*, **18**, 51–66.

NHMRC (National Health & Medical Research Council). (1988). Asthma in Australia: Strategies for reducing mortality and morbidity. Canberra.

Ormiston, L. (1979). Self-management Strategies. In R. B. Haynes, D. W. Taylor & D. Sackett (Eds), *Compliance in Health Care*. Baltimore, MD: Johns Hopkins Press, pp. 217–47.

Parcel, G., Nader, P. & Tiernan, K. (1980). A health education program for children with asthma. *J. Develop. Behav. Pediatr.*, **1**, 128–132.

Rakos, R., Grodek, M. V. & Mack, K. (1985). The Impact of a Self-Administered Behavioural Intervention Program On Pediatric Asthma. *J. Psychosom. Res.*, **29**, 101–108.

Richards, J. M., Dolce, J. J., Windsor, R. A. et al. (1989). Patient Characteristics Relevant to Effective Self-Management: Scales for Assessing Attitudes of Adults Toward Asthma. *J. Asthma*, **26**, 99–108.

Ringsberg, K. C., Wiklund, I. & Wilhelmsen, L. (1990). Education of adult patients at an "asthma school": Effects on quality of life, knowledge and need for nursing. *Eur. Respir. J.*, **3**, 33–37.

Robinson, L. D. (1985). Evaluation of an Asthma Summer Camp Program. *Chest*, January (Suppl) **88**, 105S–107S.

Rogers, E. M. (1987). The diffusion of innovations perspective. In *Taking Care—Understanding and Encouraging Self Protective Behavior*, N. D. Weistein (Ed). New York: Cambridge, pp. 79–85.

Rubin, D. H., Bauman, L. J. & Lauby, J. L. (1989). The Relationship between Knowledge and Reported Behavior in Childhood Asthma. *J. Dev. Behav. Pediatr.*, **10**, 307–312.

Rubin, D. H., Leventhal, J. M., Sadock, R. T. et al. (1986). Educational Intervention by Computer in Childhood Asthma: A Randomised Clinical Trial Testing for Use of a New Teaching Intervention in Childhood Asthma. *Pediatrics*, **77**, 1–10.

Schneider, M. R., Melton, B. H. & Reisch, J. S. (1980). Effects of a progressive exercise program on absenteeism among school children with asthma. *J. School. Health*, **50**, 92–95.

Sears, M. R. (1986). Why are deaths from asthma increasing. *Eur. J. Respir. Dis.*, **69** (Suppl. 147), 175–181.

Self, T. H., Brooks, J. B., Lieberman, P. & Ryan, M. (1983). The value of demonstration and role of the pharmacist in teaching the correct use of pressurized bronchodilators. *Canad. Med. Assoc. J.*, **128**, 129–131.

Sibbald, B., White, P., Pharoah C. et al. (1988). Relationship between psychosocial factors and asthma morbidity. *Fam. Pract.*, 5, 12–17.

Sibbald, B. (1989). Patient selfcare in asthma. *Thorax*, 44, 97–101.

Smith, J. M. (1976). The prevalence of asthma and wheezing in children. *Br. J. Dis. Chest.*, 70, 73–77.

Smith, N. A., Seale, J. P., Ley P. et al. (1986). Effects of intervention on medication compliance in children with asthma. *Med. J. Aust.*, 144, 119–122.

Snyder, S. E., Winder, J. A. & Creer, T. L. (1987). Development and evaluation of an Adult Asthma self-management program: Wheezers Anonymous. *J. Asthma*, 24, 153–158.

Strunk, R. C., Mrazek, D. A. et al. (1985). Physiologic and Psychological characteristics associated with deaths due to asthma in childhood. *JAMA*, 254, 1193–1198.

Taggart, V. S., Zuckerman, A. E., Lucas, S. et al. (1987). Adapting a self-management education program for asthma for use in an outpatient clinic. *Annals of Allergy*, 58, 173–178.

Taggart, V. S., Zuckerman, A., Sly, M. et al. (1991). You can control asthma: Evaluation of an asthma education program for hospitalised inner city children. *Patient Educ. Counsel*, 17, 35–47.

Thoresen, C. & Kirmil-Gray, K. (1983). Self Management Psychology and the Treatment of Childhood Asthma. *J. Allergy Clin. Immunol.*, 72, 596–606.

Tobin, D. L., Wigal, J. K., Creer, T. et al. (1987). The "Asthma Self-Efficacy Scale". *Ann. Allergy*, 59, 273–277.

Whitman, N., West, D., Brough, F. K. & Welch, M. (1985). A study of a self-care rehabilitation program in pediatric asthma. *Health Educ. Quart.*, 12, 333–342.

Willson, G. F. (1958). Asthma in school children. *J. Roy. Soc. Health*, 3, 274–281.

Wilson-Pessano, S. R. & McNabb, W. (1985). The role of Patient Education in the Management of Childhood Asthma. *Prev. Med.*, 14, 670–687.

Windsor, R. A., Bailey, W. C., Richards, J. R. et al. (1990). Evaluation of the efficacy and cost effectiveness of health education methods to increase medication adherence among adults with asthma. *Am. J. Pub. Health*, 80, 1519–1521.

Wolf, F. M. (1986). *Meta-analysis: Quantitative methods for research synthesis.* Palo Alto, CA: Sage Publications.

Woolcock, A., Rubinfeld, A. R., Seale, J. P. et al. (1989). Asthma management plan, 1989. *Med. J. Aust.*, 151, 650–653.

Yellowlees, P. M., Haynes, S. et al. (1988). Psychiatric morbidity in patients with life-threatening asthma: Initial report of a controlled study. *Med. J. Aust.*, 149, 246–249.

Part IV

PRACTICAL AND PROFESSIONAL ISSUES

9 Health Psychology in the USA

KENNETH A. WALLSTON
School of Nursing, Vanderbilt University, Nashville, USA

It is amazing to realize that formal recognition of the field of health psychology in the United States occurred less than 20 years ago. It is no longer correct to speak of health psychology as an "emerging" speciality within American psychology; for the last dozen or so years, health psychology has flourished as one of the most vibrant specialties within the larger discipline of psychology. Not only is it recognized as a specialty within its own right, health psychology has had a profound impact upon clinical psychology, and has played a major (if not the major) role in developing and vitalizing the interdisciplinary field called "behavioral medicine".

Because it is almost impossible to thoroughly review the breadth and depth of all of the health psychology research currently being conducted in the USA, I will not even attempt to do so in this chapter. (Such a compendium is best left to the *Annual Review of Psychology* chapter in which Rodin and Saloway last reviewed our field in 1989; the 1990 review article by Shelley Taylor in the *American Psychologist*; or to the research overviews emanating from the National Working Conference on Research in Health and Behavior, edited by Andy Baum and published in *Health Psychology* in 1989.) Instead, I will begin by reviewing the history of health psychology in the USA and end by speculating about its future. The main body of the chapter describes the state of health psychology in the early 1990s, pointing out some of the pressing issues facing our field today as I see them.

This is, admittedly, a very personal look at what is a somewhat amorphous field, seen through the eyes of an imperfect observer. It is deliverately less of a scholarly work than a "letter to friends" around to world (as an anonymous reviewer characterized an earlier draft). Also, although I recognize that the field of health psychology is older and bigger than the Division of Health Psychology within the American Psychological Association (APA), I am making the assumption that the Division represents the majority of the health psychologists in the USA. Therefore, by describing the Division, its membership, and its activities, I am comfortable in asserting that I am describing a significant aspect of the state of health psychology in the USA.

International Review of Health Psychology. Volume 2. Edited by S. Maes, H. Leventhal and M. Johnston
© 1993 John Wiley & Sons Ltd

HISTORY OF HEALTH PSYCHOLOGY IN THE USA

Table 9.1 presents a chronology of significant milestones in the history of health psychology in the USA. As is evident from this chronology, the godfather of health psychology in the USA (and, arguably, in the rest of the world as well) is William Schofield, a psychologist at the University of Minnesota's Division of Health Care Psychology. In 1969, Schofield wrote an *American Psychologist* article on the role of psychologists in the delivery of health services. In the article he demonstrated that, although only a small amount of psychological research and service in health care settings had to do with physical as opposed to mental health, there was a growing interest among psychologists in aspects of physical health. The response to that article stimulated the Board of Scientific Affairs of APA to appoint Schofield in 1973 to chair a task force on health research. The work of that task force was directly responsible for the organization of a section on health research within APA's Division 18 (Psychologists in Public Service) which, in turn, was the forerunner of the Division of Health Psychology (Division 38) within APA.

If Schofield could be considered the godfather of health psychology in the USA, there are many who could lay claim to the title of forefather. Prominent among these is George Stone. Stone began the first doctoral program in health psychology at the University of California—San Francisco, authored (along with Frances Cohen and Nancy Adler) the first handbook in the field (Stone, Cohen & Adler, 1979), and was the inaugural editor of *Health Psychology*, the official journal of Division 38. George recently retired from UCSF, having assured himself an honored place in the pantheon of giants in our field.

Another "giant" is Neal Miller, currently at Yale University, whose pioneering work set the stage for biofeedback, a technique which gave health psychologists a considerable amount of early credibility among their medical colleagues. (Miller was recently judged to be among the four most eminent contemporary American psychologists (Korn, Davis & Davis, 1991).)

Other US academicians whose research and research training have had a profound influence on the field include Joe Matarazzo of the University of Oregon who has been doing research and training in medical psychology for over 30 years; Bill Fordyce, an expert in the field of pain behavior, who recently retired from the University of Washington; David C. Glass, who is currently at the State University of New York at Stony Brook and who has conducted and stimulated a great deal of cardiovascular research; Richard Lazarus at the University of California at Berkeley whose empirical and theoretical work in stress, coping, and emotions is known throughout the world; Judy Rodin, currently the Provost of Yale University, who has made major contributions in both obesity and aging research; Tom Coates at the University of California at San Francisco who was the first health psychologist in the States to trumpet the need for behavioral research in the prevention of AIDS; and Shelley Taylor at the University of California at Los Angeles for both her work on adaptation to

Table 9.1.   History of health psychology in the USA

Date	Event
1969	William Schofield authors *American Psychologist* article calling attention to psychologists' neglect of both research and service in general medical settings.
1973	APA establishes Task Force on Health Research chaired by Schofield. Task Force holds open meeting at APA Convention in Montreal.
1976	*American Psychologist* publishes report by the Task Force on Health Research.
	Section on Health Research established as part of APA's Division 18: Psychologists in Public Service.
1977	Stephen Weiss runs for president of Health Research Section on platform of establishing separate division entirely devoted to health psychology within APA.
	First doctoral program in "health psychology" established by George Stone and colleagues at the University of California at San Francisco.
1978	APA established Division of Health Psychology (Division 38) with over 700 charter members. Joseph Matarazzo, of the University of Oregon's Health Sciences Center, is the first president.
1979	Jossey-Bass publishes *Health Psychology: A Handbook* edited by George Stone, Frances Cohen, and Nancy Adler. This was the first textbook to carry "health psychology" in the title.
	The first issue of the *Health Psychologist*, Division 38's newsletter, is published with John Linton of the University of West Virginia as editor.
1982	The journal, *Health Psychology*, begins publication as the official journal of Division 38. George Stone is the first editor.
1983	National Working Conference on Education and Training in Health Psychology held at Arden House in Harriman, New York.
1988	National Working Conference on Research in Health Psychology held in Harper's Ferry, West Virginia.

chronic illness such as cancer and for her 1986 textbook which has been widely adopted, especially at the undergraduate level.

Howard Leventhal, one of the three editors of this volume, has had a long, distinguished, and productive career as a health psychologist. His influential research and theorizing about behavioral aspects of health began when he was with the US Public Health Service, and was continued at Yale and the University of Wisconsin. Leventhal's work in self-regulation and "common-sense representations of illness" is currently being conducted at Rutgers University where he is more productive than ever. While at the University of Wisconsin in Madison, Leventhal initiated an innovative joint PhD program between nursing and psychology. He is responsible for opening up the field of health psychology to a host of young investigators, including the author of this review.

Much credit for the development of our field has to go to Stephen Weiss, formerly the chief of the Behavioral Medicine Branch of the National Heart, Lung and Blood Institute. Weiss not only has been instrumental in making it possible for psychologists to achieve respectability and funding from the National Institutes of Health, but he provided critical leadership in establishing the Division of Health Psychology within APA. When Weiss was drafted to run for the presidency of the Health Research Section of Division 18, his platform was simple: he would devote all his energies to establishing a separate division within APA entirely for health psychology. To do so, Weiss turned for support to two of his mentors, Joe Matarazzo and Neal Miller, both of whom were widely respected throughout the discipline of psychology. Between them they gathered pledges from over 600 APA members to join a division of health psychology if one were formed, and the rest is history. Matarazzo was the first president of the new division, Weiss was the second, and Miller was the third. (Matarazzo, by the way, has also served as the president of the entire APA, and Charles Spielberger, another person who identifies himself foremost as a health psychologist, is the past president of APA.)

WHAT IS THE DIVISION OF HEALTH PSYCHOLOGY?

One of over 45 divisions of the American Psychological Association, which now has over 70 000 members, Division 38 is the "home base" for those of us who identify ourselves as health psychologists, or those who value health psychology and want to be kept abreast of the latest developments in the field. The work of the Division is orchestrated by an Executive Committee consisting of elected officers, representatives to the APA Council, and chairs of standing and *ad hoc* committees.

The Division produces two informative publications: the journal, *Health Psychology*, which publishes six issues a year; and a newsletter, the *Health Psychologist*, which currently has three issues a year. The content of the journal, by design, is mostly empirical research reports. The journal occasionally publishes special issues on such topics as clinical health psychology (Epstein, 1988 (Ed)) and race, reactivity and blood pressure regulation (Anderson & Shumaker, 1989 (Eds)). The current editor of *Health Psychology* is Karen Matthews of the University of Pittsburgh who took over the editorship from Neil Schneiderman of the University of Miami in 1988. (Both Matthews and Schneiderman have also served as presidents of Division 38.)

The newsletter contains reports from the president and the divisional committees, and, on occasion, brief articles by members for the benefit of the membership. For example, in 1988, Sheldon Cohen of Carnegie-Mellon University wrote an outstanding piece on how to get a research grant funded by the NIH, and, more recently, he followed that up with an article on what to do when your grant is "approved but not funded" (Cohen, 1990). Although it takes one editor, 10 associate editors, and over 30 contributing editors to put together *Health Psychology*, publishing the newsletter has been mostly a one-man operation. John Linton of West Virginia University Medical Center has been the editor of the newsletter since its inception.

Two of the division's committees have recently inaugurated their own publications: *Update on Women's Health Issues* and *Update on Children's Health Issues*, both of which contain brief synopses of research within the domain of the committees' interests. Members of these and other committees also frequently contribute columns to the *Health Psychologist* to keep the membership abreast of current issues.

In addition to its publications, major activities of the Division involve putting on the health psychology program at the annual APA Convention and putting together national consensus conferences on such important issues as how best to educate/train health psychologists, and what should be the research agenda in health psychology. (A national conference on Behavioral and Sociocultural Perspectives on Ethnicity and Health, sponsored by the Division and organized by Norman Anderson of Duke University, was held during the fall of 1992.)

WHO ARE THE HEALTH PSYCHOLOGISTS IN THE USA?

The leadership in Division 38 has come mainly from academically-based health psychologists, with a balance between persons trained initially as clinical, experimental, or social psychologists. The leadership, however, has not been strictly representative of the membership of the Division, most of whom are not academically based scientists.

In 1988, B. Kent Houston, on behalf of the Division of Health Psychology, surveyed its membership which, at that time, consisted of slightly fewer than 2500 APA members. A total of 1149 members responded, 804 males (70%) and 345 females (30%). The respondents averaged 43 years of age (range: 25–77), and all but 49 (an embarrassing 96.3%) were White. Ninety-four and a half per cent held PhD degrees. When asked about their professional activity in health psychology, 65.2% indicated they are practitioners, 54.7% are researchers, 49.7% are teachers or supervisors, and 25% said they are administrators. (The fact that the percentages add up to over 100 signifies that many health psychologists fulfill multiple roles.) They carry out all this activity in academic settings (28.7% in universities, 26.2% in medical schools or centers), independent practices (22.8%), and hospitals, clinics, or community mental health centers (14.6%). Interestingly, only one out of four of the respondents (25.8%) viewed themselves predominantly as a health psychologist; 61% labeled themselves as a health psychologist second and some other kind of psychologist first. (The survey didn't ask, but most likely a majority of the members are clinical psychologists, followed by a large number of social psychologists, with the remainder being split among counseling, developmental, community, cognitive, educational, and physiological psychologists. It is only a relatively recent phenomenon, to be discussed below, to have persons trained generically as health psychologists.)

Approximately two-thirds of those surveyed indicated that they also hold membership in a non-APA health-related association. By far, the greatest overlap is with the Society of Behavioral Medicine; 37.2% of those surveyed (and 55.6% of those who view themselves primarily as health psychologists) are members of SBM. The organization with the next highest number of health psychologists is the American Public Health Association.

Today, the membership in the Division of Health Psychology is over 3700 strong, a figure which includes student and non-APA member affiliates, some of whom reside outside the USA. Because one can most certainly be a health psychologist without being a member of Division 38, I estimate that there are currently between 4500 and 5000 practicing health psychologists in the USA, with, perhaps, another 300–500 in training to become health psychologists.

WHERE ARE THE HEALTH PSYCHOLOGISTS IN THE USA?

The largest concentration of health psychologists in the USA (and, I would guess, the world) is in Pittsburgh, Pennsylvania. In fact, Pittsburgh is the Mecca of health psychology. Most are affiliated with the University of Pittsburgh or Carnegie-Mellon University. A few years back, a survey conducted by the Rand McNally Company named Pittsburgh "America's 'most livable' city." (Health psychologists, of all people, know the importance of a good quality of life!)

While no other single locale in the USA is blessed with quite as many health psychologists as Pittsburgh, one can find active groups of health psychologists all over the country. The state with the most health psychologists is California which, coincidentally, is the most populous state. Health psychologists are located up and down the entire California coast, from San Diago and Los Angeles in the South to San Francisco and Palo Alto in the North. Many are affiliated with Stanford University or the vast and prestigious University of California system, but an increasing number of health psychologists have a connection with the California School of Professional Psychology, a free-standing, private institution with campuses in four cities.

Not surprisingly, a large number of health psychologists reside in the states of New York, Texas, Florida, and Massachusetts. A significant number can also be found within the metropolitan area of Washington, DC, our capital city. Many work for the National Institutes of Health or other governmental agencies, or are affiliated with one of the universities in the Washington area. (One Washington area health psychologist deserving of special note is Pat DeLeon who, as special assistant to Senator Daniel Inouye of Hawaii, has been extremely effective in helping to shape our national health policy.)

WHERE DO NEW HEALTH PSYCHOLOGISTS IN THE USA GET TRAINED?

Because of the relative newness of our specialty, most health psychologists over the age of 35 received no formal training in health psychology; they were clinical, social, or experimental psychologists who just started to do research in the area of health and learned about the field piecemeal. Even today, that model probably fits a good number of those entering the field. However, beginning with George Stone's program at UCSF in 1977, predoctoral and/or postdoctoral training in health psychology is formally available at over 50 institutions in the USA

Not all of these 50+ programs are called "health psychology"; other labels such as "medical psychology", "behavioral medicine", "behavioral immunology", etc. are used. However, if the training is principally carried out by faculty who are themselves health psychologists, the training is in health psychology. When health psychologists join colleagues from other disciplines such as medicine, nursing, health education, etc., this multidisciplinary group provides training in the multidisciplinary field called "behavioral medicine".

Health psychology is not only offered to students at the graduate and postgraduate level; many courses have been developed to teach health psychology content to undergraduates (Sarafino, 1988), and there are internships and continuing education offerings in health psychology geared toward the practicing clinician.

As with other sections of this review, space does not permit a thorough description of all of the excellent training programs in health psychology in the States. Many of these hardly qualify as "programs" in their own right, but are "tracks" or subspecialties within clinical or social psychology programs. While there may be a few courses in the curricula at these institutions which are devoted to health psychology, the majority of the training in health psychology takes place in research apprenticeships and/or practical settings supervised by health psychologists.

Only one program, however, purports to train "generic" health psychologists. That unique program is located in New York City and is a joint effort between the Ferkhauf Graduate School of Psychology of Yeshiva University and the Albert Einstein College of Medicine's Department of Epidemiology and Social Medicine. The Ferkhauf/Einstein program started out in the late 1970s to be distinguishably different from all other health psychology training programs. Its aim was to train health psychologists who would be both scientists and practitioners in this new specialty without having to be simultaneously trained as clinical psychologists.

This notion, however, soon ran into difficulty; the graduates of the Ferkhauf/Einstein program had problems getting licensed as practitioners in the State of New York because they lacked a clinical internship or its equivalent. (They couldn't get into most internship programs because their predoctoral training lacked some of the essential prerequisites for clinical internships.)

Today, the Ferkhauf/Einstein program has overcome that hurdle; it has retained its uniqueness as a program which specifically trains health psychologists, but, because it has added a required internship, its graduates are now licensable as service providers in the state of New York. As yet, however, no other program has attempted to emulate the Ferkhauf/Einstein model.

WHERE DO HEALTH PSYCHOLOGISTS IN THE USA PUBLISH THEIR WORK?

Because health psychologists in the USA are both plentiful and prodigiously productive, they publish their research findings in a vast number of journals and are prolific authors of chapters and books. There is a limit, of course, to how many papers can be published in *Health Psychology*, although steps have been taken to stretch that limit. (Beginning with volume 10 in 1991, *Health Psychology* altered its size and format, resulting in a 33% increase in the number of words/volume. In 1993, *Health Psychology* will experience a 10% increase in pages per issue.)

In addition to *Health Psychology*, three other journals which are not exclusively devoted to our specialty publish a large amount of the work done by health psychologists. These are: the *Journal of Behavioral Medicine*, the *Journal of Consulting and Clinical Psychology*, and the *Journal of Applied Social Psychology*. Together, however, these four journals only account for a fraction of the articles authored each year by health psychologists in the USA. The other articles are scattered in a wide number of outlets, ranging from the general (e.g., *American Psychologist*; *Psychological Bulletin*) to the highly specific (e.g., *Arthritis and Rheumatism*; *Pain*). (Unfortunately, a relatively new journal, the *Journal of Compliance of Health Care*, which addressed an issue of great concern to health psychologists, recently ceased publication.)

PRESENTATIONS BY HEALTH PSYCHOLOGISTS AT MAJOR NATIONAL MEETINGS

In May of 1988, Division 38 held a National Working Conference on Research in Health and Behavior. Keynote addresses were delivered by Richard Evans (of the University of Houston) and Karen Matthews, followed by overviews on what is already known in key research areas by panels of experts in those areas. The areas were: biobehavioral aspects of cardiovacular disease; psychoneuroimmunology; cancer; smoking; and health outcome models for policy analysis. The work at the conference, however, was carried out by eight task forces (covering the five areas just listed plus AIDS; child health; and practice in health psychology) all of which attempted to identify the high-priority research agendas for those eight areas. The proceedings of that conference have been published in *Health Psychology* (see Baum, 1989). The task force reports, in particular, should have a significant impact on the nature of health psychology research well into the 21st century.

Although very little health psychology content is presented at the regional psychological meetings (such as the Eastern or Midwestern Psychological Associations), the program at the annual APA convention is replete with invited addresses, symposia, and poster presentations about our field. (The

Division of Health Psychology is the primary sponsor of only some of this work; many of the other APA divisions are quite interested in topics which fall within the health psychology domain.) At the 1991 convention in San Francisco, the most prevalent topic discussed was the prevention of the spread of HIV disease and interventions aimed at helping people with HIV disease cope with their condition.

The research reported by health psychologists at the APA meetings, of course, only represents a small portion of the presentations made by American health psychologists at regional, national, and even international meetings. Not too surprisingly, a large percentage of what is presented at the annual meetings of the Society of Behavioral Medicine and the American Psychosomatic Society is work done by health psychologists. In addition, this work is well represented at the meetings of almost every specialty organization related to health and/or illness.

ISSUES CURRENTLY FACING HEALTH PSYCHOLOGY IN THE USA

A 1989 US Government report revealed that although life expectancy is increasing for white Americans, factors such as high homicide rates, AIDS, and lack of adequate medical care contribute to a lower life expectancy among black Americans. More than half of premature deaths were associated with lifestyle patterns. Health psychologists have had some success in helping white, middle- and upper-middle class Americans modify aspects of their lifestyles, and these modifications have contributed to the increase in whites' life expectancy. The challenge for health psychology in the USA, however, is to develop effective methods for modifying the lifestyles of all Americans, and, so far, we haven't come close to meeting that challenge.

Securing adequate funding for health psychology research and research training is a constant preoccupation and stressor for most academically based health psychologists. A large portion of our support has traditionally come from governmental sources, particularly the National Institutes of Health and Mental Health (NIH and NIMH). A recent (February, 1990) report from the NIH recognized the contributions of behavioral factors to health and the need to assure adequate levels of support for research in this area, while at the same time acknowledging that only a scant 4.3% of the NIH budget in fiscal year 1989 went for support of health and behavior research. This figure excludes the money appropriated for AIDS; if one includes AIDS, the percentage for health and behavior drops to 3.9 which is astonishing considering that, at this point, the only means of preventing the spread of this condition is through widespread behavior change. The Board of Directors at APA appointed a Health and Behavior Task Force in 1989 and a number of prominent health psychologists served on that task force. Also, the Science Directorate at APA made "health and behavior" its number one priority, and actively lobbied and educated Congress, federal agencies, private foundations, and private industry for research support in this area. (This focus on health and behavior within the Science Directorate, however, was shortlived. By the end of 1991, the Directorate had turned its attention to other matters.)

So far, Division 38 has managed to survive the scientist vs practitioner schism that almost destroyed the American Psychological Association a few years ago. Although close to two-thirds of health psychologists are practitioners, and approximately three-quarters of those practitioners spend at least half their time in clinical practice, the practitioners of health psychology appear to be strongly committed to strengthening the scientific basis of our field. Compared to many of their fellow clinical psychologists whose service activities monopolize their time, practicing health psychologists appear to be more likely to spend a portion of their time conducting research and keeping up with current research findings. Yet, despite this commitment to research, the leadership of the Division (all of whom have been prominent researchers) has been aware for years that more attention must be paid to the needs and interests of professional health psychologists if the Division is to continue to grow and prosper. (A new book series, under the managing co-editorship of Andy Baum of USUHS and Margaret Chesney of UCSF, is being developed specifically to address the informational needs of practicing health psychologists. The first volumes should be out by 1993.)

One of the issues of direct relevance to clinical health psychologists is whether or not psychologists in the USA should be allowed to prescribe medications, especially psychotropic medications, to clients. The issue for health psychologists goes beyond just psychotropic medications, because health psychologists deal with patients with a wide variety of medical conditions. The arguments in favor of granting psychologists this "privilege" are that it will help psychologists better serve the public, especially in rural areas where clients might not have ready access to physicians (see DeLeon, Fox & Graham, 1991). The arguments against psychologists writing prescriptions are: (1) psychologists are not trained to prescribe medications; (2) in order to give them the proper training in prescribing drugs, psychologists would have to have one or two years of highly sophisticated and technical education; (3) prescribing drugs appears to many psychologists as "too easy" a solution to complex problems; doing so would only undermine psychology's unique behavioral orientation; and (4) this would be just one more area where psychologists would be perceived by psychiatrists as threatening psychiatry's territory and resented for doing so.

Not too long ago, the majority of American health psychologists were opposed to psychologists having prescription privileges (Piotrowski & Lubin, 1989). When the matter was first brought up for discussion by the Executive Committee of Division 38, the Committee voted against a recommendation that APA pursue the matter. One of the leading advocates of psychologists having at least limited ability to prescribe drugs, however, is Pat DeLeon who is a member of APA's Board of Directors as well as a former member of the

Division's Executive Committee. Through DeLeon's influence, the Division has gone on record in favor of conducting systematic research on the issue before any ultimate policy decisions are made. If it turns out that psychologists are to be granted the right to prescribe medications, rigid guidelines will have to be developed by the profession to insure that psychologists receive the proper training to do so.

A similar practice issue to writing prescriptions is whether or not psychologists should have the ability to admit patients to hospitals. In the United States it is generally only physicians, not other health professionals, who determine which patients will be admitted to hospitals and when they will be discharged. Psychiatry, in particular, is dead set against psychologists having admitting privileges. These issues (i.e. prescription and admitting privileges for psychologists) go well beyond health psychology, but they have a definite impact on those health psychologists engaged in treating patients with medical conditions.

Another issue being hotly debated is that of accreditation. Currently, any program which wishes to claim it provides training in health psychology can do so without having to demonstrate it meets certain minimum standards. Some of the questions which are being actively discussed are: Which health psychology training programs, if any, should be accredited (i.e., predoctoral only or predoctural plus postdoctoral)? Which group should be the accrediting? Who should write the guidelines for accreditation in health psychology? An APA task force spent eight years studying the issue of accreditation of all specialties within psychology and concluded that accreditation should be opened up to any speciality which can defend its right to be considered a specialty. Division 38 has been and will continue to be very much involved in this issue, and it is inconceivable that accreditation guidelines for health psychology programs will be developed without significant input from the Division and its members.

It is only a matter of time before accreditation of health psychology programs becomes a reality in the U.S. Despite the fact that the Arden House Conference (see Stone, 1983) recommended that health psychology should offer two major training options, scientist and professional, when the time for accreditation comes there will be great pressure from the academically based health psychologists to make sure that health psychology practitioners are well grounded in scientific methods and capable of carrying out high quality applied research. This is non-controversial; what is likely to be more controversial, however, is the debate over whether we need to clearly distinguish between the practice of health psychology and that of clinical psychology, and, therefore, whether health psychology programs should train students in a different manner and content than has been the case in traditional clinical programs. What has happened in the USA is that many of the formerly "traditional" clinical psychology programs have added training in health psychology as one of the options for their students. In fact, in a recent survey of the directors of APA accredited clinical psychology programs (Sayette & Mayne, 1990), it was determined that the number one research area among clinical psychology faculty was health psychology/behavioral medicine, and that behavioral medicine clinics ranked number two (just behind family therapy) as places where students could receive specialty training in clinical psychology.

Gil Levin, the founder of the health psychology program at Ferkhauf/ Einstein, believes that health psychology should look more toward counseling than clinical psychology for models of training practitioners (G. Levin, personal communication, May, 1990). Others would probably support training in community psychology and/or public policy. (In his farewell address to his colleagues at UCSF in March, 1990, George Stone pointed out that the field was overly concerned with the health of individual persons with very little consideration of other elements of the system such as the behavior of providers, health organization administrators, health policy makers, and so on.) Still others would argue that the answer for health psychology lies with a closer identification with public health (see the recent article by Stokols, 1992, and the volume by Winett, King & Altman, 1989). All these viewpoints have merit, but the fact of the matter is that, within psychology in the USA, clinical psychology is the dominant specialty and none of the other areas (e.g., counseling, community, public health) have the same degree of clout and respect.

The final, but perhaps most important, issue facing health psychology in the USA has to do with a need to balance the number of people being trained as health psychologists with in the availability of positions for those people. Up until now, health psychology has embraced those who wanted to become health psychologists with open arms; the motto was (and still is), "the more, the merrier", and no one has been terribly concerned about who will pay the salaries of all these health psychologists. Fortunately, so far, the jobs have been there for those who want them (although one doesn't find all that many listings for non-clinical health psychologists in the "positions available" section of the *APA Monitor*), but many of those jobs are highly dependent on "soft" money (i.e., research grants) and/or are non-tenure-track positions in medical centers. Because health psychology is a relatively new field, many health psychologists in tenured academic positions are young themselves, and won't be vacating those positions for years to come.

THE FUTURE OF HEALTH PSYCHOLOGY IN THE USA

The NIH Working Group on Health and Behavior is developing a long-term plan to increase levels of support over the next 10 years in four general categories of health and behavior research: (a) behavioral epidemiology; (b) development, maintenance, and change of health-related behaviors; (c) basic biobehavioral mechanisms; and (d) behavioral interventions to prevent and treat illness or to promote health. Although this is good news for American health psychologists, the USA budgetary process is highly political, and there are no guarantees that this long-term plan will be actualized. In the meantime, health psychologists in the USA continue to cultivate sources of support other than the federal government, such as foundations, corporations and even the citizenry itself. The issues that health psychologists concern themselves with are ones that the public understands and cares deeply about. Good health is the number one value in American society even though Americans do not always follow good health practices (Smith and Wallston, 1992).

At some point, the field must come to grips with its "boundaries", but what those boundaries encompass seems almost limitless. For example, health psychologists in the U.S. have embraced cigarette smoking as "their" risk behavior of choice, perhaps because of its linkage to heart disease and cancer. Interestingly, however, far fewer health psychologists study alcohol or drug abuse as health risk behaviors; those American psychologists who do work in the alcohol/drug area are less likely to label themselves as health psychologists than those who work in the smoking area. Inevitably, all issues of substance abuse which affect the health of human beings will come to be seen as within the purview of health psychology. Also, a number of health psychologists have gotten involved in the even newer field of sports psychology, particularly those who have an interest in understanding and promoting exercise behavior. One of the newest divisions within APA is the Division of Peace Psychology. Although few health psychologists currently think of themselves as peace psychologists, working to eliminate war is probably one of the most effective primary prevention avenues by which to promote health and forestall death.

A recent development has been the approval of a new specialty in health psychology by the American Board of Professional Psychology. (This was due to the efforts of the American Board of Health Psychology whose current president is Cynthia Belar of the University of Florida.) It is conceivable that sometime in the future American health psychologists might need to become "board certified" in order to be reimbursed for their services to the public, but it will at least be health psychologists who determine the criteria for that certification.

My prediction is that instead of health psychology and clinical psychology going off in different directions, they will begin to look more and more similar. Clinical psychologists will not concern themselves strictly with "mental" health/psychopathology, just as health psychologists do not devote all their attention to "physical" health/pathology. At the same time, I agree with Taylor (1990) that the diversity within health psychology in the USA and around the world will continue to grow by leaps and bounds.

> Asking "What's new in health psychology?" will be like asking "What's new in psychology or in medicine?"—queries that can be answered in only the most general and superficial ways. (Taylor, 1990, p. 47.)

REFERENCES

Anderson, N. B. & Shumaker, S. A. (Eds.) (1989). Special issue on race, reactivity, and blood pressure regulation. *Health Psychology*, 8 (5), 483–628.

APA Task Force on Health Research (1976). Contributions of psychology to health research: Patterns, problems, and potentials. *American Psychologist*, **31**, 263–274.

Baum, A. (Ed.) (1989). Proceedings of the National Working Conference on research in health psychology. *Health Psychology*, **8** (6), 629–784.

Cohen, S. (1988). Getting your grant funded by NIH. *Health Psychologist*, **10** (2), 3.

Cohen, S. (1990). Funding your unfunded PHS grant proposal. *Health Psychologist*, **12** (3), 6.

DeLeon, P. H., Fox, R. E. & Graham, S. R. (1991). Prescription privileges: Psychology's next frontier? *American Psychologist*, **46**, 384–393.

Epstein, L. (Ed.) (1988). Special issue on clinical health psychology. *Health Psychology*, **7** (6), 497–589.

Korn, J. H., Davis, R. & Davis, S. F. (1991). Historians' and chairpersons' judgments of eminence among psychologists. *American Psychologist*, **46**, 789–792.

Piotrowski, C. & Lubin, B. (1989). Prescription privileges: A view from health psychologists. *The Clinical Psychologist*, **42**, 83–84.

Rodin, J. & Saloway, P. (1989). Health psychology. *Annual Review of Psychology*, **40**, 533–579.

Sarafino, E. P. (1988). Unergraduate health psychology courses. *Health Psychologist*, **10** (3), 2.

Saytette, M. A. & Mayne, T. J. (1990). Survey of current clinical and research trends in clinical psychology. *American Psychologist*, **45**, 1263–1266.

Schofield, W. (1969). The role of psychology in the delivery of health services. *American Psychologist*, **24**, 565–584.

Smith, M. S. & Wallston, K. A. (1992). How to measure the value of health. *Health Education Research, Theory & Practice*, **7**, 129–135.

Stokols, D. (1992). Establishing and maintaining healthy environments: Toward a social ecology of health promotion. *American Psychologist*, **47**, 6–22.

Stone, G. C. (Ed) (1983). National Working Conference on education and training in health psychology. *Health Psychology*, **2** (Suppl.). Hillside, NJ: Erlbaum.

Stone, G. C., Cohen, F. & Adler, N. E. (1979). *Health Psychology: A Handbook*. San Francisco, CA: Jossey-Bass.

Taylor, S. E. (1990). Health psychology: The science and the field. *American Psychologist*, **45**, 40–50.

Winett, R. A., King, A. C. & Altman, D. G. (1989). *Health Psychology and Public Health: An Integrative Approach*. New York: Pergamon Press.

Index

International Review of Health, Psychology

Contents of Volume 1

SUBSCRIPTION NOTICE

*T*his Wiley product is updated annually to reflect important changes in the subject matter. If you purchased this copy directly from John Wiley & Sons, we will have already recorded your subscription and will inform you of new volumes.

If, however, you made your purchase from a bookseller and wish to be notified of future volumes, please complete the information opposite and return to Wiley (address printed overleaf).

WILEY
Publishers Since 1807

INTERNATIONAL REVIEW OF HEALTH PSYCHOLOGY
Volume 2

Please send me details of previous volume:

❏ **Volume 1 1992**

Please complete details below:

NAME: ....

ADDRESS: ....

....

....

COUNTRY: ....

☎ ....

A critical review of developments in health psychology...

Complete your reference library...

Are you missing Volume 1 from this important series?
To obtain full details please return the card above.

INTERNATIONAL REVIEW OF HEALTH PSYCHOLOGY

Editors

S. MAES
Leiden University, The Netherlands

H. LEVENTHAL
Rutgers University, USA

M. JOHNSTON
University of St. Andrews, UK

CONTENTS:
- ● **General concepts and Methodology**
- ● **Health Behaviour and Health Promotion**
- ● **Illness Behaviour and Health Care**
- ● **Practical and Professional Issues**

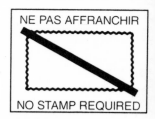
REPONSE PAYEE
GRANDE-BRETAGNE

Sarah Stevens (MARKETING)
John Wiley & Sons Ltd.
Baffins Lane
CHICHESTER
West Sussex
GREAT BRITAIN
PO19 1YN